Tom Snyder Productions®

Windows Macintosh!
Versions XP, X, 2001, 2000, 98, & 97!

Word Workshop
for Teachers™

by Janet Caughlin

Easy-to-Use Guide
- **Create newsletters, brochures, and mail-merge letters to communicate with parents**
- **Use tables to create rubrics and assignment sheets**
- **Make professional looking math worksheets**
- **Create Web Quest sheets and Web pages**

Lessons Using Word across the Curriculum
Loads of lesson ideas and templates to help meet your curriculum objectives!

Student Project Ideas
Customizable student presentations included!

Mac/Win Template CD-ROM Included!
Jam-packed with sample files you can use today!

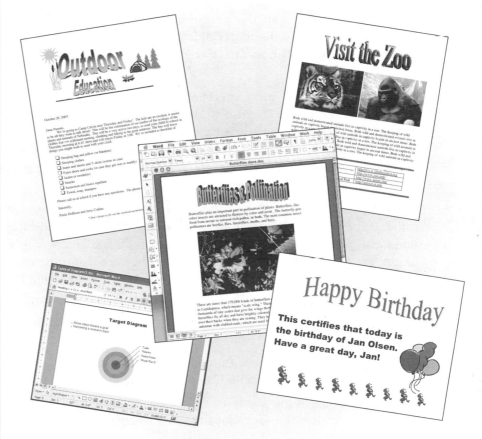

"This book is an invaluable resource for anyone using Word in the classroom."
— Jeff Ingraham
Technology Specialist, Educational Service Unit #3, Omaha, Nebraska

SCHOLASTIC

Copyright and Trademark Notice

Copyright

Trademarks

Limited Liability and Disclaimer of Warranty

Acknowledgments

This book is dedicated to my family, and especially to my husband, who has been so supportive and encouraging during this project. He understands how a book takes over my life and is still willing to share in the experience after all this time.

Special acknowledgment to Diane Wolfe, who is an educator, trainer, a Microsoft® certified user, and a friend. I appreciate all the time and effort she spent helping me make this book both accurate and relevant.

Special thanks to Jeff Ingraham, Larry Wade, and Dr. George Conrad, fellow educators and trainers who shared their knowledge.

Special thanks to Marc Albert, who helped me define the book and spent hours researching and contributing to the content.

A special thank you to the teachers who contributed their lessons to this book. They show that educators are a family that always helps one another. Thank you also to the students who contributed their files. For security reasons their names are not listed below.

Gary Schlapfer	*Fremont Middle School, Fremont, Nebraska*
Diane Johnson	*Fremont Middle School, Fremont, Nebraska*
Joanne Lehman	*Fremont Elementary Schools, Fremont, Nebraska*
Jan Kruse	*Fremont Elementary Schools, Fremont, Nebraska*
Ruth Follen	*Fremont Elementary Schools, Fremont, Nebraska*
Sharon Carlson	*Fremont Middle School, Fremont, Nebraska*
Laurie Holben	*Howard Elementary School, Fremont, Nebraska*
Annette Johnson	*Washington Elementary School, Fremont, Nebraska*
Paula Grinvalds	*Valley Elementary School, Valley, Nebraska*
Krista Mead	*Banfield Elementary School, Austin, Minnesota*
Lorna McCloud	*Jackson Elementary School, Colorado Springs, Colorado*
Diane Wolfe	*Educational Service Unit #2, Fremont, Nebraska*
Sandi Snyder	*Shickley High School, Shickley, Nebraska*
Melissa Burns Johnston	*Anahuac Middle School, Anahuac, Texas*

Contents

How Teachers Use *Word*

How Students Use *Word*

Appendix

Introduction
Detailed Contents

What Is *Word* and Why Should a Teacher Want to Use It?

Microsoft Word is the most popular word-processing program in use today. Why? Maybe it's because of the incredible looking documents you can create. Or maybe it's the unique features that make creating documents quick and easy. Using *Word,* you can create anything from simple signs and worksheets to professional-looking newsletters and brochures.

Word is a visual program, using buttons and menus to access its formatting and editing features. *Word* also provides intuitive help. For example, as you type, the program marks unknown words and grammatical errors with wavy lines. It also corrects common typos and repeats paragraph formatting. If you type "teh," *Word* will change it to "the." If you begin a paragraph with a number, e.g., 1., in the next paragraph, *Word* will type the "2." and indent as you did in the previous paragraph. Sometimes this help feature can be overwhelming for the new user, but *Microsoft* allows you to customize *Word* to meet your needs. You can turn off features and change the options and toolbars, so a primary-level student or a beginning computer user can easily use the program to write a story and include graphics. Don't worry, anything you change can be changed back.

Word is also very powerful. You can hyperlink documents to other *Word* files, to *PowerPoint* presentations, *Excel* worksheets and charts, or even Web pages on the Internet. If you create a large document, like a handbook, you can insert bookmarks to hyperlink the table of contents directly to the sections and back. You can even create Web pages with *Word*.

With *Word* it's easy to insert graphics into a document. Almost any graphic, including movies and still pictures from digital cameras or scanners, can be added to your files. Visual learners in your classroom will certainly appreciate this capability.

Parts of a Flower

A set of drawing tools is included with *Word*. Using these tools, you can create visual worksheets and quizzes that will aid student learning and understanding.

You'll find that *Word* is a tool that not only makes your job easier, it makes teaching and learning an exciting adventure!

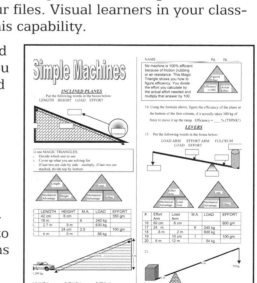

While *Word* is easy to use, questions will still arise. *Word Workshop for Teachers* is designed to answer them for you in an easy-to-read fashion. It also contains ideas on using *Word* in the classroom.

About This Book

Word Workshop for Teachers was written by a teacher to help colleagues make better use of their valuable time. After all, who has less time and more things to do than a teacher?

This book is not a manual written in technical and hard-to-understand language. Rather, it is a guide that you can go to for help whenever the need arises. Flip through the book. You'll notice actual pictures of what should be on your computer monitor as you work through the activities. Don't worry about your typing skills; many of the activities don't require much typing. Just open a file from the CD-ROM that is included with the book and follow the step-by-step directions. If the pictures on your monitor match the ones in the book, congratulations, you've done it right! If it doesn't look quite right, go back a step or two and try it again. In no time at all, you'll be producing professional-looking documents!

Please note that this book assumes that you know the basics of your Windows or Macintosh computer. Though Windows and Macintosh basics are discussed briefly in this chapter, the intent of this book is to help you learn to use *Word*.

Some fellow teachers will be there to help you. Be sure to read the helpful messages next to them.

Here's how to fix it!   Don't worry if you make a mistake! Julia will tell you how to fix it. It's probably a common mistake and easy to fix!

Here's more information!   Do you need more instructions? Mary will give you more information or tell you the page where you can find a more detailed explanation.

Warning!   Be sure to follow the directions *exactly* here!

Here's a faster way!   This is a faster way to do it!

Contacting the Author

This book is constantly being shaped by the educators who use it and share their experiences. As a teacher and trainer, I know that a big part of the value of any tutorial resource is in the tutorial's accessibility and flexibility. Please feel free to contact me at janetcaughlin@aol.com if you need help or have comments or questions. I also invite you to visit the official Workshop Books Web site, created especially for you, at www.workshopbooks.com. You'll find the latest information about this book and all the other software tutorials in the Workshop Books series, as well as lots more about the in-person training seminars I do with these books.

Windows and Macintosh Commands

Microsoft has done a fabulous job making *Word* truly cross-platform. As a result, it is easy to include both Windows and Macintosh commands on the same page. Most things in the Windows menus are found in the Macintosh menus, though there are a few differences. Some things are found only on the Windows platform, some only on the Macintosh platform. For example, the File menu in ⊞ *XP*, *2000*, and *97* shows Options in the Tools menu. The File menu in *X* , *2001,* and *98* shows Preferences. ⊞ *XP* allows you to use a Task Pane to perform tasks. *X* and *2001* users can use a Formatting Palette to format text and graphics. *X* and *2001* allow you to do terrific things with pictures like removing red-eye and scratches, or cutting out portions of pictures.

In this book, the Windows command is given first, followed by the Macintosh command. Screen shots are shown from both Windows and Macintosh. The similarity of the screens will allow you to work easily with either platform.

Different Versions of *Word*

This book covers the ⊞ *XP*, *2000, 97* and *X, 2001,* and *98* versions of *Word*. The command for ⊞ *XP* is given first. If a command is different in other versions, it is given next. If a particular screen is significantly different in three versions, all three are shown with a label identifying the version. If a feature is available only on one platform or version, you'll see a message like this:

** X, 2001**	*This section is for Word X, 2001 users only. Users of other versions go to your section of this activity.*

After launching *Word*, how do you know which version you are using?

Windows: Click the Help menu and choose About Microsoft *Word*.

Macintosh: Click the Apple menu and choose About Microsoft *Word*.

Word files can be opened on either a Windows or a Macintosh computer as long as files are saved on a Windows-formatted disk. The extension ".doc" needs to be added to Macintosh files if you are going to use them on a Windows computer. The versions covered are completely compatible although some features are not included in all versions. See the Appendix for information about the compatibility of earlier versions.

Version of Office	Symbol Used
WINDOWS	
XP (also known as 2002)	⊞
2000	⊞
97	⊞
MACINTOSH	
X	
2001	
98	

Opening Files to Complete Activities

Many activities in this book are designed to work together with the sample files on the CD-ROM. The files on the CD-ROM are organized in folders by chapter of this book. For example, if you are doing an activity from the Learning to Use *Word* chapter, you'll find the files in the Learning to Use *Word* folder. You can also find graphics in the Pictures folder and movies in the Movies folder.

Windows Basics

Using the Mouse

Windows computers use a mouse for many functions, including opening files and folders, accessing menus, and sizing graphics. You'll see an arrow on the computer screen. This is the pointer. The mouse moves the pointer around the screen. To use the mouse, hold it with your palm over the round end and the cord up by your fingertips. As you move the mouse, the pointer will move in the same direction on the screen. If you run out of room on the mouse pad (a common problem for new users), just pick up the mouse and set it down at the other end of the mouse pad so that you have more room to move.

The pointer changes shape according to what you are doing.

- If you are at the Desktop (the opening screen), the pointer is shaped like an arrow.

- If you are typing text in *Word,* the cursor is a blinking vertical line. When you move the mouse, a separate "I-beam" pointer will move. If you click the mouse, the cursor moves to the place where the I-beam is.

- If you are in the Drawing mode, the pointer is shaped like a plus sign. Spreadsheets have a fat, cross-shaped pointer.

- If the computer is doing something that takes a while, such as sorting or moving a large graphic, the pointer changes into an hourglass.

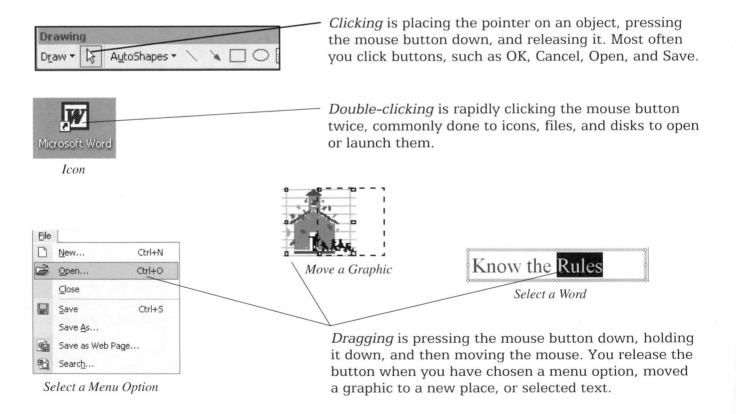

Clicking is placing the pointer on an object, pressing the mouse button down, and releasing it. Most often you click buttons, such as OK, Cancel, Open, and Save.

Icon

Double-clicking is rapidly clicking the mouse button twice, commonly done to icons, files, and disks to open or launch them.

Move a Graphic

Select a Word

Select a Menu Option

Dragging is pressing the mouse button down, holding it down, and then moving the mouse. You release the button when you have chosen a menu option, moved a graphic to a new place, or selected text.

Interpreting the XP Desktop

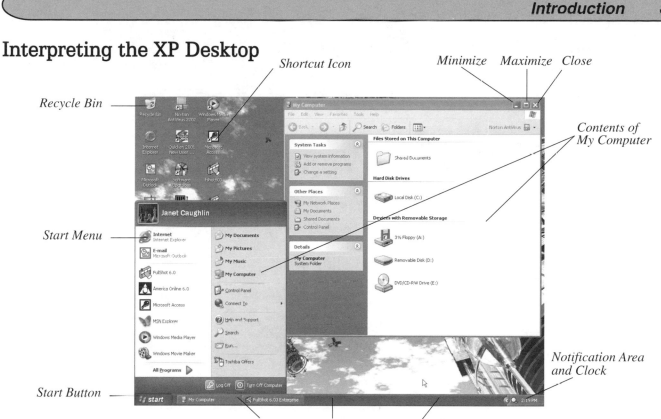

Recycle Bin

Shortcut Icon

Minimize   Maximize   Close

Contents of My Computer

Start Menu

Notification Area and Clock

Start Button

Open Programs and Windows in the Taskbar

Below is a description of elements shown above, starting with the Recycle Bin in the upper left corner and going counterclockwise around the screen.

- **Desktop:** The screen you see when you first start the computer. Just like in your office, you can see and use the trash can, and open your files (from the hard drive).

- **Recycle Bin:** A trash can where you can move things to be deleted from your computer or floppy disk.

- **Start Menu:** Lets you launch programs, find files and programs, and shut down the computer.

- **Start Button:** Makes the Start Menu appear.

- **Taskbar:** A strip that runs along the bottom of the window. It contains very useful items, including the Start button on the left, the Open Programs and Windows area in the middle, and the Notification Area and Clock on the right. The name of programs and windows you have open appear in the middle. If you click a program/window name in the Taskbar, it moves to the front so that you can use it. This allows you to move between open programs.

- **Notification Area:** Shows icons that tell you what your computer is doing and lets you change settings. A printer icon appears during printing, a speaker appears if you have a sound card, etc.

- **My Computer:** Choose this from the Start menu to reveal the hard drive, floppy drive, CD-ROM drive, etc. Double-clicking an icon reveals the files on that drive. Double-click a file to open it.

- **Close:** Exits a program or closes a window.

- **Maximize:** Enlarges a window to fill the screen.

- **Minimize:** Makes a program disappear from the screen, but does not close the program. You can click the program name in the Taskbar to use it again.

- **Shortcut Icons:** Can be double-clicked to open files and programs.

Interpreting the 2000 and 98 Desktop

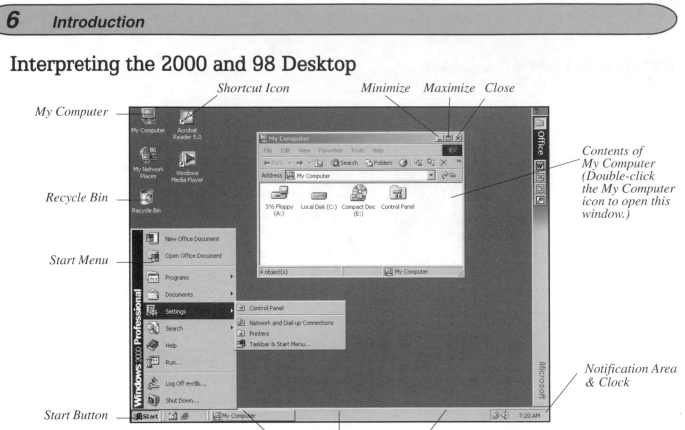

Below is a description of elements shown above, starting with My Computer in the upper left corner and going counterclockwise around the screen.

- **Desktop:** The screen you see when you first start the computer. Just like in your office, you can see and use the trash can, and open your files (from the hard drive).

- **My Computer:** Double-click to reveal the hard drive, floppy drive, CD-ROM drive, etc. Double-clicking an icon reveals the files on that drive. You can then double-click a file to open it.

- **Recycle Bin:** A trash can where you can delete things from your computer or floppy disk.

- **Start Menu:** Lets you launch programs, find files and programs, and shut down the computer.

- **Start Button:** Makes the Start Menu appear.

- **Taskbar:** A strip that runs along the bottom of the window. It contains very useful items, including the Start button on the left, the Open Programs and Windows area in the middle, and the Notification Area and Clock on the right. The name of programs and windows you have open appear in the middle. If you click a program/window name in the Taskbar, it moves to the front so you can use it. This allows you to move between open programs.

- **Notification Area:** Shows icons that tell you what your computer is doing and lets you change settings. A printer icon appears during printing, a speaker appears if you have a sound card, etc.

- **Close:** Exits a program or closes a window.

- **Maximize:** Enlarges a window to fill the screen.

- **Minimize:** Makes a program disappear from the screen, but does not close the program. You can click the program name in the Taskbar to use it again.

- **Shortcut Icons:** Can be double-clicked to open files and programs.

Search XP

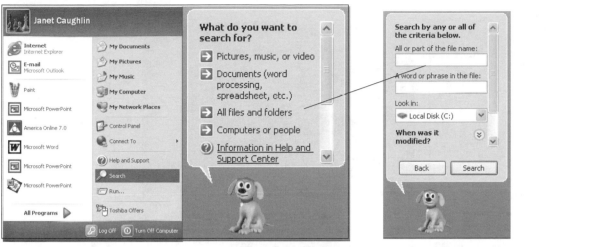

Search locates files and folders. This feature is handy if you can't remember where things are. You can choose the drive(s) to search and then search by file name, the date a file was modified, or other criteria.

Search 2000

Help XP

Help locates information on topics about which you want to learn more. Type the first few letters of the word you want in the Search box. Then click the entry at the bottom that matches your topic. Information on that topic will appear.

Help 2000

Shut Down XP

Turn Off or Shut Down
prepares your computer to be
turned off. Choose Turn Off
or Shut Down, then Turn Off
or Shut Down again.

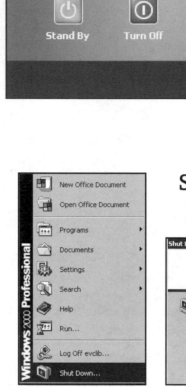

Shut Down 2000

My Computer XP

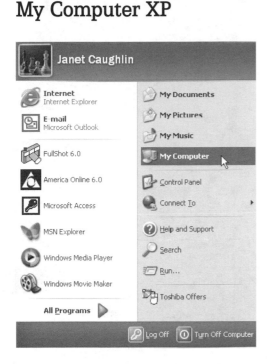

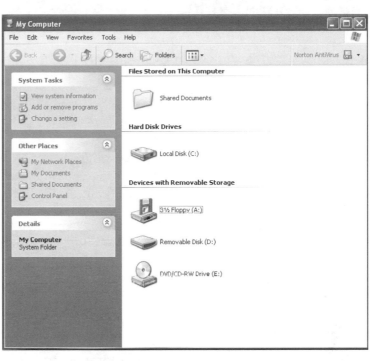

My Computer contains icons of the hardware attached to your computer: floppy drives, hard drives, and anything else attached to your computer, e.g., a CD-ROM drive, scanner, zip drive, or digital camera.

My Computer 2000

Windows Explorer XP

Windows Explorer shows you folders on your computer in a tree form. All the sub folders and files in each folder are shown.

Windows Explorer 2000

- You can open a folder and copy or move files by dragging them to the new location.

- You can create shortcuts on the Desktop by dragging a file from Explorer to the Desktop. This shortcut will save time in opening files.

The example shows a Windows Explorer window.

- The left side shows the folders on the hard drive.

- The right side shows the files in the My Documents folder (the selected one).

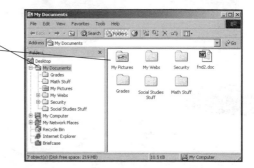

Saving Files

Saving a New File

When you save a new file from within a program, you must name the file and decide where you want it to be saved. Here are some basic instructions on how to do this.

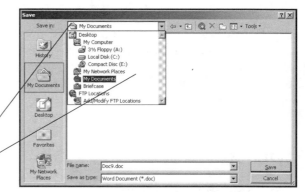

1. Click the **File** menu and choose **Save** or press ⌨CTRL ⌨S.

2. **Type a file name** in the File Name box. Be sure the name identifies the contents of the file.

3. Click the **arrow** in the **Save In box** and navigate to the location where you want to save your file. You can choose to save on the hard drive (C:), the floppy drive (A:), or in a folder on either drive. (You can't save to the CD-ROM drive.)

4. Click **Save**. Once you've done this, you can simply press ⌨CTRL ⌨S, or click the **File** menu and choose **Save** at any time to save changes to your file.

Saving a Previously Created File

This lets you save a file with another name, which is helpful if you want to change your document but preserve the original. It also enables you to save a file to a different location. For example, if you are using one of the template files on the CD-ROM that comes with this book, you need to save the file to a location on your hard drive, since you cannot save files to a CD-ROM. Depending on the situation, you may choose to change the file name, the location, or both. Here's how:

1. Click the **File** menu and choose **Save As**.

2. Type a **new file name** in the Save As box. Be sure the name identifies the contents of the file.

3. Click the **Save In** box at the top of the Save As window and navigate to the location where you want to save your file. You can save on the hard drive (C:), the floppy drive (A:), or in a folder on either drive. (You cannot save to the CD-ROM drive.)

4. Click **Save**. Your old file is preserved, and you now have a new file.

Macintosh Basics

Using the Mouse

Macintosh computers use a mouse for many computer functions including opening files and folders, accessing menus, and sizing graphics. You'll see an arrow on the computer screen. This is the pointer. The mouse moves the pointer around the screen. To use the mouse, hold it with your palm over the round end and the cord up by your fingertips. As you move the mouse, the pointer will move the same direction on the screen. If you run out of room on the mouse pad (a common problem for new users), just pick up the mouse and set it down at the other end of the mouse pad so that you have more room to move.

The pointer changes shape according to what you are doing.

- If you are at the Desktop, the pointer is shaped like an arrow.

- If you are typing text in a text box in *Word,* the cursor is a blinking vertical line. When you move the mouse, a separate "I-beam" pointer will move. If you click the mouse, the cursor moves to the place where the I-beam is.

- If you are in the Drawing mode, the pointer is shaped like a plus sign. Spreadsheets have a fat, cross-shaped pointer.

- If the computer is doing something that takes a while, such as sorting or moving a large graphic, the pointer will change into a watch or a spinning beach ball.

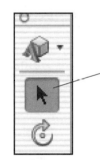

Clicking is placing the pointer on an object, pressing the mouse button down, and releasing it. Most often you click buttons, such as OK, Cancel, Open, and Save.

Double-clicking is rapidly clicking the mouse button twice, commonly done to icons, files, and disks to open or launch them.

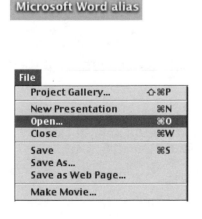

Microsoft Word alias

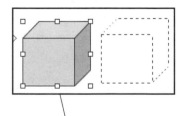

Dragging is pressing the mouse button down, holding it down, and then moving the mouse. You release the button when you have chosen a menu option, moved a graphic to a new place, or highlighted a block of text.

File	
Project Gallery...	⇧⌘P
New Presentation	⌘N
Open...	⌘O
Close	⌘W
Save	⌘S
Save As...	
Save as Web Page...	
Make Movie...	

Interpreting the Desktop (Finder) OS X

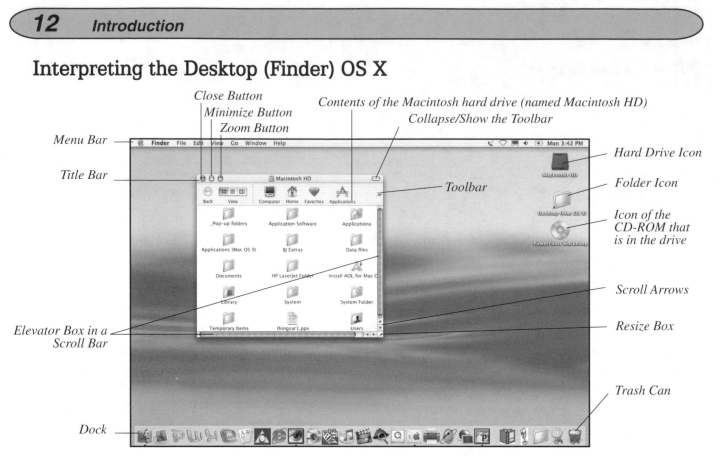

Below is a description of elements shown above, starting with the Title Bar in the upper left corner and going counterclockwise around the screen.

- **Desktop:** The screen you see when you first start the computer. Just like in your office, you can see and use the trash can, and open your files (from the hard drive).
  Note: To the layperson, the Desktop and the Finder are the same thing. The two terms are used interchangeably in this book, even though to a computer expert they are different things.

- **Title Bar:** Shows the name of your file or window. Click the title bar and drag it to move the window.

- **Elevator Box:** Allows you to jump instead of scroll. Click and drag the box to a desired location, or click above or below it to jump in preset increments.

- **Dock:** Allows you to move between programs without closing them. A triangle under an icon means the program is open. You can double-click a program icon to launch the program.

- **Trash Can:** Click and drag items to the Trash Can. Then choose Empty Trash from the Finder menu to delete the contents of the trash. You can also remove disks or CD-ROMs from the computer by dragging them to the Trash Can. This does not delete any files. It just ejects the disk. ("Eject" from the File menu or a right-click does the same thing.)

- **Resize Box:** Click and drag this to change the size of the window.

- **Scroll Arrows:** Let you see files and folders inside a window. If you want to see something at the top of the window, click the top arrow.

- **Collapse/Show toolbar:** Collapses or shows the toolbar portion of the window.

- **Zoom Button:** Lets you jump between small and large window sizes. Click in the box. Click it again. Click the Resize and the Zoom boxes. They work the same in applications like *Word*.

- **Minimize Button:** Lets you "shrink" windows to the right end of the Dock.

- **Close Button:** Click in it to close the window.

The Menu Bar OS X

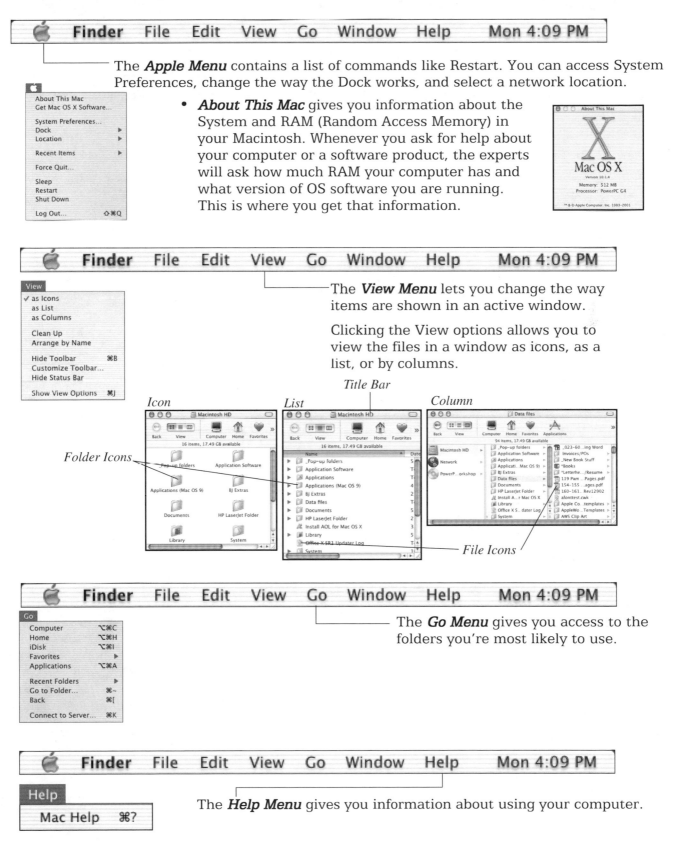

The **Apple Menu** contains a list of commands like Restart. You can access System Preferences, change the way the Dock works, and select a network location.

- **About This Mac** gives you information about the System and RAM (Random Access Memory) in your Macintosh. Whenever you ask for help about your computer or a software product, the experts will ask how much RAM your computer has and what version of OS software you are running. This is where you get that information.

The **View Menu** lets you change the way items are shown in an active window.

Clicking the View options allows you to view the files in a window as icons, as a list, or by columns.

Title Bar

Icon   *List*   *Column*

Folder Icons

File Icons

The **Go Menu** gives you access to the folders you're most likely to use.

The **Help Menu** gives you information about using your computer.

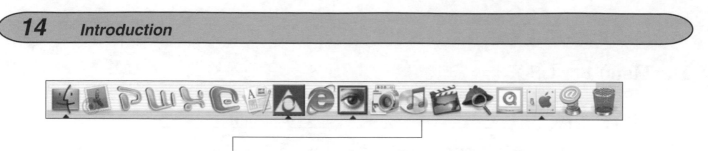

The ***Dock*** lets you switch from one application program to another or to the Finder (Desktop). A triangle under an icon means the program is open. You can double-click a program icon to launch the program.

Saving Files

Saving a New File

When you save a new file, you must tell the computer the name of the file and where you want it to be saved.

1. Choose **Save** from the **File** menu, or press [⌘][S].

2. Type a file name in the Save As box. Be sure the name identifies the contents of the file.

3. Click and hold down the **arrow** of the **Where pull-down menu**, and then navigate to the location where you want to save your file. You can choose to save on the hard drive, a floppy disk, or in a folder in either of these places. (You can't save to a CD-ROM.)

4. Click **Save**.

5. Once you've done this, you can simply press [⌘][S], or click the **File** menu and choose **Save** at any time to save changes to your file.

Saving a Previously Created File

This lets you save a file with another name, which is helpful if you want to change your document but preserve the original. It also enables you to save a file to a different location. For example, if you are using one of the template files on the CD-ROM that comes with this book, you will need to save the file to a location on your hard drive, since you cannot save files to a CD-ROM. Depending on the situation, you may choose to change either the file name or the location, or both. Here's how:

1. Click the **File** menu and choose **Save As**.

2. **Type a new file name** in the Save As box. Be sure the name identifies the contents of the file.

3. Click and hold down the **arrow** of the **Where pull-down menu** and navigate to the location where you want to save your file. You can choose to save on the hard drive, a floppy disk, or in a folder in either location. (You can't save to a CD-ROM.)

4. Click **Save**. Your old file is preserved, and you now have a new file.

Interpreting the Desktop (Finder) OS 9.x

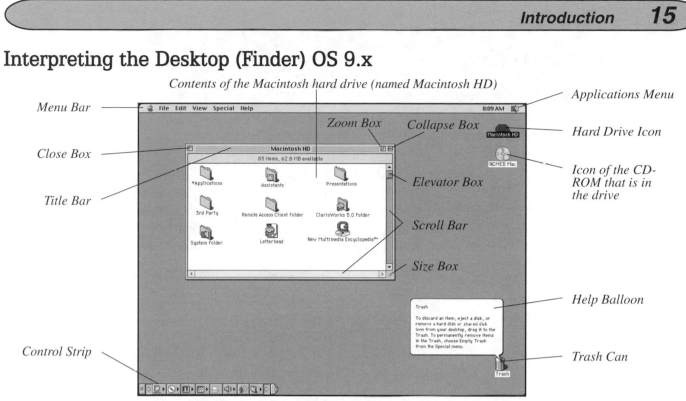

Contents of the Macintosh hard drive (named Macintosh HD)

Below is a description of elements shown above, starting with the Close Box in the upper left corner and going counterclockwise around the screen.

- **Desktop:** The screen you see when you first start the computer. Just like in your office, you can see and use the trash can, and open your files (from the hard drive).
  Note: To the layperson, the Desktop and the Finder are the same thing. The two terms are used interchangeably in this book, even though to a computer expert they are different things.

- **Close Box:** Click in it to close the window.

- **Title Bar:** Shows the name of your file or window. Click the title bar and drag it to move the window.

- **Control Strip:** A quick and easy way to change some of your computer settings.

- **Trash Can:** Click and drag items to the Trash Can. Then choose Empty Trash from the Special menu to delete the contents of the trash. You can also remove disks or CD-ROMs from the computer by dragging them to the Trash Can. This does not delete any files. It just ejects the disk. ("Put Away" from the File menu does the same thing.)

- **Help Balloons:** Provide onscreen help as you move your cursor. To turn them on, choose Show Balloons from the Help menu. To get rid of them, choose Hide Balloons from the Help menu.

- **Size Box:** Click and drag this to change the size of the window.

- **Scroll Bars:** Let you see files and folders inside a window. If you want to see something at the top of the window, click the top arrow.

- **Elevator Box:** Allows you to jump instead of scroll. Click and drag the box to a desired location, or click above or below it to jump in preset increments.

- **Collapse Box:** Lets you "roll up" windows so that only the title bar shows. Click it again to unroll the window.

- **Zoom Box:** Lets you jump between small and large window sizes. Click in the box. Click it again. Play with the Size and the Zoom boxes. They work the same in applications like *Word*.

- **Applications Menu:** Allows you to move between programs without closing them. This is a good way to see which applications are open.

The Menu Bar OS 9.x

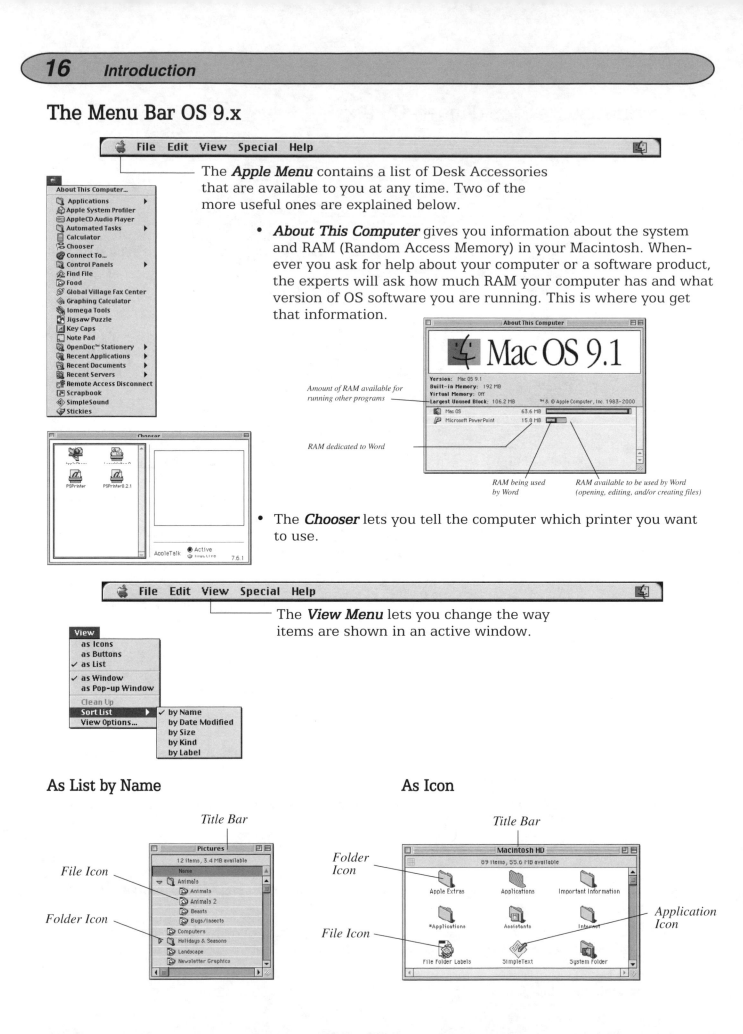

The **Apple Menu** contains a list of Desk Accessories that are available to you at any time. Two of the more useful ones are explained below.

- **About This Computer** gives you information about the system and RAM (Random Access Memory) in your Macintosh. Whenever you ask for help about your computer or a software product, the experts will ask how much RAM your computer has and what version of OS software you are running. This is where you get that information.

Amount of RAM available for running other programs

RAM dedicated to Word

RAM being used by Word

RAM available to be used by Word (opening, editing, and/or creating files)

- The **Chooser** lets you tell the computer which printer you want to use.

The **View Menu** lets you change the way items are shown in an active window.

As List by Name

Title Bar

File Icon

Folder Icon

As Icon

Title Bar

Folder Icon

File Icon

Application Icon

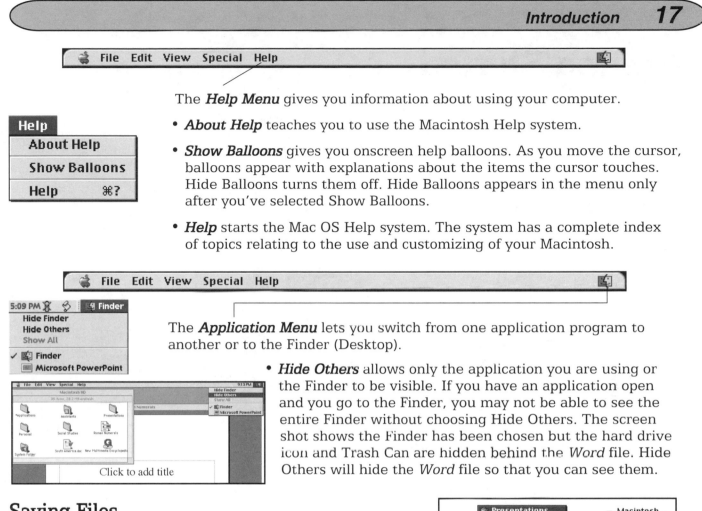

The *Help Menu* gives you information about using your computer.

- *About Help* teaches you to use the Macintosh Help system.

- *Show Balloons* gives you onscreen help balloons. As you move the cursor, balloons appear with explanations about the items the cursor touches. Hide Balloons turns them off. Hide Balloons appears in the menu only after you've selected Show Balloons.

- *Help* starts the Mac OS Help system. The system has a complete index of topics relating to the use and customizing of your Macintosh.

The *Application Menu* lets you switch from one application program to another or to the Finder (Desktop).

- *Hide Others* allows only the application you are using or the Finder to be visible. If you have an application open and you go to the Finder, you may not be able to see the entire Finder without choosing Hide Others. The screen shot shows the Finder has been chosen but the hard drive icon and Trash Can are hidden behind the *Word* file. Hide Others will hide the *Word* file so that you can see them.

Saving Files

Saving a New File

When you save a new file, you must tell the computer the name of the file and where you want it to be saved.

1. Click the **File** menu and choose **Save**, or press ⌘ S.

2. **Type a file name** in the Save As box. Be sure the name identifies the contents of the file.

3. Click the **arrow** or **name** at the top of the dialog box, and then navigate to the location where you want to save your file. You can choose to save on the hard drive, a floppy disk, or in a folder in either of these places. (You can't save to a CD-ROM.)

4. Click Save. Once you've done this, you can simply press ⌘ S, or click the **File** menu and choose **Save** at any time to save changes to your file.

Saving a Previously Created File

This lets you save a file with another name, which is helpful if you want to change your document but preserve the original. It also enables you to save a file to a different location. For example, if you are using one of the template files on the CD-ROM that comes with this book, you will need to save the file to your hard drive, since you cannot save files to a CD-ROM.

1. Click the **File** menu and choose **Save As**.

2. Follow steps 2-4 above. Your old file is preserved, and you now have a new file.

Getting Started

Word is part of a suite of programs called *Microsoft Office,* so it is usually found in a folder called Microsoft Office. Following are instructions on how to launch the program (also called an application) and do some basic things to get you started. You will need to be familiar with these basics to do the activities in the Learning *Word* section.

Launching the Program

Windows

Here are two ways to launch the program:

* Your computer may have shortcuts to programs on the Desktop. If so, **double-click** the Microsoft *Word* **shortcut** to launch the program.

* Or click **Start** in the lower left corner of the Desktop. Then drag up to **All Programs,** (Programs in earlier versions) and **drag right and down** to select Microsoft *Word.*

Word Shortcut (Windows)

Launching Word from the Start menu

Macintosh

Here are two ways to launch the program:

* Your computer may have a set of aliases to programs on the Desktop. If so, **double-click** the Microsoft *Word* **alias** to launch the program.

* Or locate the actual program on the hard drive and **double-click** the Microsoft *Word* icon. It's usually in the Applications folder.

Word Alias (Macintosh)

Launching Word from the program icon

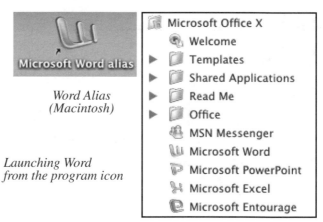

Creating a *Word* File

This is the screen you'll see if you open Microsoft *Word* using one of the methods above. You'll be ready to start typing a new document.

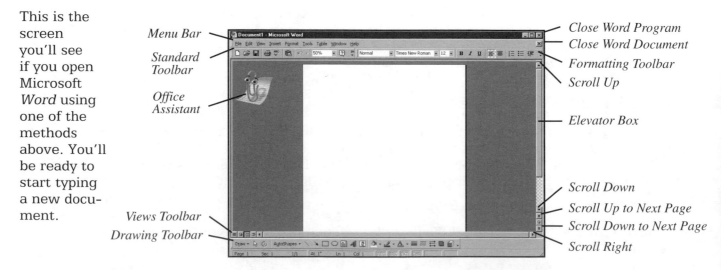

Menu Bar

Standard Toolbar

Office Assistant

Views Toolbar

Drawing Toolbar

Close Word Program

Close Word Document

Formatting Toolbar

Scroll Up

Elevator Box

Scroll Down

Scroll Up to Next Page

Scroll Down to Next Page

Scroll Right

Creating a *Word* File from within the Program

Here's how to create a file if you have already started *Word*.

1. Click the **New** icon

   or

   press [CTRL][N] (Windows) [⌘][N] (Macintosh)

   or

   if you're using XP click **Blank Document** on the **Task Pane**

   to get a new *Word* file.

2. Click the **File** menu and choose **New** to see more choices. You can click the tabs, e.g., **Letters and Faxes** tab, to open a template.

Opening a *Word* File

There are several ways to open a file.

* Click the **Open** icon on the toolbar.

   or

* Click the **File** menu and choose **Open.**

   or

* Press [CTRL][O] (Windows) [⌘][O] (Macintosh).

   or

* If you're using XP, click **More Documents** on top of the **Task Pane**

From there, navigate to the file you wish to open and double-click it.

Note: *Word* will open files from all earlier versions of the program. If you don't see the file you want to open, choose All Files from "Files of type" at the bottom of the window (called "List files of Type" on Macintosh). You must do this to open files saved as templates, outlines, or Web pages.

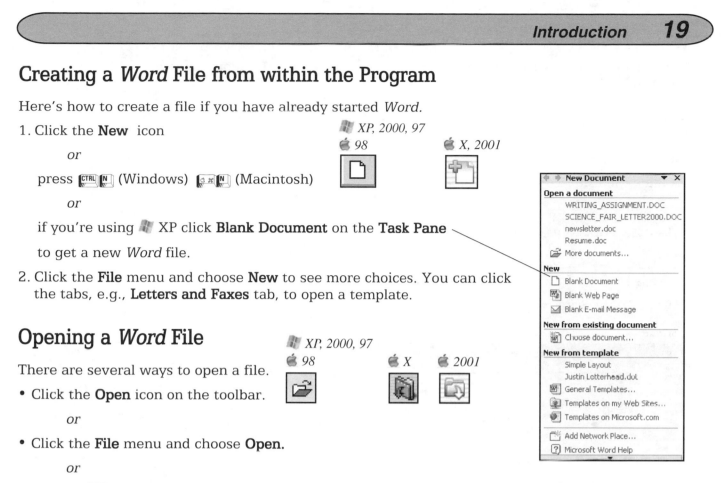

Saving a File

Saving a *Word* file works just like saving a file in any word-processing program.

1. Click the **Save** icon on the toolbar.

   or

   Click the **File** menu and choose **Save.**

   or

   Press [CTRL][S] (Windows) [⌘][S] (Macintosh).

2. Name your file.

3. Navigate to where you want to save the file.

4. Click **Save.**

Note: If you want people with earlier versions of *Word* to be able to open your file, you need to use the drop-down menu next to the words **"Save as type"** ("Save File as Type" on Macintosh) and select the appropriate version.

For more detailed instructions on saving files, see page 10 for Windows and page 14 for Macintosh.

Printing a File

The basics of printing a *Word* file are easy. Simply do one of the following:

1. Click the **Print** icon on the toolbar.

> *or*

Choose **Print** from the **File** menu.

> *or*

Press ⌨️ (Windows) ⌨️ (Macintosh).

2. Click **OK** or **Print.**

Windows

Macintosh

Word Help

One of the best things about *Word* is its built-in help features. If you are in the middle of something and can't figure out how to finish it, you can ask the Office Assistant by clicking its button (or pressing F1 on Windows). You can also access the Help menu and dig deeper into a topic using Contents, Index, or Find. These options are found in all versions. As you browse these pages, you'll see many similarities and a few differences in the help features for Windows and Macintosh.

The Office Assistant

The Office Assistant is a quick way to access help. If you are in the middle of a procedure and you're not sure what to do next, ask the Assistant. **You can type your question in plain language and click Search.** The Assistant will present a list of topics. Click the blue button next to your chosen topic or redefine your question.

The help topic you chose appears.

If the Office Assistant isn't visible, you can access it by clicking the Assistant button on the Standard Toolbar. On Windows, you can also press F1.

To hide the Assistant, right-click the Assistant (Control-click for Macintosh) and then click Hide or click the Close button.

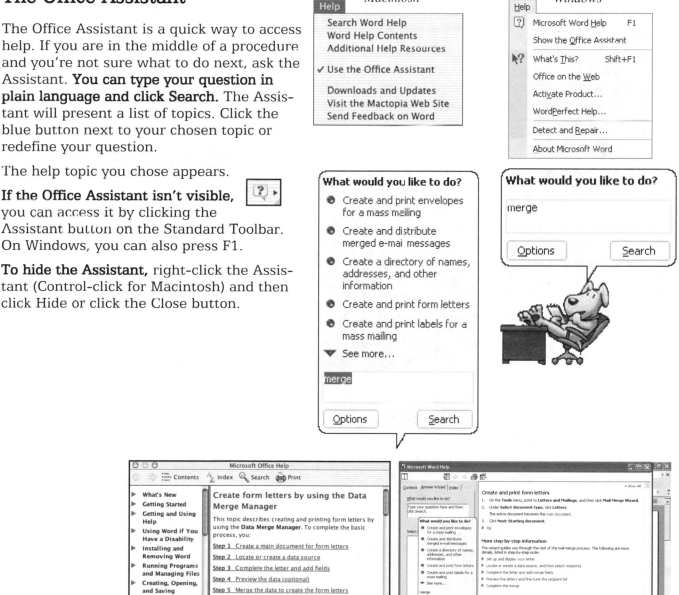

If you don't want the Assistant to guess which Help topics you want, right-click the Assistant (Control-click for Macintosh), and then click Options. On the Options tab, clear the Guess Help topics check box.

Here's a useful trick: If you don't like the "Paperclip Face" or "Computer Face" Assistant, **you can choose another face!** Right-click the Assistant (or Control-click on Macintosh), and then click Choose Assistant. On the Gallery tab, click Next or Back until you find an Assistant you like! You'll need to place the *Microsoft Office* CD-ROM in the drive to complete this process.

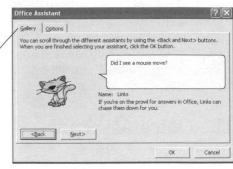

Button Help

If you are using a Windows computer you can press Shift-F1 to access Help. The pointer changes to an arrow with a question mark. Click a button to see what it does. When you click, an explanation window appears.

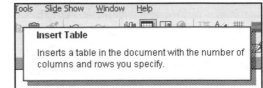

Contents

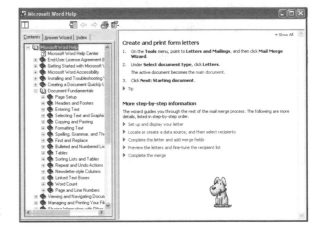

The Wizard gives you help in the **Answer Wizard** tab. Additional help can be accessed by clicking the **Contents** tab. **Contents** gives you a detailed list of help topics. It is arranged in an outline format, with book icons indicting major topics. Clicking or double-clicking a book reveals subtopics. You can also click the plus (+).

A closed book has topics hidden behind it. Double-click (single-click on a Macintosh) to open and the hidden subtopics will drop below it. You can also click the plus (+).

An open book contains topics as well as closed books.

Double-click a book and then double-click a topic to obtain information. On a Macintosh computer, click once to see an explanation window.

Click an arrow to get additional information.

Index

Click the **Index** tab. Windows users type a topic in the keywords section. Macintosh users click a letter to begin the process.

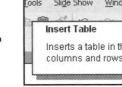

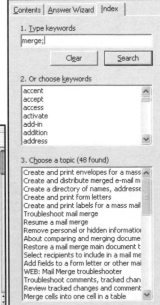

Word Toolbars

Word lets you click a button on a toolbar to perform a task. You can also use menu commands, but you may find it faster to click a button on the toolbar. For example, you can click the Save icon or click the File menu, then drag to the Save command. Try both methods and see which one appeals to you.

Standard Toolbar

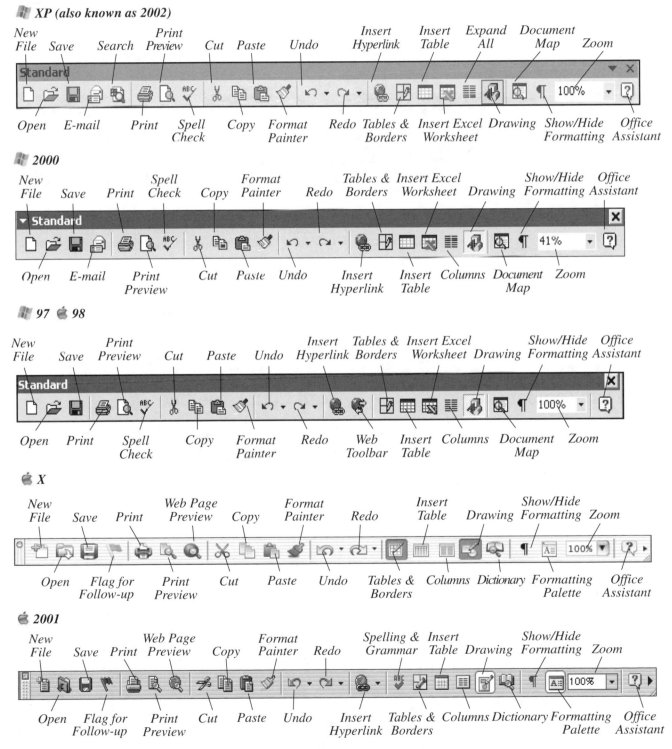

Formatting Toolbar

🪟 XP (also known as 2002)

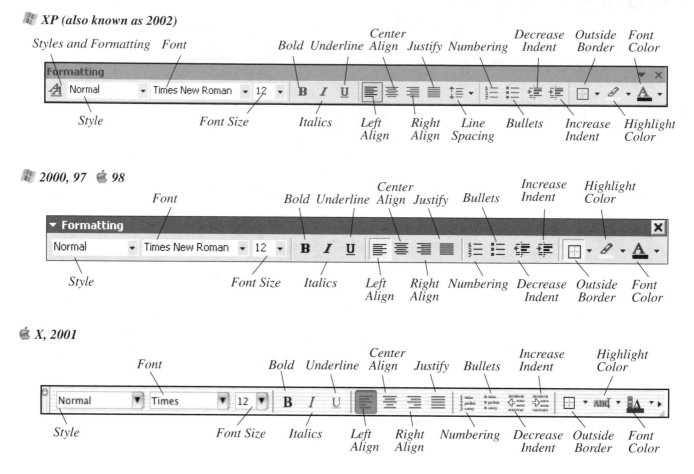

Styles and Formatting   Font   Bold   Underline   Center Align   Justify   Numbering   Decrease Indent   Outside Border   Font Color

Style   Font Size   Italics   Left Align   Right Align   Line Spacing   Bullets   Increase Indent   Highlight Color

🪟 2000, 97 🍎 98

Font   Bold   Underline   Center Align   Justify   Bullets   Increase Indent   Highlight Color

Style   Font Size   Italics   Left Align   Right Align   Numbering   Decrease Indent   Outside Border   Font Color

🍎 X, 2001

Font   Bold   Underline   Center Align   Justify   Bullets   Increase Indent   Highlight Color

Style   Font Size   Italics   Left Align   Right Align   Numbering   Decrease Indent   Outside Border   Font Color

AutoText Toolbar

(All versions)

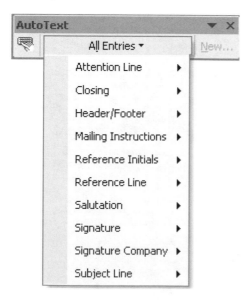

Word Count Toolbar

🪟 XP

Movie Toolbar

🍎 X, 2001

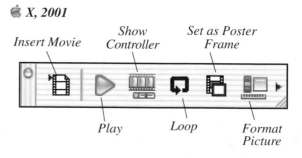

Insert Movie   Show Controller   Set as Poster Frame

Play   Loop   Format Picture

WordArt Toolbar

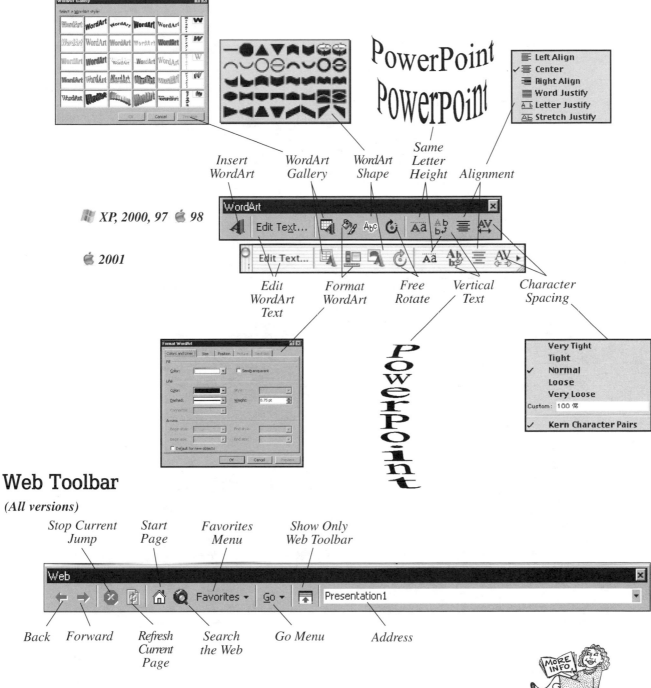

Insert WordArt · **WordArt Gallery** · **WordArt Shape** · **Same Letter Height** · **Alignment**

🪟 *XP, 2000, 97* 🍎 *98*

🍎 *2001*

Edit WordArt Text · **Format WordArt** · **Free Rotate** · **Vertical Text** · **Character Spacing**

Web Toolbar

(All versions)

Stop Current Jump · **Start Page** · **Favorites Menu** · **Show Only Web Toolbar**

Presentation1

Back · **Forward** · **Refresh Current Page** · **Search the Web** · **Go Menu** · **Address**

If you can't find a toolbar on your screen, click the View menu, drag to choose Tools, then click the toolbar you need. You can also right-click in the menu bar or on the toolbar at the top of the screen.

Drawing Toolbar

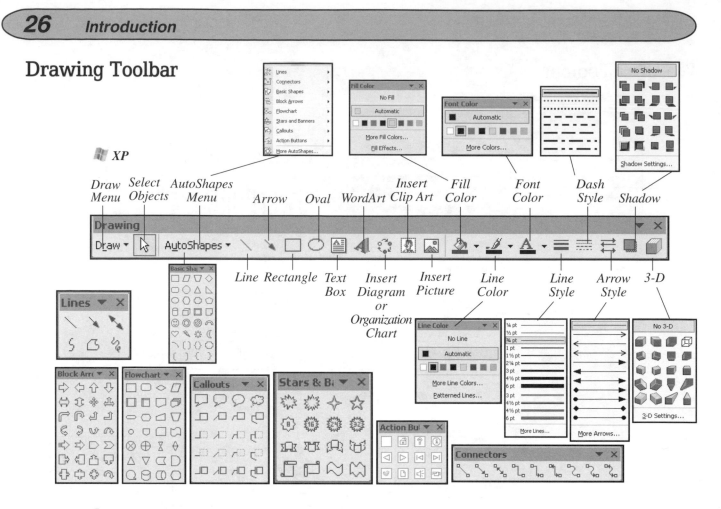

XP

Draw Menu · Select Objects · AutoShapes Menu · Arrow · Oval · WordArt · Insert Clip Art · Fill Color · Font Color · Dash Style · Shadow

Line · Rectangle · Text Box · Insert Diagram or Organization Chart · Insert Picture · Line Color · Line Style · Arrow Style · 3-D

2000, 97   98

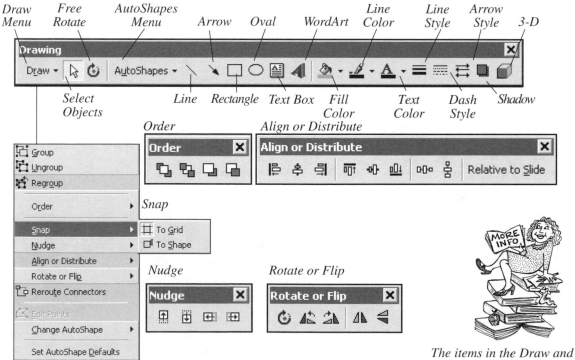

Draw Menu · Free Rotate · AutoShapes Menu · Arrow · Oval · WordArt · Line Color · Line Style · Arrow Style · 3-D

Select Objects · Line · Rectangle · Text Box · Fill Color · Text Color · Dash Style · Shadow

Order · Align or Distribute

Snap

Nudge · Rotate or Flip

The items in the Draw and AutoShapes menus are the same in all versions, so check them out.

Drawing Toolbar

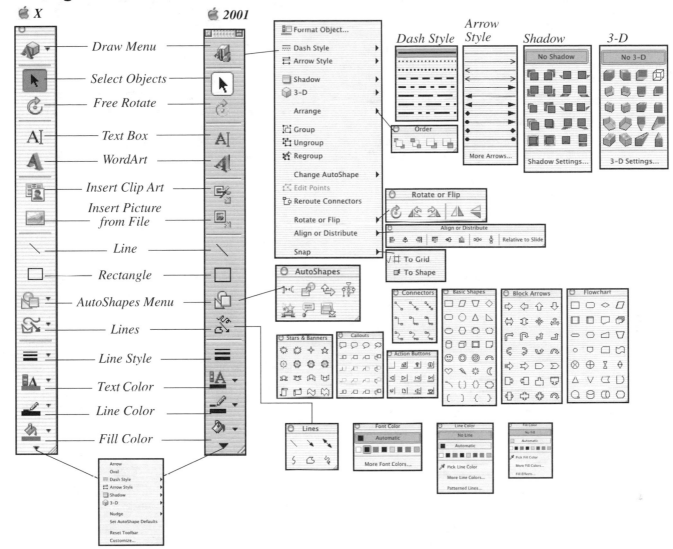

Draw Menu	
Select Objects	
Free Rotate	
Text Box	
WordArt	
Insert Clip Art	
Insert Picture from File	
Line	
Rectangle	
AutoShapes Menu	
Lines	
Line Style	
Text Color	
Line Color	
Fill Color	

Shadow Settings Toolbar

(All versions)

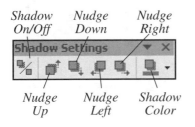

Shadow On/Off — Nudge Down — Nudge Right

Nudge Up — Nudge Left — Shadow Color

3-D Settings Toolbar

(All versions)

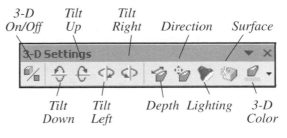

3-D On/Off — Tilt Up — Tilt Right — Direction — Surface

Tilt Down — Tilt Left — Depth — Lighting — 3-D Color

Picture Toolbar

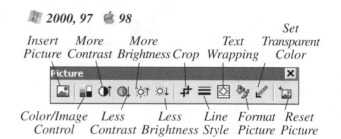

XP

Insert Picture · More Contrast · More Brightness · Crop · Line Style · Text Wrapping · Set Transparent Color

Color · Less Contrast · Less Brightness · Rotate Left · Compress Picture · Format Picture · Reset Picture

2000, 97 98

Insert Picture · More Contrast · More Brightness · Crop · Text Wrapping · Set Transparent Color

Color/Image Control · Less Contrast · Less Brightness · Line Style · Format Picture · Reset Picture

X

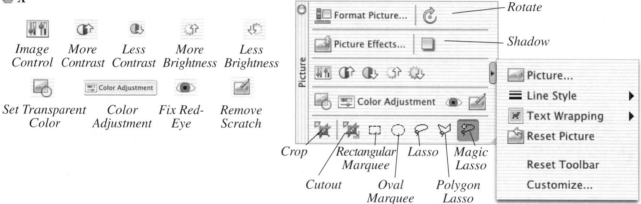

Image Control · More Contrast · Less Contrast · More Brightness · Less Brightness

Set Transparent Color · Color Adjustment · Fix Red-Eye · Remove Scratch

Format Picture... — Rotate

Picture Effects... — Shadow

Color Adjustment

Picture...
Line Style
Text Wrapping
Reset Picture
Reset Toolbar
Customize...

Crop · Cutout · Rectangular Marquee · Oval Marquee · Lasso · Polygon Lasso · Magic Lasso

2001

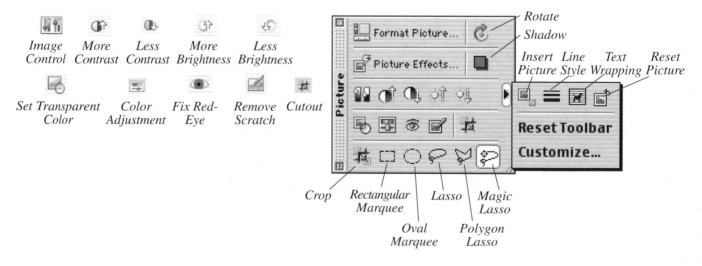

Image Control · More Contrast · Less Contrast · More Brightness · Less Brightness

Set Transparent Color · Color Adjustment · Fix Red-Eye · Remove Scratch · Cutout

Format Picture... — Rotate, Shadow

Picture Effects...

Insert Picture · Line Style · Text Wrapping · Reset Picture

Reset Toolbar
Customize...

Crop · Rectangular Marquee · Oval Marquee · Lasso · Polygon Lasso · Magic Lasso

Tables and Borders Toolbar

Reviewing Toolbar

Mail Merge Toolbar

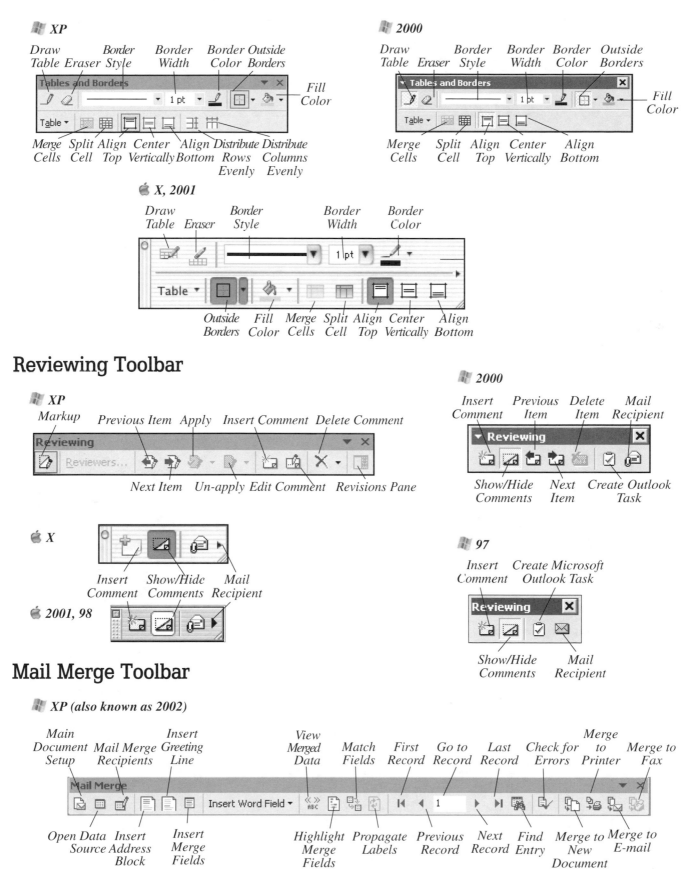

Mail Merge Toolbar

🪟 *2000, 97* 🍎 *98*

View
Merged *Previous* *Next* *Mail* *Merge to* *Start Mail* *Edit Data*
Data *Record* *Record* *Merge* *New* *Merge* *Source*
Helper *Document*

▼ Mail Merge ✕

Insert Merge Field ▾ | Insert Word Field ▾ | 《》ABC | ◀ | ◀ | 1 | ▶ | ▶ | | | | Merge... | |

First *Go to* *Last* *Check for* *Merge* *Find*
Record *Record* *Record* *Errors* *to* *Record*
Printer

🍎 *X, 2001*

Data Merge Manager
▼ Main Document
Create ▾ | Main document: Document1 Micro
Merge type: Form Letters
▼ Data Source
Get Data ▾ 🖳 ☑ ☑ ☝
Data: Student Information
▶ Word Field
▼ Merge Field
Drag and drop into document:

Last_Name	First_Name	Combined_Name
Phone	Special_1	Special_2
Special_3	Get_to_School	Safety_Patrol
	City_State_Zip	
Address		Mom
	Dad	
Mom_Phone	Title	Dad_Phone

▼ Preview
《》ABC | ◀ | ◀ | 1 | ▶ | ▶ | {a}
▼ Merge
🖳 🖳 | Query Options...
All ▾
From: | To:

🪟 *2000, 97* 🍎 *98*

◀ ▶ Mail Merge ▾ ✕

Select document type

What type of document are you
working on?

⦿ Letters
◯ E-mail messages
◯ Envelopes
◯ Labels
◯ Directory

Letters

Send letters to a group of people.
You can personalize the letter that
each person receives.

Click Next to continue.
Step 1 of 6
➡ Next: Starting document

Task Pane 🪟 2000 only

◀ ▶ New Document ▾ ✕
O ✓ New Document
Clipboard
Search
Insert Clip Art
Styles and Formatting
Reveal Formatting
Mail Merge
Translate
New from existing document
📄 Choose document...
New from template
Simple Layout
Justin Letterhead.dot
📄 General Templates...
📄 Templates on my Web Sites...
📄 Templates on Microsoft.com
📄 Add Network Place...
❓ Microsoft Word Help

◀ ▶ New Document ▾ ✕
Open a document
WRITING_ASSIGNMENT.DOC
SCIENCE_FAIR_LETTER2000.DOC
newsletter.doc
Resume.doc
📂 More documents...
New
📄 Blank Document
📄 Blank Web Page
✉ Blank E-mail Message
New from existing document
📄 Choose document...
New from template
Simple Layout
Justin Letterhead.dot
📄 General Templates...
📄 Templates on my Web Sites...
📄 Templates on Microsoft.com
📄 Add Network Place...
❓ Microsoft Word Help

◀ ▶ Basic Search ▾ ✕
Search for:
Search text:
[ ]
Search | Restore
❓ Search Tips...
Other Search Options:
Search in:
Selected locations ▾
Results should be:
Selected file types ▾
Fast searching is currently disabled
Search options...
See also
🔍 Advanced Search
🔍 Find in this document...

◀ ▶ Insert Clip Art ▾ ✕
Search For
Search text:
schppl
Search | Restore
Other Search Options
Search in:
All collections ▾
Results should be:
Multiple media file types ▾
See also
🖼 Clip Organizer...
🌐 Clips Online
❓ Tips for Finding Clips

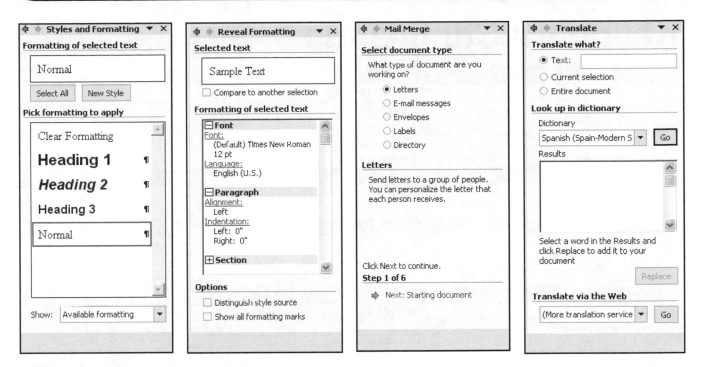

Task Pane <img> X, 2001 only

Keyboard Commands

File & Window Commands	Windows Keys	Macintosh Keys
Open file	Control+O	Command+O
Save file	Control+S	Command+S
Print file	Control+P	Command+P
Print preview (on/off)	Control+Alt+I	Command+Alt+I
Close window	Control+W	Command+W
Undo/Redo	**Windows Keys**	**Macintosh Keys**
Undo an action	Control+Z	Command+Z
Redo an action	Control+Y	Command+Y
Layout Views	**Windows Keys**	**Macintosh Keys**
Page layout view	Control+Alt+P	Command+Option+P
Outline view	Control+Alt+O	Command+Option+O
Normal view	Control+Alt+N	Command+Option+N
Set Line Spacing	**Windows Keys**	**Macintosh Keys**
Single-space lines	Control+1	Command+1
Double-space lines	Control+2	Command+2
Set 1.5-line spacing	Control+5	Command+5
Align Paragraphs	**Windows Keys**	**Macintosh Keys**
Center a paragraph	Control+E	Command+E
Justify a paragraph	Control+J	Command+J
Left align a paragraph	Control+L	Command+L
Right align a paragraph	Control+R	Command+R
Change Font & Size	**Windows Keys**	**Macintosh Keys**
Change font	Control+Shift+F	Command+Shift+F
Increase font size	Control+Shift+>	Command+Shift+>
Decrease font size	Control+Shift+<	Command+Shift+<
Increase font size by 1 point	Control+] or Control+ in XP	Command+]
Decrease font size by 1 point	Control+[or Control+ in XP	Command+[
Change case	Shift+F3	Shift+F3 or Command+Option+C
All caps	Control+Shift+A	Command+Shift+A
Small caps	Control+Shift+K	Command+Shift+K
Format Text	**Windows Keys**	**Macintosh Keys**
Bold	Control+B	Command+B
Italics	Control+I	Command+I
Underline	Control+U	Command+U
Underline words but not spaces	Control+Shift+W	Command+Shift+W
Double underline	Control+Shift+D	Command+Shift+D
Subscript	Control+ Equals Sign	Command+Equals Sign
Superscript	Control+Shift+Plus Sign	Command+Plus Sign
Edit Text	**Windows Keys**	**Macintosh Keys**
Copy text	Control+C	Command+C
Paste text	Control+V	Command+V
Copy format	Control+Shift+C	Command+Shift+C
Paste format	Control+Shift+V	Command+Shift+V
Insert page break	Control+Shift+Enter	Command+Shift+Return
Find & replace	Control+F	Command+F
Find again (after closing window)	Control+Alt+Y	Command+Option+Y
Soft return	Shift+Enter	Shift+Return
Insert Footnote/Endnote/Comment	**Windows Keys**	**Macintosh Keys**
Insert footnote	Control+Alt+F	Command+Option+F
Insert endnote	Control+Alt+E	Command+Option+E
Insert comment	Control+Alt+M	Command+Option+A

Learning *Word*

Detailed Contents

Word Editing Basics

A Sample Field Trip Letter

Microsoft *Word* is easy to learn. This activity takes you through a quick tour of a *Word* document and shows you how to make frequently used edits.

This Activity Covers the Following Topics

- Opening a File
- Editing Text
- Formatting Text
- Setting Tabs
- Justifying the Text
- Previewing the Document
- Inserting a Letterhead
- Drawing a Rectangle in the Letterhead
- Saving the File
- Printing the File

Opening a File

1. **Launch** *Word*. The screen you see when you launch depends on the version you are using. Find your version and follow the directions.

   XP users click **Open a document on** the Task Pane. You can also click the **Open icon** on the Standard toolbar or **press** [CTRL][O] (Windows).

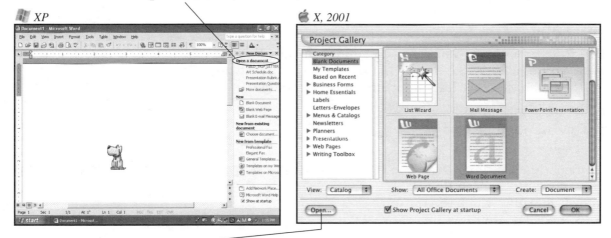

   X and 2001 users click the **Open** button in the lower left corner.

   2000, 97 and 98 users click the **Open icon** on the Standard toolbar or **press** [CTRL][O] (Windows) [⌘][O] (Macintosh).

2. Open the file "Field Trip Letter" from the "Learning Word" folder on the CD-ROM that came with this book. Turn to page 19 for additional help with opening files.

Editing Text

1. **Double-click** the word **kids** in the first line. The entire word becomes highlighted. **Type** the word **students**, but *don't press the delete key first*. Notice that as you start typing, the word kids is deleted and replaced with students.

2. Click *immediately* **after the word animal** in the second line in the sentence reading "They have researched where animal live...." **Type** the letter **s** to make the word plural.

3. Click *immediately* **after the word family** in the next line. This also needs to be plural. Press the **Backspace** key (**Delete** for Macintosh) to erase the **y** and **type ies**.

Formatting Text

1. The places toured by the students will be easier to see if they are emphasized. You're going to italicize this text. Click in front of the **L** in **Lied Jungle**. Hold down [SHIFT] and click the mouse after the second **o** in the word **Zoo**. This highlights everything between the click and the shift-click (Lied Jungle at the Henry Doorly Zoo in this case). This is the *Click Shift-Click* method of highlighting text.

2. Click the **Italic** button on the toolbar at the top of the screen or **press** [CTRL][I] (Windows) [⌘][I] (Macintosh).

3. Using the *Click Shift-Click* method, **italicize Gifford Farm.**

4. Scroll down until all the activities for the field trip are visible on your screen. **Double-click Activity**. **Bold** and **underline** the word. Then **bold** and **underline** the words **Begin** and **Leave**. **Hint:** You can make both changes in quick succession.

   Click the boldface button [B] then the underline button [U] or **press** [CTRL][B] then [CTRL][U] (Windows) [⌘][B] then [⌘][U] (Macintosh).

Setting Tabs

1. Click in front of the **L** in the word **Load** under the heading **Activity**. While holding the mouse button, drag the mouse down and to the right to **select (highlight) the entire schedule**.

2. Click the **1/2"** mark on the ruler. This inserts a **Left** justified **tab** at that location. [L] [↱]

3. You can change the type of tab you insert by clicking the **Tab Box** button to the left of the ruler. Click the button **twice** to choose a right justified tab. [↲] [↰]

   You'll learn more about tabs on page 60.

4. Click the **4 1/2" and 5 1/2"** marks on the ruler to insert **Right** justified tabs at those locations.

The numbers in the screen shot to the right correspond to the directions above.

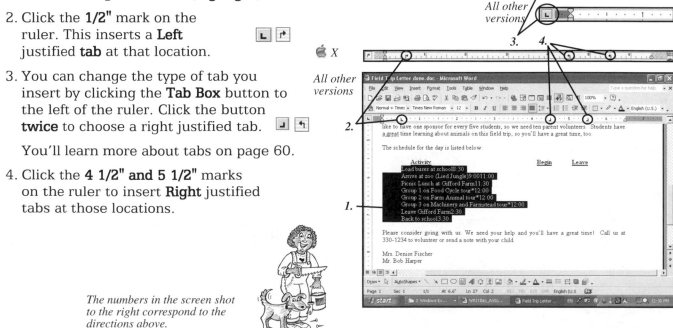

5. Place the **I-beam** pointer to the **left** of the **8** in **8:30** on the first line of the activities. **Click** to move the cursor to that location. **Press TAB**. 8:30 moves to the right under **Begin. Tab the rest of the activities**. For Arrive at zoo you need to click before each time and press tab. Press the Tab key two times for Leave Gifford Farm.

The schedule for the day is listed below:

Activity	Begin	Leave
Load buses at school	8:30	
Arrive at zoo (Lied Jungle)	9:00	11:00
Picnic Lunch at Gifford Farm	11:30	
Group 1 on Food Cycle tour*	12:00	
Group 2 on Farm Animal tour*	12:00	
Group 3 on Machinery and Farmstead tour*	12:00	
Leave Gifford Farm		2:30
Back to school	3:30	

Please consider going with us. We need your help and you'll have a great time! Call us at 330-1234 to volunteer or send a note with your child.

Justifying the Text

Click the **Edit** menu and choose **Select All,** or **press CTRL A** (Windows) **⇧⌘A** (Macintosh) to highlight the entire document. Click the **Justify** button on the **Formatting toolbar** to justify the letter. 🍎 X, 2001 users, find this on the Formatting Palette.

Previewing the Document

XP, 2000, 97
🍎 98   🍎 X, 2001

1. Click the **Print Preview button** on the **Standard toolbar**. You can see that only two-thirds of the page is taken up by the letter. This will allow a letterhead to be inserted at the top.

2. Click the **Close button** on the toolbar at the top of the window.

3. Type the **current year** in the date. **Click** to the **left of the M** in **May. Press ENTER** (Windows) **RETURN** (Macintosh) **five times** to move the text down the page.

Inserting a Letterhead

1. **Click the "I-Beam" two lines down from the top margin.** Click the **Center Text** button.

2. Click the **Bold** button or **press CTRL B** (Windows) **⇧⌘B** (Macintosh) to boldface the text you are about to type.

Mrs. Denise Fischer
Mr. Bob Harper
Valley Public Schools

May 2,

3. Click the **Font Size** box `24 ▾` on the **Formatting toolbar** and choose **24 Point**.

4. Type the letterhead text shown above or type your name, a colleague's name, and your school name. Press **ENTER** (Windows) **RETURN** (Macintosh) at the end of each line. The text will be centered, 24 point, and bold because you just chose those text formatting options.

5. **Click to the left of the M in Mrs. Denise Fischer** (or the first name that you typed). **Press ENTER** (Windows) **RETURN** (Macintosh) to move the line down.

XP, 2000, 97
🍎 98   🍎 X, 2001

Drawing a Rectangle in the Letterhead

1. Click the **Rectangle** tool on the **Drawing toolbar. Move the pointer to the letterhead text** you just created. It turns into a plus + shape.

XP, 2000, 97   🍎 X   🍎 2001
🍎 98

Click this button on the Standard toolbar if the Drawing toolbar isn't visible.

This portion of the pointer must be to the left and above the text.

2. Starting at the **upper left corner, draw a rectangle around the 3 lines containing the teachers and school names**. The text will disappear behind the filled-in square. (Don't panic!)

3. Click the **Draw** menu at the bottom of the screen. 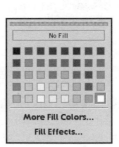 X, 2001 users the menu is on the left side of the screen. Choose **Order**, and then **Send Behind Text**. Your words reappear!

4. Click the arrow to the right of the **Fill Color** icon in the **Drawing toolbar** and choose a **Fill Color**. The box fills with that color.

> **Mrs. Denise Fischer**
> **Mr. Bob Harper**
> **Valley Public Schools**

5. **Click somewhere in the letter to deselect the square**. (The handles – small squares or circles on the corners – disappear.)

6. **Draw another rectangle outside of the first one.** Again, it covers the text. This time instead of moving the rectangle behind the text you're going to make it transparent.

7. Choose **No Fill** from the top of the **Fill Color palette**. The text and the previous box appear because the new box is now transparent.

8. Choose **Whole Page** from the **Zoom box** on the **Standard toolbar**. The letter appears on the screen reduced so that the whole page is shown. If you need to make any changes, you can make them in this size or return to a larger size using the Zoom box.

Saving the File

You did it! Click the **File** menu and choose **Save As** to save your file. Save it on your hard drive or floppy disk.

Printing the File

Click the **Print** button, click the **File** menu and choose **Print**, or **press** [CTRL][P] (Windows) [⌘][P] (Macintosh) to print your file.

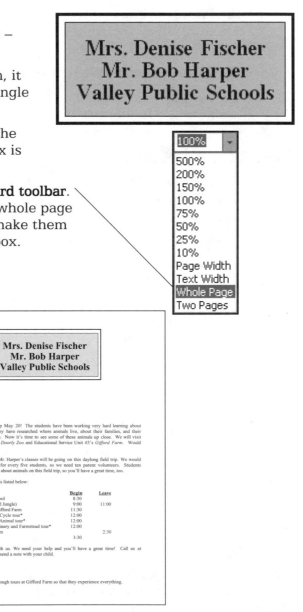

Résumé

Create a Great Résumé

You should keep your résumé updated because you never know when you'll need to use it. Résumés aren't just for jobs, they are also needed if you apply for a grant or honor. *Word* makes it easy to create professional-looking résumés and the directions below show you how.

> ### This Activity Covers the Following Topics
> - Selecting, Boldfacing, and Changing the Size of Text
> - Changing Margins, Setting Tabs
> - Showing Formatting Characters
> - Indenting Text
> - More Tabs
> - Finding and Changing Text
> - Drawing Lines for Emphasis
> - Previewing the Document
> - Creating a Résumé Using the Templates and the Wizard

Selecting, Boldfacing, and Changing the Size of Text

1. Open the file "Résumé" from the "Learning Word" folder on the CD-ROM that came with this book.

2. Place the **arrow pointer in the left margin** on the same line as the words Jolene Peterson. Click the mouse to select the name **Jolene Peterson**.

> **Jolene Peterson**
> 204 Park Avenue South Phoenix, Arizona 50326 H 602-559-2654

3. Click the **Bold button** on the **Formatting toolbar** or press [CTRL][B] (Windows) [⌘][B] (Macintosh). ⌘ X, 2001 users, click the **Formatting palette button** on the **Standard toolbar**.

4. Click the **Font Size** box on the **Formatting toolbar** and choose **24**.

5. Click the **Center** button on the **Formatting toolbar**. ⌘ X, 2001 users can find this in the **Alignment and Spacing** section of the **Formatting palette**.

6. Continuing down the page, select and **boldface** the titles **Career Objective**, **Employment Experience**, **Related Experiences**, **Sponsored:**, **Coaching:**, **Education**, **Professional Organizations**. See pages 40 and 41.

Changing Margins, Setting Tabs

1. Click the **File** menu and choose **Page Setup** (Macintosh users click the **Format** menu and choose **Document**). On the **Margins tab**, select the **1** in the box next to the word **Left**. Type **.85** to change the left margin from 1" to .85". Press the **Tab** key and do the same on the **right** margin. **Click OK**.

2. Select the **address** and **phone number** lines. These lines need tabs to set the information apart in an attractive manner. Click a **left tab** at **2 3/4"**. Click a **right tab** close to the **right margin marker**. Turn to the Setting Tabs section of the previous activity if you need help.

All other versions

⌘ X

3. Click in front of the **P** in Phoenix in the first address line and press 🄣. **Click** in front of the **H** by the **home phone** number and press 🄣. **Do the same in the second line.**

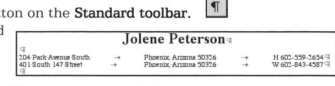

Jolene Peterson		
204 Park Avenue South	Phoenix, Arizona 50326	H 602-559-2654
401 South 147 Street	Phoenix, Arizona 50326	W 602-843-4587

Showing Formatting Characters

1. Click the **Show/Hide Formatting Characters** button on the **Standard toolbar.** ¶

   Formatting characters appear. The same command will hide the characters. A bullet (•) appears between each word to show the Spacebar was pressed. An arrow (→) indicates the Tab key was pressed, and a paragraph mark (¶) means [ENTER] (Windows) [RETURN] (Macintosh) was pressed.

Jolene Peterson¶		
¶ 204 Park Avenue South →	Phoenix, Arizona 50326 →	H 602-559-2654 ¶
401 South 147 Street →	Phoenix, Arizona 50326 →	W 602-843-4587 ¶
¶		

2. The text under the headings **Employment Experience** and **Related Experiences** need tabs set into the ruler to align it in a readable and attractive manner. **Select all the text under these headings.** The formatting characters show you the Tab key was pressed when the file was created, but the tabs are no longer in the ruler. This was done so that you can see how the tabs affect the document when they are put in the ruler. You don't have to spend time pressing the Tab key.

   Click the **Show/Hide Non-Printing Characters** button ¶ to hide the characters.

3. Click a **left tab** at **1"**. As discussed in the previous step, the text will move because the Tab key was pressed when the file was created.

Indenting Text

The Related Experiences section would look much better if the second lines of multiline experiences are indented so they line up on the tab.

Related Experiences		Related Experiences	
1987-1988	Curriculum revision	1987-1988	Curriculum revision
1986-1987	Rewrote curriculum	1986-1987	Rewrote curriculum
1986-Present	Strong background i the curriculum	1986-Present	Strong background the curriculum
1989-Present	"Developing Thinki	1989-Present	"Developing Thinki
1986-1987	Critical and Creative	1986-1987	Critical and Creative
1989-Present	Trained in and imple	1989-Present	Trained in and imple
1987-1988	Authored and impler	1987-1988	Authored and impler
1986-1987	Conducted Gifted W	1986-1987	Conducted Gifted W
	1986 University of N		1986 University of N
	1986 Creighton Univ		1986 Creighton Univ
	1987 Yutan Public S		1987 Yutan Public S
1970-present	Reading Coordinator of materials	1970-present	Reading Coordinator of materials

1. **Select the text** under **Related Experiences** again.

2. Drag the **bottom triangle** (Hanging Indent marker) of the left margin marker on top of the tab you set in the last step. The indent marker has two parts. The ⌂ affects the position of text that wraps to the next line. The ▽ affects the position of the first character. (You'll learn more about hanging indents on page 61.)

   The text that wrapped to a second line is indented (lined up) on the indent marker.

More Tabs

The Sponsored and Coaching sections need tabs to improve their readability and appearance.

Sponsored:		Coaching:	
Elementary Student Council 10 years		Volleyball 3 years	
7th Grade Class 2 years		Track 10 years	
8th Grade Class 1 year			
9th Grade Class 5 years			
Cheerleaders 2 years			
Education		**Professional Organizations**	
College:	University of Nebraska Lincoln	Phi Delta Kappa	
Degree:	Master of Education 1986	Association for Supervision and Curriculum	
Major:	Curriculum and Instruction, Gifted Education	Arizona Association for the Gifted Arizona State Education Association National Education Association	
College:	Wayne State College		
Degree:	Bachelor of Arts in Education 1969		
Major:	Elementary Education		

1. **Select** the headings and text under **Sponsored:** and **Coaching:**. Click a **left tab** at **3"**.

2. **Select** the **headings and text** under **Education** and **Professional Organizations**. Click **left tabs** at **3/4"** and **3 1/2"**.

Finding and Changing Text

1. To change the name on the résumé, click the **Edit** menu and select **Replace** or **press** [CTRL][H] (Windows) [⌘][H] (Macintosh).

2. A dialog box appears. Type **Jolene Peterson** in the **Find what** box. Press the **Tab** key. Type **your name** in the **Replace with** box.

3. Click the **Find Next** button. The computer finds the name. If the dialog box covers up the name, click and drag on the dark or striped title bar to move the box so that you can see behind it.

When the computer selects the name Jolene Peterson, click the **Replace** button. It replaces Jolene's name with yours!

4. Click the **Find Next** button to see if there are any other occurrences of Jolene's name. When there are no others, click **Close**.

Windows   Macintosh X   Macintosh 9, 8, 7

Drawing Lines for Emphasis

1. Scroll to the **top of your document**. Choose the **Straight Line** tool from the **Drawing** toolbar.

3. Hold down **SHIFT** and **drag the cursor** just above the address lines to **draw a line from margin to margin**. The Shift key forces a straight line. Release the mouse button before the Shift key. Do the **same below the address lines**. *Note:* Use the arrows on the keyboard to move the line up and down.

Previewing the Document

XP, 2000, 97
98   *X, 2001*

1. Click the **Print Preview button** or click the **File** menu and choose **Print Preview** so that you can see the entire document.

2. Click the **Print icon** or **Close** in the new **toolbar**.

Creating a Résumé Using the Templates and the Wizard

1. Click the **File** menu and choose **New**.

2. **XP** users, click **General Templates** in the **New from template** section of the **Task Pane**. Click the **Other Documents tab**. You can choose a résumé template or use the Resume Wizard.

XP

2000, 97 and 98 users, click the **Other Documents tab**. You can choose a résumé template or use the Resume Wizard.

X, 2001 users click the **File menu** and choose **Project Gallery** and then click the **Home Essentials**, and **Resumes**. You can choose a résumé template.

3. **Click a few templates** to see how they look.

Letterheads

Create Your Own Stationery

It's easy to make attractive and professional-looking letterhead stationery using *Word*. Follow these directions to make your own!

> ### This Activity Covers the Following Topics
> * Changing the Margins
> * Inserting a Text Box
> * Inserting WordArt
> * Inserting Clip Art
> * Saving as a Template
> * Using a Template

Changing the Margins

Letterhead text and graphics do not start 1" from the top of the page in stationery you buy. Instead, they usually start closer to the top. The default *Word* document has 1" top and bottom margins and 1.25" side margins. The first thing to do when creating letterheads is to change the margins.

1. Create a new *Word* document.

2. Click the **File** menu and choose **Page Setup** (Macintosh users click the **Format** menu and choose **Document**).

3. Give the document a **Top** margin of **.5"** and side margins of **1"**. Click **OK**.

4. Press ⏎**ENTER** (Windows) ⏎**RETURN** (Macintosh) **10** times to move the cursor down. The space above the carriage returns will contain the letterhead text and graphics. You'll begin typing at the cursor location. This can be modified later if needed.

Inserting a Text Box

XP, 2000, 97
98   *X, 2001*

1. Click the **Text Box** icon or click the **Insert** menu and choose **Text Box**.

2. Drag to **draw a text box** in the upper left corner of the page. Type **Notes from**.

3. Select the text. Choose **18** from the **Font Size** box. `18 ▾`

4. The text box is outlined with a thin line. You're going to remove it. Click the arrow next to the **Line Color icon** and choose **No Line**.

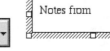

Inserting WordArt

1. Click the **WordArt icon** or click the **Insert** menu, choose **Picture**, and then **WordArt**.

Special letterheads for students to use can be created to motivate them, e.g., spelling lists, math worksheets.

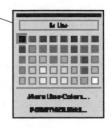

2. Double-click a **WordArt style** you like.

3. Type **your name** in the highlighted text box. Click **OK**.

4. Click the **Arrow** tool on the **Drawing toolbar**. Drag the two elements to an attractive arrangement.

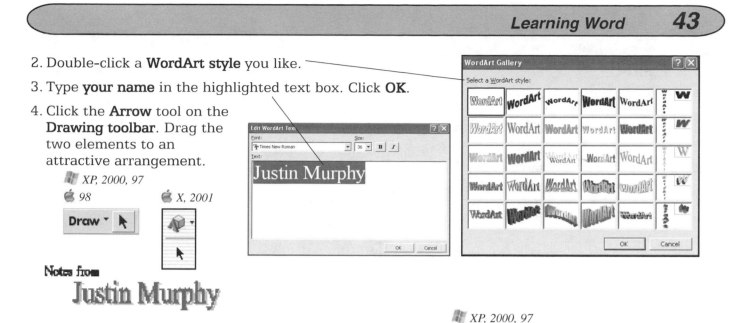

XP, 2000, 97

98   *X, 2001*

Notes from

Justin Murphy

Inserting Clip Art

XP, 2000, 97

98   *X*   *2001*

1. Click outside of the text box, then click the **Clip Art icon** or click the **Insert** menu, choose **Picture**, and then **Clip Art**. The clip art palette appears. When Microsoft *Office* or *Word* is installed, a small number of clip art images are loaded. There are tons of good clip art images on the *Office* CD-ROM that are not loaded. You must have the *Office* CD-ROM in the drive to access these images. Ask your computer specialist to install them onto your computer.

XP | *This section is for Word XP users only. Users of other versions go to your section of this activity.*

Find the section that covers YOUR version of Word. Follow the directions for that section.

2. The **Insert Clip Art task pane** appears. Click **Clip Organizer** at the bottom of the screen.

3. Click the **+** next to the **Office Collections folder**. A list of clip art folders appears.

4. Click a **folder**. Images appear on the right side. Click the arrow on the bar to the right.

5. Choose **Copy** to duplicate the image.

6. Click the *Word* document behind the Clip Organizer.

7. **Right-click** and choose **Paste**.

8. **Right-click** the image and choose **Format Picture**. Click the **Layout tab** and choose **In front of text**.

9. Drag the picture so that the letterhead looks great. Turn to **Saving As a Template** on page 45.

Notes from *Justin Murphy*

2000 *This section is for Word 2000 users only. Users of other versions go to your section of this activity.*

2. Click a **folder** image (e.g., **Academic**). Clip art with a matching theme appears providing a palette of choices. Click the **image you wish to use**.

3. A graphic menu appears. Click the **top choice** to insert the clip art, then close the window (click the X) in the title bar. You may click  to go back to the previous screen.

4. **Right-click** the image and choose **Format Picture**. Click the **Layout tab** and choose **In front of text**.

5. Drag the picture so that the letterhead looks great. Turn to **Saving As a Template** on page 45.

Notes from  Justin Murphy

 97 ● 98 *This section is for Word XP 97 and 98 users only. Users of other versions go to your section of this activity.*

2. Click a **category** from the left side (e.g., **Academic**). Clip art with a matching theme appear providing a palette of choices. **Double-click** the **image you wish to use**.

3. Drag the picture so that the letterhead looks great. Turn to **Saving As a Template** on page 45.

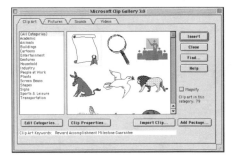

Notes from
 Justin Murphy

 ● X, 2001 *This section is for Word X and 2001 users only. Users of other versions go to your section of this activity.*

2. Click a **category** from the left side (e.g., **Academic**). Clip art with a matching theme appears providing a palette of choices. **Double-click** the **image you wish to use**.

3. **Right-click** the image and choose **Format Picture**. Click the **Layout tab** and choose **In front of text**.

4. Drag the picture so that the letterhead looks great. Turn to **Saving As a Template** on page 45.

Notes from
Justin Murphy

Most schools purchase Office without buying a CD-ROM for each computer. To use all the images, you need to borrow the CD-ROM from the computer administrator or ask to have the clip art images loaded on your computer or on a server.

Saving As a Template

Word gives you the option of saving a file as a template. When you open a template, a copy of the original file is opened, preventing the original document from being altered.

1. Click the **File** menu and choose **Save As**.

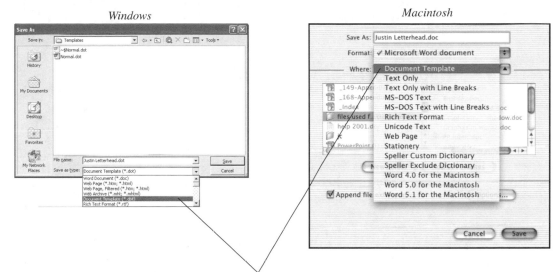

Windows   *Macintosh*

2. Click the **Save File as Type** (**Format** on Macintosh computers) menu and choose **Document Template**.

3. Give the file a **name you'll recognize as the name of your letterhead**. The file is saved in the templates folder.

Using a Template

XP, 2001, 97 98

1. Click the **File** menu and choose **New**.

2. XP users, click **General Templates** from the **New from template** section of the **Task Pane**. 2000, 97 and 98 users, skip this step.

3. Click the **General Templates tab**. **Double-click the file** to open it.

X, 2001

1. Click the **File** menu and choose **Project Gallery**.

2. Click **My Templates**. **Double-click the file** to open it.

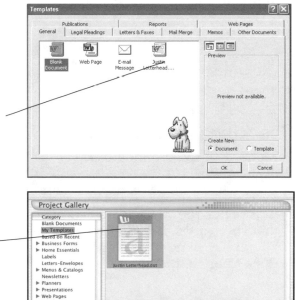

Spelling and Grammar Check

Learn to Check Spelling and Grammar

Spelling and grammar checkers will never replace our brains, but they can help us find many mistakes. This activity will show you how to use the spelling and grammar checkers in *Word*.

> ### This Activity Covers the Following Topics
> * Checking Spelling for One Word
> * Checking Grammar for One Word
> * Checking Spelling for the Document
> * Checking Grammar
> * Spelling and Grammar Options

Checking Spelling for One Word

You can check a single word for spelling or grammar as you type by right-clicking the word (Macintosh users **CTRL**-click.). *Word* underlines a word with a red wavy line if it thinks the word is misspelled. It underlines the word with a green wavy line if it thinks there is a grammatical error.

1. Open the file "Spell Check Assign" from the "Learning Word" folder on the CD-ROM that came with this book. Words that the spell checker doesn't recognize have a wavy red line under them. Grammatical errors have a wavy green line.

2. **Right-click** the misspelled word "**buton**" at the beginning of the fourth line (Macintosh users **CTRL**-click) and **choose the correct spelling**.

If you don't see wavy red and green lines, the Spelling and Grammar option has been turned off. Turning Off Automatic Spelling and Grammar Checking on page 52 tells you how to turn it back on.

Checking Grammar for One Word

1. **Right-click** the grammatically incorrect word **when** at the beginning of the second sentence (Macintosh users **CTRL**-click). Choose **About This Sentence** from the choices.

2. **Right-click** the word again and choose **Grammar**. Notice that the word *Capitalization* appears above the sentence. You already know what's wrong, but this is a reminder. Click **Change**, then **Close**.

Checking Spelling for the Document

Click the **Spell Check** button or click the **Tools** menu and choose **Spelling and Grammar** (Windows users can also press F7). Use the commands on the next page to check the spelling and grammar in the document.

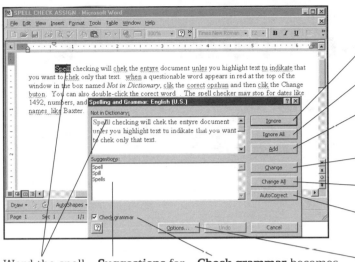

Ignore the spell checker suggestions because the word is spelled correctly.

Ignore All suggestions because the word is spelled correctly.

Add this word to the user dictionary, so the spell checker will recognize it as a correctly spelled word. Use this feature for names and unusual words you use frequently.

Change the unknown word to the selected suggestion or double-click the correct spelling.

Change All words spelled this way to the selected suggestion.

AutoCorrect lets you add a selected word to the AutoCorrect list.

Options lets you customize Spelling and Grammar checking.

Word the spell checker doesn't recognize.

Suggestions for correct spelling.

Check grammar becomes inactive if the check is removed.

Checking Grammar

If the Office Assistant is visible, an explanation of rules for the suggestion is shown.

Capitalization
Capitalize the first word of a sentence.

• Instead of: it usually snows in November.
• Consider: It usually snows in November.

• Instead of: does this book belong to you or to the library?
• Consider: Does this book belong to you or to the library?

Ignore the suggestions and leave it as typed.

Ignore Rule and leave it as typed.

Next Sentence moves to the next sentence and makes no changes.

Change accepts the suggestion or you can double-click the suggestion.

Undo the change you just made.

Sentence with a possible grammar error.

Indication of the type of grammar error.

Suggested correction for the error.

If the Office Assistant isn't visible, click the icon.

Spelling and Grammar Options

1. Click the **Options** button and explore the options. You may wish to change items to customize this feature to meet your needs.

2. Press [ENTER] (Windows) [RETURN] (Macintosh) or click **OK** when the window tells you it is finished.

You can turn off automatic spell checking of the document. Turn to page 52 to see another way to access these options and others.

Word checks the document to match the tone you choose.

Microsoft Word
The spelling and grammar check is complete.
OK

Human Brain
Not Yet Obsolete

Eye halve a spelling chequer,
It came with my pea sea.
It plainly marques four my revue
Miss steaks eye kin knot sea.

Eye strike a key and type a word,
And weight four it two say
Whether eye am wrong oar write;
It shows me strait a weigh.

As soon as a mist ache is maid,
It nose bee fore two long,
And eye can put the error rite;
Its rare lea ever wrong.

Eye have run this poem threw it.

Author Unknown

*As you can see, relying on spelling and grammar
checkers, and not proofreading, will cause problems!*

Use the Thesaurus

Learn to Use the Thesaurus

Word has a built-in thesaurus that is easy to access and easy to use!

> ### This Activity Covers the Following Topics
> - Replacing a Word
> - Looking Up a Word Within the Thesaurus

Replacing a Word

1. Open the file "Common Nouns" from the "Learning Word" folder on the CD-ROM that came with this book.

2. ▩ 2000, 97 and 98 users, skip to step 3. **Right-click** the word **car**, choose **Synonyms**, then **van**. Macintosh users [CTRL]-click. Car is replaced with van.

3. **Double-click** the word **house**. Click the **Tools** menu and then **Thesaurus** (▩ 97 and 98 users, click the **Tools** menu, choose **Language**, and then **Thesaurus**) (Windows users can also press [SHIFT]F7; Macintosh users can also press [⌘][OPTION][R]). Users of all versions except ▩ 97 can also right-click the word and choose **Synonyms**.

4. A list of meanings for the word **house** appears on the left side. Both nouns (n.) and verbs (v.) are shown. Synonyms for the word are on the right. Click the word **home** on the right side. New synonyms appear on the right side.

5. Click **residence** in the right column. Click **Replace**, and **residence** appears in the document.

Looking Up a Word Within the Thesaurus

1. **Right-click** the word **sack** and choose **Synonyms**, then **Thesaurus**. (▩ 97 and 98 users, **double-click** the word, then click the **Tools** menu, choose **Language**, and then **Thesaurus**.)

   A list of meanings are on the left side. Synonyms for **sack** are on the right with the word **bag** selected.

2. Click **Look Up** to find synonyms for **bag**.

3. Click **a synonym** in the list on the right. Click **Replace**.

Customize *Word*

Make *Word* Easier for Beginners

Word has many unique features that make it one of the best-known word-processing programs in the world. It is a very visual program. Many formatting and editing features are available as buttons as well as in the menus. *Word* also provides intuitive help. For example, as you type, *Word* marks unknown words and grammatical errors with wavy lines. It also corrects common typos, and repeats paragraph formatting (e.g., if you type "teh," *Word* will change it to "the"). If you begin a paragraph with a number (e.g., 1., in the next paragraph *Word* will type the "2"), and indent as you did in the previous paragraph. Sometimes this help can be overwhelming for the new user. *Microsoft* allows you to customize *Word* to meet your needs. Don't worry, anything you change can be turned back on! In this activity you'll add frequently used buttons, create a button bar for primary-level students, try some of these unique text features, and then turn them off and on.

> ### This Activity Covers the Following Topics
> - Adding a Button to a Toolbar
> - Removing Buttons
> - Creating a New Toolbar for Primary Students
> - Viewing Only the Primary Students Toolbar
> - Changing Icons to a Large Size
> - Turning Off Automatic Spelling & Grammar Checking
> - Changing the Text Selection Options
> * Changing the Graphic Options ⊞ XP Only
> - Changing the Overtype Mode
> - Changing the View Options
> - Using AutoCorrect
> - Adding an AutoCorrect Entry
> - Using AutoFormat
> - Apply As You Type
> - Ordinals with Superscript
> - Changing the Default to 1" Margins

Adding a Button to a Toolbar

As you use *Word*, you'll find that there are certain activities that you do over and over. You can perform some of these activities more quickly if you click them in the Standard, Formatting, or Drawing toolbars (these toolbars are usually visible on the screen). It is easy to add frequently used buttons to the toolbars.

1. Create a new *Word* document. Click the **View** menu, choose **Toolbars**, and then **Customize**. You're going to add a clip art button to the Standard toolbar.

2. Click the **Commands tab**.

3. Many of the categories match menu titles. You would click the Insert menu to insert clip art, so click **Insert** from **Categories** to find the clip art button in **Commands**.

4. Scroll down in the **Commands** section until you find the **Clip Art** command.

5. Drag the **Clip Art** icon up to the **Standard toolbar**.

Before   *After*

6. Adding frequently used Formatting commands can make using *Word* faster. Click **Format** from **Categories**.

7. Drag **Change Case, Double-Spacing, and Drop Cap** into the **Formatting toolbar**. Click **Close.**

8. Click the **Double-Spacing** button and type two lines of text (without pressing ⌨ENTER (Windows) ⌨RETURN (Macintosh)). The text is double-spaced.

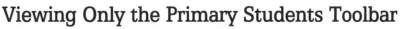

Removing Buttons

If there are buttons that you never use, you may wish to remove them to simplify the toolbar. Don't worry, any buttons you remove can be added again later.

Press ⌨ALT (Windows) ⌨⌘ (Macintosh) and drag the **Change Case** button down from the toolbar.

Creating a New Toolbar for Primary Students

The toolbar may be the easiest way for beginners and students in primary grades to manipulate *Word*. The **Standard toolbar** contains so many buttons that it may be confusing.

1. Click the **Tools** menu and choose **Customize**. Click the **Toolbars tab**.

2. Click **New.** Name the new toolbar **Primary Grades**. Click **OK**. A new toolbar appears. It is shaped like a square and only a few letters of the name appear. It grows as you add buttons.

4. Click the **Commands** tab.

5. **Drag buttons** beginners will use **onto the toolbar**.

Viewing Only the Primary Students Toolbar

1. Click the **View** menu and choose **Toolbars**.

2. **Remove the checks from all toolbars** except **Primary Grades**.

3. Click the blue title bar (striped in Macintosh) and **drag the title bar into the proper place** above the document if necessary. *Note:* This simplified toolbar can be modified at any time.

Changing the Icons to a Large Size

1. Large icons can help some students. Click the **View** menu and choose **Toolbars**, then **Customize**.

2 Click the **Options tab (Appearance** in 2001) and click **Large icons**. Click again to return the icons to their regular size. Click **Close**.

Creating toolbars specific to your students' abilities can save time and frustration for both the students and yourself.

Turning Off Automatic Spelling and Grammar Checking

1. Open the file "Spell Check Assign" from the "Learning Word" folder on the CD-ROM that came with this book. Because it has so many errors, the paragraph is filled with red and green wavy lines. Documents your students type may look like this too, which makes concentrating on their writing difficult. You can turn them off and students can check the spelling and grammar when they are finished writing.

2. ⊞ XP 2000, 97 users, click the **Tools menu** and choose **Options**. ⬤ 98 users choose **Preferences**. ⬤ 2001 users, click the **Edit** menu and choose **Preferences**. ⬤ X users, click the **Word** menu and choose **Preferences**.

3. Click the **Spelling & Grammar tab**.

4. Click the box next to **Check spelling as you type** to remove the check mark and click **OK**.

5. Type a **misspelled word** and press the **Spacebar**. No wavy red line appears. You can still check the spelling when you want to. You can remove **Check grammar as you type** by removing the check at the bottom of the window.

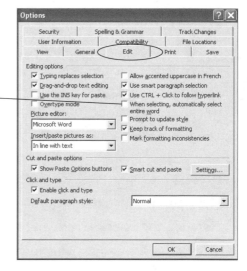

Changing the Text Selection Options

1. Open the **Options** or **Preferences** as you did above. Click the **Edit tab**. The *Word* default is to select an entire word whenever you drag in any part of it. You can change this to select only part of it (e.g., select the Mon in Monday so that you can change it to Tuesday). Here's how you do it.

2. Click **When selecting, automatically select entire word** to remove the check mark.

Changing the Graphic Options ⊞ XP Only

1. Click the **Edit tab**. The *Word* default is to insert or paste graphics as in-line graphics. The graphic pushes text to the right and *Word* sees it as a letter or a word. ⊞ XP allows you to change this option.

2. Click the **arrow** to the right of **In line with text** and choose **In front of text**. Click **OK**.

3. **Insert a piece of clip art or paste a picture** into the document. The graphic will be surrounded with white circle handles to indicate it is floating. You can move it anywhere on the page. If you have text in the document, the graphic floats in front of the text. You can format the picture so that text wraps around it as you like. Turn to page 75 to learn more about text wrapping.

These options remain turned off until you turn them back on. This action will affect every document you create, not just this document.

Changing the Overtype Mode

If you click in the middle of a line and type text, the old text moves to the right and the new text is inserted. This is called the Insert mode. If the old text is "eaten" instead of moving to the right as you type the new text, you are in the Overtype mode. Students have been known to change to the Overtype mode as a prank. Here's how you fix it.

1. Open the **Options** or **Preferences** as you did on page 52. Click the **Edit tab**.

2. A check in the **Overtype mode** box means you are in the overtype mode.

3. A quicker way to change modes uses the **Status Bar** at the bottom of the screen. Double-click **OVR** to switch between modes. You can also press the Insert button on the keyboard.

| Page 1 | Sec 1 | 1/1 | At 2.7" | Ln 5 | Col 5 | REC | TRK | EXT | OVR |

Changing the View Options

1. Open the **Options** or **Preferences** as you did on page 52. Click the **View tab**.

2. Make sure both the **Horizontal scroll bar** and **Vertical scroll bar** are checked. Students have been known to remove the checks from these boxes. It can really confuse users if the scroll bars are missing.

Using AutoCorrect

The AutoCorrect feature in *Word* automatically detects and correct spelling, typographical, grammar, and capitalization errors. For example, if you type studnet, and press the Spacebar, AutoCorrect replaces your word with student.

1. Create a new *Word* document. Type **tthe**. While looking at the screen, press the Spacebar. **The** appears because tthe is one of the common typos entered into the AutoCorrect feature. The word is capitalized because **Capitalize first letter of sentence** is a default in **AutoCorrect**.

2. Type **DOg**. Again, look at the screen and press the Spacebar. **Dog** appears.

Adding an AutoCorrect Entry

1. By adding to the AutoCorrect list, you can make *Word* type frequently used words for you (for example, the name of your school). Click the **Tools** menu and choose **AutoCorrect Options** (**AutoCorrect** in some versions).

2. Type **jj** in the **Replace** box.

3. Type **Jefferson High School** in the **With** box.

4. Click **Add** and then **OK**.

5. Type **jj**. **While looking at the screen**, press the **Spacebar**. Jefferson High School appears.

Using AutoFormat

The AutoFormat feature in *Word* "memorizes" formatting in a paragraph and repeats it in the next.

1. Create a new *Word* document.

2. Type **1. Red** and press [ENTER] (Windows) [RETURN] (Macintosh). "2." appears because AutoFormat copies the format you defined in the previous line.

Apply As You Type

1. Click the **Tools** menu and choose **AutoCorrect Options** (**AutoCorrect** in some versions).

2. Click the **AutoFormat As You Type** tab.

3. Click the box next to **Automatic numbered lists** to remove the check mark. Click **OK**.

4. Type **1. Red** and press [ENTER] (Windows) [RETURN] (Macintosh). The number 2 will not appear because you removed the check mark from Automatic numbered lists.

Ordinals with Superscript

Word automatically corrects a number of things when you type. This is usually helpful, but if you don't like it, you can turn off these defaults in the AutoCorrect menu. Here is an example that shows you how.

1. Create a new *Word* document.

2. Type **1st** and press [ENTER] (Windows) [RETURN] (Macintosh). The "st" changes to superscript.

3. Click the **Tools** menu and choose **AutoCorrect**.

4. Click the **AutoFormat As You Type** tab.

5. Click the box next to **Ordinals (1st) with superscript** to remove the check mark.

6. Click **OK**.

7. Type **1st** again to see the difference.

Changing the Default to 1" Margins

Most word processors have 1" margins as a default. *Word* has 1.25" left and right margins. If you prefer the standard 1" margins, you can change the default so that a new document has 1" margins.

1. Click the **File** menu and choose **Page Setup** (Macintosh users click the **Format** menu and choose **Document**).

2. Type **1"** in the **Left** and **Right** margin boxes.

3. Click the **Default** button. Click **Yes** when the message asks you if you want to change the default settings.

   All new documents will have 1" margins.

Show Formatting Characters

Now You Can See How Things Happen

Microsoft *Word* will show you not only every letter you pressed while typing, it will also show you where you pressed the Spacebar, Tab key, and Return key. This is called "Showing the Non-Printing Characters." You activate this feature by using the mouse or key commands.

> ### This Activity Covers the Following Topics
> - Preparing the Text
> - Showing the Formatting Characters

Preparing the Text

Open the file "Field Trip Letter Done" from the "Learning Word" folder on the CD-ROM that came with this book.

Showing the Formatting Characters

1. Click the **Show/Hide Non-Printing Characters** button ¶ on the **Standard toolbar**.

2. Using the **Non-Printing Character Key** on the right, interpret the text to see which keys were pressed. Notice the tab characters where you inserted tabs.

3. When you are finished, click the **Show/Hide Non-Printing Characters** button ¶ to hide the characters.

Formatting Character Key

→	Tab key was pressed
•	Spacebar was pressed
¶	Enter/Return was pressed

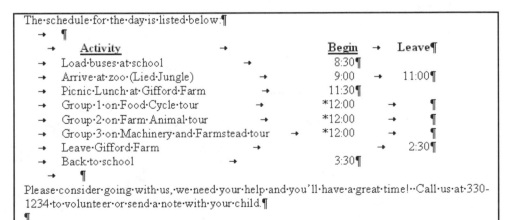

```
The·schedule·for·the·day·is·listed·below:¶
  →   ¶
    →   Activity          →           Begin  →   Leave¶
  →   Load·buses·at·school          →       8:30¶
  →   Arrive·at·zoo·(Lied·Jungle)       →       9:00   →   11:00¶
  →   Picnic·Lunch·at·Gifford·Farm      →       11:30¶
  →   Group·1·on·Food·Cycle·tour     →       *12:00   →       ¶
  →   Group·2·on·Farm·Animal·tour    →       *12:00   →       ¶
  →   Group·3·on·Machinery·and·Farmstead·tour   →   *12:00   →       ¶
  →   Leave·Gifford·Farm          →               →   2:30¶
  →   Back·to·school            →       3:30¶
  →   ¶
Please·consider·going·with·us,·we·need·your·help·and·you'll·have·a·great·time!··Call·us·at·330-
1234·to·volunteer·or·send·a·note·with·your·child.¶
¶
```

When students ask for help with a Word *document, click the **Show/Hide Non-Printing Characters** button to see which keys they have pressed. This solves the* ¶ *mysterious "I never touched a key and look what it did!" dilemma.*

Change the Case of Text

Make *Word* Correct Your Capitalization Errors

Have you ever been typing along, then stopped to look at the monitor only to find that you had the Caps Lock key down and everything was capitalized? Or have you ever told a student, "I'm sorry, you'll have to type the whole thing over again because it's all caps!"? *Word* makes it easy to change the case of text.

> ## This Activity Covers the Following Topics
> - Changing Text from Caps to Sentence Case
> - Changing Text from Sentence Case to Title Case
> - Changing Text from Title Case to tOGGLE cASE

Changing Text from Caps to Sentence Case

1. Create a new *Word* document.

2. Press ⌐CAPS LOCK⌐. Type the following text: "**DON'T YOU HATE IT WHEN YOU TYPE A WHOLE PARAGRAPH AND THEN DISCOVER THE CAPS LOCK KEY WAS PRESSED?**"

3. Select the text.

4. Click the **Format** menu and choose **Change Case**.

5. Click **Sentence Case**. Click **OK**.

> Don't you hate it when you type a whole paragraph and then discover the caps lock key was pressed?

Changing Text from Sentence Case to Title Case

1. Click the **Format** menu and choose **Change Case**.

2. Click **Title Case.** Click **OK**.

> Don't You Hate It When You Type A Whole Paragraph And Then Discover The Caps Lock Key Was Pressed?

Changing Text from Title Case to tOGGLE cASE

1. Click the **Format** menu and choose **Change Case**.

2. Click **tOGGLE cASE.** Click **OK**.

> dON'T yOU hATE iT wHEN yOU tYPE a wHOLE pARAGRAPH aND tHEN dISCOVER tHE cAPS lOCK kEY wAS pRESSED?

3. Click the **Format** menu and choose **Change Case**.

4. Click **lowercase**. Click **OK**.

5. Click the **Format** menu and choose **Change Case**.

6. Click **UPPERCASE**. Click **OK**.

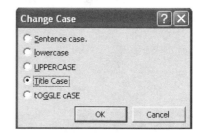

Use Comments

Use Comments to Give Feedback on Papers

Instead of handwriting feedback on student papers, use the Comments function of *Word* to type it. Students will love getting electronic feedback!

> ## This Activity Covers the Following Topics
> * Inserting Comments
> * Inserting an Audio Comment
> * Editing the Document
> * Viewing the Comments
> * Deleting a Comment

Inserting Comments

1. Open the file "Writing Assignment" from the "Learning Word" folder on the CD-ROM that came with this book.

2. **Double-click** the word **good** in the second paragraph.

3. Click the **Insert** menu and choose **Comment**.

4. The comments dialog box appears on the screen. The cursor is blinking in the **Comments From** box. Type **The word "well" is the correct choice**.

5. In XP, the comments are typed in the margin with a dotted line leading to the word in the Print Layout or Web Layout views. Jump to step 7 below.

> say both of her names out loud. She is tall and thin. She ha
> and dresses very good[JC1]. I am always proud to say she is r
> really mad sometimes, but I guess that is the way it is with a
> She works at JC Penny.
>
> ments From: [All Reviewers] [Close]
>
> [JC1]The word :well: is the correct choice

XP in Print Layout or Web Layout view

> named Mary Alice. I think it is a pretty name, but my mom really hates her
> She says it is old fashioned and ugly. I think it sounds pretty when you
> r names out loud. She is tall and thin. She has brown hair and hazel eyes
> :ry good. I am always proud to say she is my mom. She makes me really
> :s, but I guess that is the way it is with all mothers and daughters. She
> enny.
>
> **Comment:** The word "well" is the correct choice

All other users Click **Close**. The word "good" is highlighted in color to indicate a comment has been inserted.

6. Move the pointer over the word **good** without clicking the mouse button. The comment you inserted appears.

7. Click the word "**not**" in the third paragraph. This is a really long sentence that needs to be fixed.

8. Click the **Insert** menu and choose **Comment**. Type this comment: "**Try improving this sentence. Read it out loud and see if it is easy to read. Making it into two sentences may be a good idea.**" Click **Close** unless you're using XP.

> My mother is nar~~~ ~~~~~~ ~~~~ ~~~~ ~~ ~~~ pretty
> **Janet Caughlin:**
> middle name. Sh The word "well" is the correct gly. I
> say both of her n: choice. : thin.
> and dresses very good. I am always proud to say she i
> mad sometimes, but I guess that is the way it is with al
> works at JC Penny.
>
> but he is very pessimistic. When people meet him and ask him how he is (the way people
> always do) he always says, "Terrible, like always" and then they don't know what to say
> because they don't know if he means it or not[JC2]. He works for Union Pacific.
>
> My sister is Heather. She is 4 years older than me so she thinks she knows everything.
> She has long brown hair and brown eyes and is very pretty. She plays volleyball and
> softball and goes to the university. She lives at home, but I don't see her very often
> because of school and her job. She works at target[JC3].
>
> Comments From: All Reviewers [Close]
> [JC2]Try improving this sentence. Read it
> out loud and see if it is easy to read. Making
> it into two sentences may be a good idea.
> [JC3]Read this paragraph out loud. You'll
> notice that almost every sentence begins
> with the word "She." See what you can do
> to add variety. Target is a name so it needs a
> capital letter.

9. 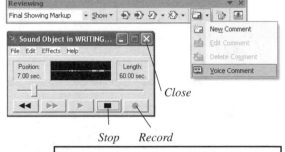 XP users, go to Inserting an Audio Comment below. Other users, click the last word in the fourth paragraph. Insert this comment: Click the **red record** button and **read** this comment: **Read this paragraph out loud. You'll notice that almost every sentence begins with the word she. See what you can do to add variety. Target is a name, so it needs a capital letter**. Go to Editing the Document instructions on this page.

Inserting an Audio Comment XP only (if you have audio input capabilities)

1. Click **after the last word in the fourth paragraph**. Click the **New Comment arrow** on the **Reviewing toolbar** and choose **Voice Comment**. If you don't see the toolbar, click the **View menu**, choose **Toolbars**, and then **Reviewing**.

2. Click the **red record** button and **read** this comment: **Read this paragraph out loud. You'll notice that almost every sentence begins with the word she. See what you can do to add variety. Target is a name, so it needs a capital letter**. Click the **Stop button**, and then click the **Close button**.

Close

Stop   Record

Editing the Document

1. So far, you've been the teacher who made suggestions. Now you're going to be the student who makes the edits. Move your **pointer over good** to see the comment.

2. **Click** to the **left of the word, good**, and **type the suggested word, well**. Both well and good are on the line. Sometimes it helps students to keep the comment until the changes are made in case they need to refer to it again.

3. **Click between** the word **good** and the **period**. Press the **Backspace** key (Macintosh users press the **Delete** key) to delete the comment and the original word.

    XP users, **double-click** the **Audio Comment icon** to hear the suggested edit, and then make the changes.

Viewing the Comments

1. There is another way to view comments. All comments will show in this method. Click the **View** menu and choose **Comment**.

2. Read the **second comment** and **fix the sentence**.

Deleting a Comment

Now that you've fixed the sentence, you no longer need the comment, but you don't want to delete the selected word.

1. **Right-click** the **comment** (Macintosh users `CTRL`-click).

2. Choose **Delete Comment**. The comment and the highlighting are removed.

Students will be eager to do Peer Editing if they can use the Comments function in Word to do it!

If the comments don't show when you move your pointer over the word, click the Tools menu and choose Options (Preferences in Macintosh versions). Click the View tab, and then Screen Tips.

Format Painter

Jazz Up a Worksheet

Formatting a document can be very time-consuming, especially if you make several changes to enhance the text. Using Format Painter can make this task incredibly easy and fun. This activity will show you how fun and easy formatting can be.

> **This Activity Covers the Following Topics**
> - Formatting the Text
> - Using Format Painter

Formatting the Text

1. Open the file "American Artists" from the "Learning Word" folder on the CD-ROM that came with this book.

2. Select the name "**John James Audubon.**"

3. Click the **Format** menu and choose **Font**.

4. Choose **Bold** from **Font style**, **16** from **Size**, and **Small caps** from **Effects**. Click **OK**.

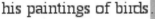

Using Format Painter

1. The name John James Audubon really stands out now, so you need to make the other artists look the same. With the name John James Audubon selected, **double-click** the **Format Painter** icon. The pointer changes to an "I-beam" with a paintbrush ("I-beam" with a + on Macintoshes) to indicate you are in the Format Painter.

2. Click "**John**" in John Singleton Copley. The word is formatted like the previous artist.

3. Select **Singleton Copley**. The words have the same format.

4. **Format** the **other artists' names** using **Format Painter**.

5. Click the **Format Painter icon** to turn Format Painter off.

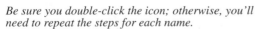

Be sure you double-click the icon; otherwise, you'll need to repeat the steps for each name.

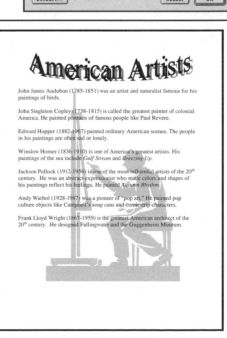

Set Tabs

Learn to Create a Schedule

Tabs can be frustrating until you learn to use them. Different tabs allow you to move text in different ways. This lesson will show you how they work.

This Activity Covers the Following Topic
- Setting Tabs

Setting Tabs

1. Open the file "Setting Tabs" from the "Learning Word" folder on the CD-ROM that came with this book.

2. **Highlight the text** under the heading **Different Types of Tabs & What They Do**.

3. Click the **1/2"** mark on the ruler. A left tab is inserted ⌊.

4. Click the **Tab Box** again to choose a **Center tab** ⊥.

5. Click the ruler's **2"** mark to insert the **Center** tab.

6. Click the **Tab Box,** and then a **Right tab** under the **3 1/2"** mark ⌟.

7. Click a **Decimal tab** under the **4 1/2"** mark on the ruler ⊥.

Left Tab

Center Tab

Right Tab

Decimal Tab

Bar Tab

Different Types of Tabs & What They Do

left	center	right	1.2345
lef	center	righ	12.345
le	center	rig	123.45
l	center	ri	1234.5
left	center	r	12345
lef	center	right	12345
le	cent	righ	1234
l	cen	rig	123
left	ce	ri	12
lef	c	r	1

When typing new documents, text won't move just because you set tabs in the ruler. You need to press the Tab key inside the text to move it. In this lesson, the text moved because tabs were put into the document by pressing the Tab key in front of each section when it was originally typed. The tab icons were then removed from the ruler. This allowed you to immediately see how different types of tabs change text location after you inserted them.

Notice how the text is aligned under each tab marker. The text under the Left tab is aligned on the left side. The text under the Center tab is centered under the tab. The text under the Right tab is aligned on the right side. The text under the Decimal tab is aligned on the decimal point. A vertical line appears under the bar tab.

8. **Scroll** down until the word **Schedule** is the top line on the screen. **Highlight the text under** the title **Schedule**.

9. Click a **Right** tab at **1 1/2"**, a **Left tab** at **2"**, and a **Decimal** tab at **4"**.

10. ⊞ XP, 2000 and X, 2001 users, click a **Bar** tab at **1 3/4"** and **3 1/2"**. ▮

Schedule

8:15	Nebraska History	20
9:09	American History	17
10:07	American History	19
11:00	Lunch	100
11:27	Nebraska History	17
12:24	Plan	
1:16	Geography	16
2:05	Geography	15

To remove a tab, drag the tab marker below the ruler and release the mouse.

Indent Text

Make a List That Wraps

You can tell *Word* to indent text for you. It saves you time and makes your documents look great. It's so easy!

> ### This Activity Covers the Following Topics
> - Indenting the First Line
> - Creating a Hanging Indent

Indenting the First Line

1. Create a **new** *Word* document.

2. Drag the **top triangle** (First Line Indent marker) of the **left margin marker** to the .5" mark on the ruler.

3. Type the **text in the screen shot below**. Read as you type to learn about this technique.

> The top triangle of the left margin marker controls the first character in a paragraph. If you move the top triangle to the right, all paragraphs will be indented without pressing the Tab key. When there is too much text to fit on one line, the words will wrap back to align with the bottom triangle. This will continue until you press the Enter/Return key.
> The first line after you press the Enter/Return key will be indented because it is controlled by the top triangle. Isn't this an easy way to indent all paragraphs?

Creating a Hanging Indent

1. Create a **new** *Word* document.

2. Drag the **bottom triangle** (Hanging Indent marker) of the **left margin marker** **one ruler mark to the right**. **Hint**: Place the pointer arrow on the triangle, not the rectangle.

3. Type **1**. Press `TAB`, then type the rest of the **text in the screen shot below** for point number 1. Do not press `ENTER` (Windows) `RETURN` (Macintosh) until the end of the sentence because it will cause the next line to return to the left margin.

4. **Type** the rest of the **text**. Read as you type to learn about this technique. Be sure to press `TAB` after each number and period!

> It is easy to make a list and indent text using Microsoft Word. Follow the directions below.
>
> 1. Place the mouse on the bottom triangle of the left margin marker. Drag it one ruler mark to the right.
> 2. Type "1." Press the Tab key to position the first line. The cursor will move under the triangle you just moved. Start typing. When there is too much text to fit on one line, the words will wrap to this marker. As you can see, the bottom triangle acts as a tab and also controls the text that wraps. Press Enter/Return.
> 3. After you press the Enter/Return key, the cursor moves under the top triangle because it controls the first character in a paragraph.
> 4. This is great for making lists.

Leader Tabs

Create a Short-Answer Test

Leader tabs draw a line from text to a tab location. For example, in tables of contents they are used to draw a dotted line from the title of the section to the page number. This activity will help you make a checklist and a form, using leader tabs to draw the lines.

> ### This Activity Covers the Following Topics
> - Preparing *Word* for This Activity
> - Changing Apply As You Type
> - Creating Leader Tabs
> - Using Leader Tabs
> - Creating a Form Using Leader Tabs

Preparing *Word* for This Activity

Word has some helpful options including AutoFormat. However, occasionally you need to turn them off to create a document. In this activity you will learn how to create a "short-answer" test with "answer" lines. To make *Word* draw the lines, you must modify the AutoFormat options.

Changing Apply As You Type

1. Create a new *Word* document.

2. Click the **Tools** menu and choose **AutoCorrect Options**.

3. Click the **AutoFormat As You Type** tab.

4. Click the box next to **Automatic numbered lists** to remove the check mark.

5. Click **OK**.

Creating Leader Tabs

1. Click the **Tab Box** 3 times to choose a **Decimal** tab.

2. Click the **1"** mark on the ruler to insert the **Decimal** tab.

3. Drag the **bottom triangle** (Hanging Indent marker) of the left margin marker to the **1 1/4"** mark.

4. Click the **Format** menu and choose **Tabs**.

5. Click the **radio button** next to **4** ____ in the **Leader** section of the box. This choice draws a line when you press the [TAB] key.

6. Click **Set**, and then **OK**.

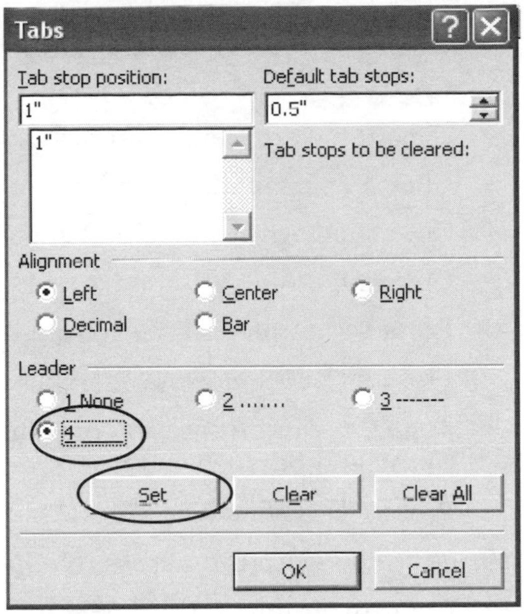

```
Tabs                                        [?][X]

Tab stop position:          Default tab stops:
1"                          0.5"                [▲▼]
┌─────────────────┐
│ 1"          [▲] │          Tab stops to be cleared:
│                 │
│             [▼] │
└─────────────────┘
Alignment ─────────────────────────────────────
   (•) Left          ( ) Center        ( ) Right
   ( ) Decimal       ( ) Bar
Leader ────────────────────────────────────────
   ( ) 1 None        ( ) 2 .......     ( ) 3 -------
   (•) 4 _____

        (   Set   )    (  Clear  )    ( Clear All )

                          [  OK  ]     [ Cancel ]
```

Using Leader Tabs

1. Press [TAB]. A line (leader) is drawn (see the screen shot below).

2. Press the **Spacebar twice**.

3. Type **9**.

4. Type **A leader tab will draw a line to the left of the tab position when the Tab key is pressed**.

5. Press [ENTER] (Windows) [RETURN] (Macintosh) **twice**.

6. Press [TAB]. A line (leader) is drawn.

7. Press the **Spacebar**.

8. Type **10**. *Note:* You only press the Spacebar twice if you are typing a single-digit number. The spaces take the place of the first digit. If you don't press the Spacebar, the lines for single-digit numbers will be longer than those for double-digit numbers.

9. **Type the text in the screen shot** below.

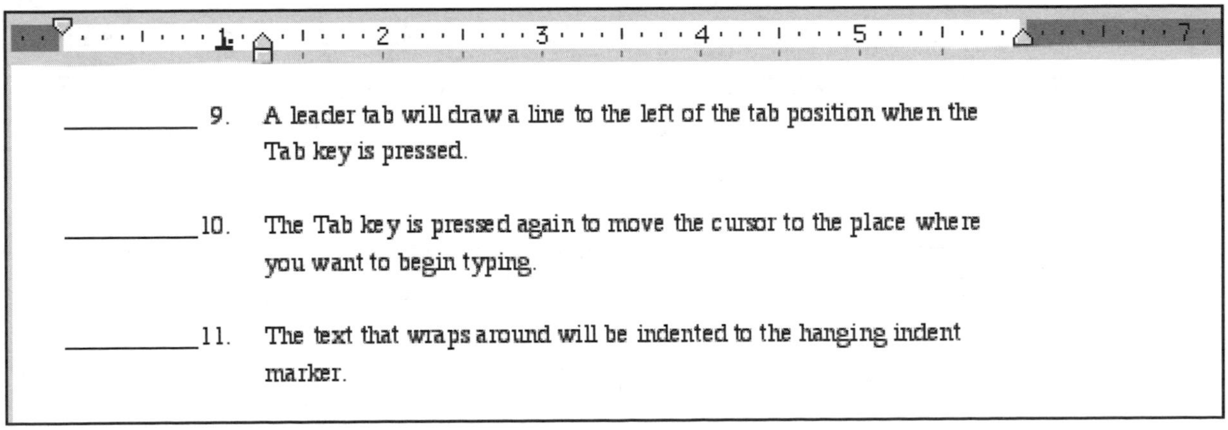

```
▽ · · · I · · · 1 · △ · I · · · 2 · · · I · · · 3 · · I · · · 4 · · I · · · 5 · · · I · · · △ · · · I · · · 7 ·

_____  9.   A leader tab will draw a line to the left of the tab position when the
                 Tab key is pressed.

_____ 10.   The Tab key is pressed again to move the cursor to the place where
                 you want to begin typing.

_____ 11.   The text that wraps around will be indented to the hanging indent
                 marker.
```

Creating a Form Using Leader Tabs

1. Create a new *Word* document.

2. Type the word **Name** and press the **Spacebar**.

3. Click a **Left** tab just to the **left of the right margin marker**.

4. Click the **Format** menu and choose **Tabs**.

5. Click the radio button next to **4 ___**. Click **Set**, and then **OK**.

6. **Press** [TAB]. A line is drawn from the space to the tab marker.

7. Press [ENTER] (Windows) [RETURN] (Macintosh) **twice**.

8. Type the word **Address**. Press the **Spacebar**. **Press** [TAB] to draw another line. The line goes to the end because you inserted that tab in step 2.

9. Press [ENTER] (Windows) [RETURN] (Macintosh) **twice**.

10. Type the word **City**. Press the **Spacebar**.

11. Click a **Left** tab on the **3 1/2"** mark.

12. Click the **Format** menu and choose **Tabs**.

13. **Select** the **3 1/2"** tab.

14. **Click** in the **solid line** radio button. Click **Set**, then **OK**.

15. Press [TAB]. A line is drawn.

16. **Type** the word **State** and press the **Spacebar**.

17. Click a **Left** tab on the **4 3/4"** mark.

18. Click the **Format** menu and choose **Tabs**.

19. **Select** the **4 3/4"** tab.

20. Click the **solid line** radio button. Click **Set**, then **OK**.

21. Press [TAB] to draw a line.

22. **Type** the word **Zip** and press the **Spacebar**.

23. Press [TAB] to draw a line. The line goes to the end because you inserted that tab in step 2.

24. Good job! Press [CTRL][S] (Windows) [⌘][S] (Macintosh) or click the **File** menu and choose **Save as** to save your file.

This has many steps, but it's easy–so don't get nervous!

Page Numbers, Headers/Footers

Put Automatic Page Numbers in a Document

You can automatically insert information such as the page number, title, and date on every page in a header or footer. A *header* appears at the top of every printed page in a document. A *footer* appears at the bottom of every page. This saves you time and give your document a finished, professional appearance. This activity will shows you how it all works.

> ### This Activity Covers the Following Topics
> • Inserting Automatic Page Numbers
> • Inserting a Page Break
> • Inserting a Header
> • Inserting a Fixed Date
> • Inserting a Changing Date
> • Using the Header and Footer Toolbar

Inserting Automatic Page Numbers

You can insert automatic page numbers anywhere in a document, but they usually appear in a header or footer.

1. Open the file "Field Trip Letter Done" from the "Learning Word" folder on the CD-ROM that came with this book.

2. Click the **Insert** menu and choose **Page Numbers**. The default **Position** for page numbers is **Bottom of page** and that's what we want.

3. The default **Alignment** is Right. Click the **arrow** and choose **Center**.

4. Click **OK**. **Scroll** to the **bottom of the page**. The number is light gray but it will print in black. The number is in a **footer,** so it will appear on the bottom of every page.

Inserting a Page Break

1. You can create a new page in a document. **Click at the beginning of the first paragraph**. You're going to insert a page break.

2. Click the **Insert** menu and choose **Break**.

    ⊞ XP, 2000, 97 and 98 users – The Break dialog box appears with **Page Break** selected. Click **OK**. The text after the cursor moves to a new page.

     X, 2001 users choose **Page Break**.

3. **Scroll down** to check out the footers. You'll see **1** on the **bottom of page 1**, and **2** on the bottom of **page 2**.

⊞ *XP 2000, 97,*
 98

 X, 2001

Page Break	
Column Break	⇧⌘↵
Section Break (Next Page)	
Section Break (Continuous)	
Section Break (Odd Page)	
Section Break (Even Page)	

Inserting a Header

1. Click the **View** menu and choose **Header and Footer**. The cursor is blinking in a header box at the top of the page.

2. Type **your name** in the header, then click **Close**. Your name appears at the top of each page.

Inserting a Fixed Date

1. **Select the date** at the top of the page.

2. Click the **Insert menu** and choose **Date and Time**. Click **OK**. Today's date appears in the place of the previous date. Choose the **date form in the screen shot**.

Inserting a Changing Date

Do you send out the same field trip announcements or letters every year? If you insert a changing date into the document, the current date will appear every time you open it. That way you won't have to manually change it.

1. **Select the date** at the top of the page.

2. Click the **Insert** menu and choose **Date and Time**. Click to insert a check mark in **Update Automatically**. Click **OK**. The date will look the same, but it will always show the date that you open the file.

Using the Header and Footer Toolbar

1. There are some great options on the Header and Footer toolbar. Click the **View menu** and choose **Header and Footer**.

2. Click the **Switch Between Header and Footer button on the toolbar**. The cursor moves to the footer at the bottom of the page.

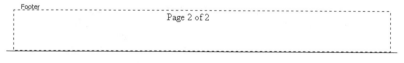

3. **Delete the page number**. You're going to put in a better one.

4. **Look at the ruler** at the top of the page. You'll see that a **center tab is set** in the middle of the footer and a right tab is set near the right margin. **Press** [TAB] to move the cursor to the middle of the footer box.

5. Click **Insert AutoText** in the **Header and Footer toolbar** and choose **Page X of Y**. Scroll to view both footers.

    Footer
    Page 2 of 2

6. **Experiment with the other buttons** in the toolbar.
   Click **Close** when you're finished.

The header and footer appear in a light gray color but they will print normally.

Create a Math Worksheet

Make a Fractions Worksheet for Your Class

Word has a built-in equation editor, so you can make professional-looking math worksheets. Follow these directions to make a math worksheet. You may need to install Microsoft Equation before you can complete this activity.

This Activity Covers the Following Topics
- Creating an Equation
- Editing the Equation
- Creating Other Fractions
- Modifying the Defaults

Creating an Equation

1. Create a new *Word* document.

2. Click the **Insert** menu and choose **Object**. There are many choices, so type **mi** to jump to the choices beginning with the letter m.

Microsoft Equation does not install automatically. You'll need to do a custom install.

3. Scroll down and choose **Microsoft Equation 3.0** and click **OK**. The Equation Editor toolbar appears.

4. Click the **second option from the left** in the **bottom row**, then choose the **first option on the left**.

5. Two boxes representing the number positions in a fraction appear. Type **2** and then press [TAB] to move the cursor down to the bottom box. Type **4**. (Macintosh types the text inside the Equation Editor box).

$$\frac{2}{4}$$

6. **Click outside the equation box** in the *Word* document (Macintosh users click the **Close** box in the upper left corner). The fraction appears on the page.

$$\frac{2}{4}$$

Editing the Equation

1. **Click** the **newly created fraction**. Handles appear. **Drag a corner handle** to increase the size of it.

2. You may find it easier to use the fraction if you can move it anywhere on the page. To do this, you need to convert fraction from an in-line graphic to a floating one. **Right-click** (Macintosh users [CTRL]-click) the fraction and choose **Format Object**.

3. Click the **Layout tab** and choose **In front of text**. Click **OK**. Now you can move the fraction around the page. You can also do this by clicking the Text Wrapping button on the Picture toolbar.

4. Double-click the **fraction**. The Equation Editor appears. Change the fraction.

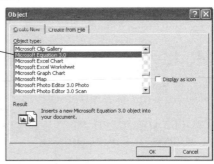

Creating Other Fractions

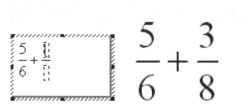

1. Click the **Insert** menu and choose **Object**, then **Microsoft Equation**, and click **OK**.

2. Again, choose the **fraction**. You're going to create a fraction addition problem. **Create a fraction**, then **click to the right of the fraction** and type **+**. Then **choose another white fraction** and **create a fraction**. **Click outside the box** (Macintosh users click the Close box.). The fractions appear as one graphic object.

$$\frac{5}{6} + \frac{3}{8}$$

3. **Double-click** the new fraction **problem**. It returns to the Equation Editor box. **Click to left of the first fraction** and type **1**. The fraction is too large for the whole number. Delete the whole number and click outside the box (Macintosh users click the **Close** box.)

4. Click the **Insert** menu and choose **Object**, then **Microsoft Equation**, and click **OK**.

5. Choose the **small black fraction** to the right of the previous one. You can tell by the size of the boxes that this fraction will be smaller.

6. **Create a fraction, click to the left** of the fraction, and type a **whole number**. **Click outside the box** (Macintosh users click the Close box.).

$$1\frac{5}{8}$$

7. Click the **Insert** menu and choose **Object**, then **Microsoft Equation**, and click **OK**.

8. Choose the same equation menu, but choose the **left icon on the bottom row**.

9. **Create** this division problem.

$$9\overline{)560}$$

Modifying the Defaults

If you are going to use the Equation Editor frequently, you can change the settings for the components so that you don't have to format each problem individually.

1. Click the **Insert** menu and choose **Object**, then **Microsoft Equation**, and click **OK**.

2. The menu changes when the Equation toolbar appears. Click the **Size menu** at the top of the screen (the menu bar changed to an Equation Editor menu) and choose **Define**.

3. The default font size is 12 pt. but you probably want a larger size for worksheets. Change the size in the **Full** box to **18** and click **OK**. **Apply** changes the default to your new choice.

4. Click the **Style menu** and choose **Define**. **Click each box** and see the choices. Click **OK**.

5. Click the **Format menu** and choose **Spacing**. **Click each box** and see the choices. Click **OK**.

📄 Document1 - Microsoft Word

File   Edit   View   Format   Style   Size   Window   Help

Sizes

Full	12 pt	
Subscript/Superscript	7 pt	
Sub-Subscript/Superscript	5 pt	
Symbol	18 pt	
Sub-symbol	12 pt	

$$(1+B)^2$$
$$\sum_{p=1} \mathbf{X}_{n_k}^{kp}$$

OK   Cancel   Apply   Defaults

Styles

Style	Font		Bold	Italic
Text	Times New Roman		□	□
Function	Times New Roman		□	□
Variable	Times New Roman		□	☑
L.C. Greek	Symbol		□	☑
U.C. Greek	Symbol		□	□
Symbol	Symbol		□	□
Matrix-Vector	Times New Roman		☑	□
Number	Times New Roman		□	□

OK   Cancel

Spacing

Line spacing	150%
Matrix row spacing	150%
Matrix column spacing	100%
Superscript height	45%
Subscript depth	25%
Limit height	25%

$$x = a$$
$$y = c$$

OK   Cancel   Apply   Defaults

Draw a Border

Make a Classroom Rules Poster

Borders can make simple text suitable for framing. They can also be used to emphasize text. *Word* provides many border options, allowing you to give your document just the right look.

> ### This Activity Covers the Following Topics
> - Preparing the Text
> - Indenting the List
> - Inserting a Graphic Border
> - Adding a Plain Page Border
> - Removing a Page Border
> - Adding a Shaded Title Border

Preparing the Text

1. Open the file "Golden Rule" from the "Learning Word" folder on the CD-ROM that came with this book. This file contains some "good sense" rules for cooperation. You're going to jazz it up to post it in your classroom.

2. It is easier to add borders if you can see the entire document. Click the **Zoom Box** on the **Standard toolbar** and choose **Whole Page**. You can see that much of the page is blank. You'll change that. Click the **Zoom Box** and choose **Whole Page**.

3. Press **CTRL A** (Windows) **⌘ A** (Macintosh) or choose **Select All** from **Edit** to select the text.

4. Choose a font that seems exactly right for the message of the text by clicking the **Font Box** or click the **Format menu** and choose **Font**. `Verdana ▾`

5. Click the **Font Size box** and choose **24** point. *Note:* Fonts are not all the same size. `24 ▾` If 24 point seems too large or the text moves to another page, you may need to choose a smaller size. Try the keyboard command **CTRL [** (Windows) **⌘ [** (Macintosh) to decrease the font size.

6. Select the **title** only and make it **larger**, then click the **Center** button ▤. Click the **Zoom Box** on the **Standard toolbar** and choose **Whole Page** to see how the text fits on the page. **Look at the screen shots below** so that you know how much space your text should take.

Indenting the List

1. **Select the text** under the title. The text on some lines wraps onto another line. It would look better if it was aligned under the first word of the rule.

2. Click a **Decimal tab** to align the numbers properly. `▭···ı·⊔·ı·1·ı···ı·2` **Note**: More information about inserting Decimal tabs can be found on page 60.

3. Drag the **bottom triangle** of the **Left Margin marker** to the **right of the tab** to align the text. `▭·ı···ı·⊔·△··ı···ı·2` **Note**: More information about using this hanging indent can be found on page 61.

Inserting a Graphic Border

1. Click the **Zoom box** on the **Standard toolbar** and choose **Whole Page**.

2. Click the **Format** menu and choose **Borders and Shading**.

3. Click the **Page Border** tab.

4. Click **Box** under **Setting**.

5. Click the menu under **Art** and choose a border. You may need to install this first.

6. Click **OK**.

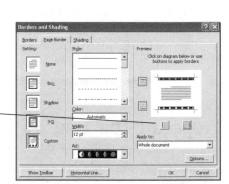

You don't have to border all sides. Click the Border boxes to see what they do.

Adding a Plain Page Border

1. Save the file if you like the border you just created. You're going to remove it because you don't want it for the next step. Click the **Undo button** on the **Standard toolbar** until you remove the border.

2. Click the **Format** menu and choose **Borders and Shading**.

3. Click the **Page Border** tab.

4. Click **Box** under **Setting**.

5. Choose a new **Style**.

6. Choose a new **Color** for the border and click **3 pt** from the **Width** menu. Click **OK**.

Removing a Page Border

1. Click the **Format** menu and choose **Borders and Shading**.

2. Click the **Page Border** tab and click **None** under **Setting**. Click **OK**.

Adding a Shaded Title Border

1. **Select the title** of the page **Practical Applications of the Golden Rule**. Click the **Format** menu and choose **Borders and Shading**.

2. Click the **Borders** tab and click **Box** under **Setting**.

3. Click the **Shading tab**. Choose a **light color** and click **OK**. The title is bordered and shaded. **Hint:** If your border doesn't look like the screen shot, make sure **Apply to:** in the bottom corner reads **Paragraph**.

Here's a rule-of-thumb for understanding borders: Borders are inside the margins while page borders are outside the margins.

Practical Applications of the Golden Rule

1. If you open it, close it.
2. If you turn it on, turn it off.
3. If you unlock it, lock it.
4. If you break it, repair it.
5. If you can't fix it, call someone who can.
6. If you borrow it, return it.
7. If you use it, take care of it.
8. If you make a mess, clean it up.
9. If you move it, put it back.
10. If it belongs to somebody else and you want to use it, get permission.
11. If you don't know how to operate it, leave it alone.
12. If it doesn't concern you, don't mess with it.

Bulleted Lists

Create Supply Checklists

Do you have trouble getting parents and students to follow through on supply lists you send home? Give them a list with boxes and they automatically start checking it off. In this activity you'll learn how to make all of your lists into checklists!

> ### This Activity Covers the Following Topics
> - Adding Bullets to a List
> - Adding Bullets to Part of a Document
> - Sorting the Text
> - Changing the Case of the Text
> - Adding Bullets to the List

Adding Bullets to a List

1. Open the file "School Supplies" from the "Learning Word" folder on the CD-ROM that came with this book.

2. Click the **Zoom box** on the **Standard toolbar** and choose **Whole Page**. **Select** (highlight) the **list**.

3. Click the **Format** menu and choose **Bullets and Numbering**.

4. Click the **Bulleted** tab.

5. Choose a square or round **checkbox list**. Click **Customize**.

6. Click the **Font** button and choose **22** from the **Font Size** choices.

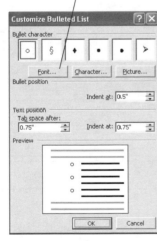

Larger boxes are more inviting to the user!

7. Click **OK**, then **OK** again.

Adding Bullets to Part of a Document

1. Open the file "Outdoor Ed Letter" from the "Learning Word" folder on the CD-ROM that came with this book.

2. **Select** (highlight) the **list of supplies in the middle of the letter**.

3. Following the directions above, **make this into a checklist**.

Sorting the Text

1. Open the file "Classroom Inventory" from the "Learning Word" folder on the CD-ROM that came with this book.

2. **Select** (highlight) the **list**.

3. Click the **Table** menu and choose **Sort**.

4. Click **OK**. The list is alphabetized. **Hint:** Numbers appear before letters when alphabetizing.

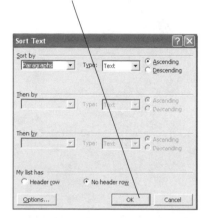

Changing the Case of the Text

This list would look better if it wasn't typed in all capital letters.

1. **Select** (highlight) the **list**.

2. Click the **Format** menu and choose **Change Case**.

3. Choose **Title Case** and click **OK**.

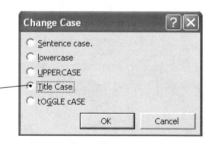

Adding Bullets to the List

1. Click the **Format** menu and choose **Bullets and Numbering**.

2. Click the **Bulleted** tab. Choose a **style** and click **Customize**.

3. Click the **Character button** (**Bullet** in X, 2001). Pictures connected to the font shown appear in a grid. Double-clicking any picture will choose it for your list. Try other fonts, especially Monotype Sorts, Webdings, Wingdings, and Symbol. **Double-click a picture**. Click **OK**.

Symbol

4. Select the **style** again, click the **Format** menu and choose **Bullets and Numbering** from the **Bulleted** tab. X, 2001 users, go to step 5. Other users, choose a **style** and click **Customize**.

5. Click the **Picture button**. Great-looking bullets appear. **Double-click a picture**. Click **OK**, then **OK** again.

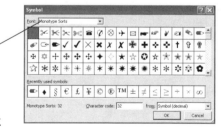

Picture

Section Breaks

Insert an Outline in Part of a Document

Have you ever wanted to put columns in just part of a document? Inserting a section break allows you to do this. Section breaks are also used to create different headers, footers, and page numbers, and to vary the number of columns in sections of a document.

> ### This Activity Covers the Following Topics
> - Learning About the Document
> - Inserting a Section Break
> - Inserting a Column Break

Learning About the Document

This letter informing parents of an upcoming assignment contains a list of items containing computer chips. It would take up less space if these items were in two columns.

1. Open the file "Computer Letter" from the "Learning Word" folder on the CD-ROM that came with this book.

2. Click on the first item in the list, **Video game**. Click the **Column button** [icon] and drag to select two columns. The entire document is in two columns, but only the list needs to be in columns. You can remedy this by inserting a section break.

3. Click the **Column button** again and reduce the columns to **one**.

Inserting a Section Break

1. Click to the **left** of the word **Video** in the list. Click the **Insert** menu and choose **Break**.

2. Choose **Continuous**. This forces the new section to begin on this line. Click **OK**. Nothing appears to happen.

3. Click the **Column button** and drag to select **two columns**. [icon]

4. The closing paragraph is at the bottom of the second column. Click to the **left** of **Your child...** and **insert a Continuous break**.

5. Click the **Column button** and select **one** column. [icon]

6. Press [ENTER] (Windows) [RETURN] (Macintosh) to insert a blank line between the columns section and the closing paragraph.

Inserting a Column Break

1. The first column has more text than the second. Click to the **left** of **Sprinkler System** at the bottom of the first column.

2. Click the **Insert** menu, choose **Break**, and then **Column break**. Click **OK**. This forces Sprinkler System to move to the second column.

Decorative Characters

Give Your Text a Formal Look

This feature in the *Word* program puts text creativity at your fingertips. Letters and numbers can become graphic works of art that set the mood for quotes or stories.

> ### This Activity Covers the Following Topics
> * Creating a Raised Initial Cap
> * Creating a Dropped Initial Cap

Creating a Raised Initial Cap

A raised initial cap is used to create a mood in a document. It is characterized by a noticeably taller first letter.

1. Create a new *Word* document.

2. Type in the following quote from Albert Einstein: **Great spirits have always encountered violent opposition**.

3. Click and drag to **select** the letter **G**.

4. Click the **Font Size** box 36 ▾ and choose **36** point. Either 24 or 36 point works well for an initial cap when you have 12-point text. The text below is 12 point and the "G" is 36 point.

5. Try different fonts until you find one that suggests the mood of the quote.

Creating a Dropped Initial Cap

A dropped initial cap is just what the name implies. The first letter is dropped below the baseline.

1. Create a new *Word* document.

2. Type the following text: **Love has been characterized by Einstein**. **He said, "Gravity cannot be held responsible for people falling in love."**

3. **Select** the text. Move the **Right Margin marker** to **1 3/4"** so that the quote will run on five lines.

4. Click the **Format** menu and choose **Drop Cap**.

5. Click **Dropped**. You can also change the Font if you wish. Click **OK**.

Learn About Graphics

Understand How Graphics Work

Graphics can add so much to a document. This activity helps you understand the wrap and editing options available in *Word*.

> ### This Activity Covers the Following Topics
> - Inserting Clip Art
> - Wrapping Square
> - Wrapping Tight Using the Toolbar
> - Wrapping Top and Bottom
> - Creating a Watermark
> - Cropping a Picture
> - Changing the Contrast and Brightness
> - Adding a Shadow
> * Inserting Another Picture
> - Using the Color/Image Control Button

Inserting Clip Art

1. Open the file "Graphics in Word" from the "Learning Word" folder on the CD-ROM that came with this book.

2. **Click at the beginning of the second paragraph.**

3. Click the **Clip Art** icon or click the **Insert** menu, choose **Picture**, and then **Clip Art**. XP users, click **Clip Organizer** at the bottom of the screen. Click the **+** next to the **Office Collections folder**. Click a **folder** from the list of clip art folders that appears. **Insert a picture**.

4. **Drag** a **corner handle** (one of the boxes surrounding the picture) **to resize** the picture so that it is **smaller than the paragraph**. See the screen shot below.

Wrapping Square

1. **Right-click** the picture (Macintosh users [CTRL]-click). Choose **Format Picture**. The Format Picture icon is also on the **Picture toolbar**.

2. Click the **Layout** tab (**Wrapping** in 97 and 98). Note that the chosen style is **In line with text** which means the graphic fits into the line like a big letter (e.g., Q. 97 and 98 users will find that **None** is the default).

3. Click the **Square** option and click **OK**.

4. **Move the picture** around and watch the text wrap around the picture in a square shape.

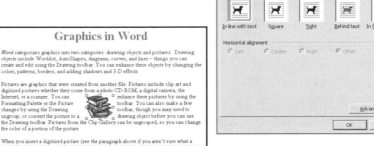

Wrapping Tight Using the Toolbar

1. Click the **Text Wrapping icon** on the **Picture toolbar** and choose the **Tight** option.

2. **Move the picture** around and watch the text wrap around the picture. The wrap is tighter than it was in the square wrapping style.

If the toolbar isn't showing, right-click anywhere in the menu bar and choose Picture from the list of toolbars. You can also click the View menu, choose Toolbars, and then Picture.

Wrapping Top and Bottom

1. Click the **Text Wrapping icon** on the **Picture toolbar** and click the **Top and Bottom** option. X, 2001 users, click the arrow on the right side of the toolbar to see the Text Wrapping icon.

2. **Move the picture down.** The wrap is on the top and bottom and always takes up the whole line.

Creating a Watermark

1. **Right-click** the picture (Macintosh users [CTRL]-click). Choose **Format Picture** and click the **Layout** tab (Wrapping in 97 and 98). Choose the **In front of text** option (None in 97 and 98). Click **OK**.

2. Click a **corner handle** and **drag to enlarge the graph**ic so that it **covers most of the first 3 paragraphs**.

3. **Right-click** the picture (Macintosh users [CTRL]-click). Choose **Format Picture** and click the **Picture tab**. Click the **arrow in Color** in the **Image control** section and choose **Watermark** (Washout in XP). The image fades to a watermark. Click **OK**.

4. **Right-click** the picture (Macintosh users [CTRL]-click). Choose **Format Picture** and click the **Layout tab**. Choose **Behind text** and click **OK**. Now you have a watermark behind the text.

   97 and 98 users, click the **Draw** button on the **Drawing toolbar**, choose **Order**, and then **Send Behind Text**.

Cropping a Picture

1. Click the **Insert menu**, choose **Picture**, and then **From File. Navigate** to the CD-ROM that came with this book. **Double-click** the **Pictures** folder, then **Animals**, then **Birds**, then "Cardinal Male."

2. Choose the **In front of text** as the **Wrapping option** (97 and 98 users choose **None**). **Note:** If the picture has inside handles, you may need to click the **Text Wrapping button** on the **Picture toolbar** and choose **Edit Wrap Points twice**. This makes the wrap points move to the outside.

3. This picture has lots of background at the top and bottom that could be cropped out. Click the **Cropping tool** on the **Picture toolbar**.

XP, 2000, 97

98

X, 2001

4. The cursor changes to a cropping cursor. Place this cursor on the **top center handle** of the picture and **drag down to just above the bird's head**. The picture is cropped as you drag.

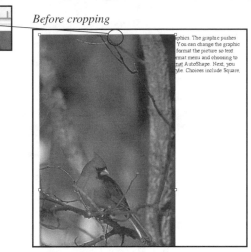
Before cropping

After cropping

5. **Crop** the **bottom** of the picture, and then move it under the text.

Changing the Contrast and Brightness

1. Click the **More Contrast button** on the **Picture toolbar**. Click it several times to see how it changes the picture.

2. Click the **Less Contrast button** on the **Picture toolbar** several times to see how it changes the picture.

3. Click the **More Brightness button** on the **Picture toolbar**. Click it several times to see how it changes the picture.

4. Click the **Less Brightness button** on the **Picture toolbar** several times to see how it changes the picture.

5. Using these four buttons, **make the picture look great**.

XP, 2000, 97
 98   X, 2001

XP, 2000, 97
 98   X, 2001

The brightness and contrast buttons can really improve pictures taken from the Internet.

Adding a Shadow

Click the **Shadow Style button** on the **Drawing toolbar** and **choose a shadow setting**.
 X, 2001 users will find the button on the **Picture toolbar**.

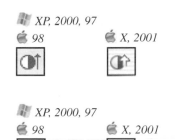

Inserting Another Picture

Click the **Insert Picture button** on the **Picture toolbar**. **Choose another picture**. X, 2001 users, find this button on the **Drawing toolbar**, too. As you see, this is a quick way to insert several pictures on a page.

XP, 2000, 97
 98   X   2001

Using the Color/Image Control Button

1. Click the picture you just inserted so that handles appear. Click the **Color button (Image Control** on Macintosh) on the **Picture toolbar**.

2. Choose **Grayscale**. This option lets you see what the image will look like if it is printed on a laser printer.

XP, 2000, 97   *X, 2001, 98*

Learn About Graphics 2

Understand How Graphics Work 2

You can make more advanced edits to graphics in *Word*. In this activity you'll learn to change the color of graphics, make special effects, crop a custom shape, and adjust color of graphics.

> ### This Activity Covers the Following Topics
> * Changing a Color in a Clip Art Image
> * Using Transparent Color
> * Using the Magic Lasso and Cutout Tools
> * Using the Color Adjustment Tool

Changing a Color in a Clip Art Image

1. Create a **new** *Word* document and **insert** a **multicolor clip art image**. You're going to change the color of a few pieces of the image.

2. ⊞ XP users, click the **Tools menu** and choose **Options**. Click the **General tab** and then click to remove the check from **Automatically create drawing canvas when inserting AutoShapes**. Click **OK**. Right-click the clip art image and choose **Edit Picture**. Other users skip to step 3.

   ⊞ *XP, 2000, 97*
   🍎 *98*   🍎 *X, 2001*

   Draw ⌄   ◻

3. Click the **Draw button** on the **Drawing toolbar** and choose **Ungroup**. The image suddenly has zillions of handles. **Click outside the image** to deselect it.

The numbers in the screen shot to the right correspond to the directions above and below.

4. **Click an element** of the clip art (in the example, the front cover of the top book). Click the **Fill Color icon** in the **Drawing toolbar** to change the color. Change any other colors you wish.

5. Click the **Select Objects arrow** on the **Drawing toolbar**. **Drag to draw a large selection box around the *entire* picture**. All the pieces become selected and the image has a zillion handles again.

   ⊞ *XP, 2000, 97*
   🍎 *98*   🍎 *X, 2001*

   Draw ⌄ ⇱   ◻

6. Click the **Draw button** on the **Drawing toolbar** and choose **Group**. The image has eight handles.

Using Transparent Color

1. Create a new *Word* document. Click the **Insert menu**, choose **Picture**, then **From File**. **Navigate** to the CD-ROM that came with this book. **Double-click** the **Pictures** folder, then **Animals**, then **Insects**, then "American Painted Lady." Set the **Wrapping Style** to **In front of text**.

2. Click the **Set Transparent Color button** on the **Picture toolbar**. This tool changes a selected color to transparent. If you have a picture that has a single colored background, you can make it transparent. However, in most photographs, what looks like

   ⊞ *XP, 2000, 97*
   🍎 *98*   🍎 *X, 2001*

a single color can actually be made from a group of colors. You can make only one color transparent, but changing this one color can really make a cool effect.

Before   *After*

3. Click a **purple color at the bottom of a flower**. Everything with the same shade turns transparent. If you don't like that effect, click the button again, and then click another part of the picture.

Using the Magic Lasso and Cutout Tools X, 2001 only

1. Create a new *Word* document. Click the **Insert menu**, choose **Picture**, then **From File**. **Navigate** to the CD-ROM that came with this book. **Double-click** the **Pictures** folder, then **Animals**, then **Mammals**, then "Bison." Set the **Wrapping Style** to **In front of text**.

2. Click the **Magic lasso button** on the **Picture toolbar**. Red handles appear around the picture. This tool magically clings to the edge of a picture so that you can select sections of it. Click **under the bison's nose**. **Without pressing the button**, move the mouse **up the edge of the nose** and **click** again. A line clings to the black edge of the nose.

Before   *After*

Click here

Begin here *Click here*

Cutout

3. Using this *click-release-move a little-click* method, draw a line around the bison's head, horn, and neck (see the finished picture). **Double-click** when you're **finished**.

4. Click the **Cutout button**. Everything around the selected area is cut out.

Using the Color Adjustment Tool X, 2001 only

1. Create a new *Word* document. Click the **Insert menu**, choose **Picture**, then **From File**. **Navigate** to the CD-ROM that came with this book. **Double-click** the **Pictures** folder, then **Animals**, then **Birds**, then "Cockatoo." Set the **Wrapping Style** to **In front of text**.

2. Click the **Color Adjustment tool**. Along with the Contrast and Brightness tools, this tool allows you to fine-tune pictures.

3. Drag the **Settings arrow** to the **left** until **one bird picture** on the bottom row **disappears**. Click **Apply**. The background and bird are a lighter color.

4. Use other options in the Color Adjustment tool, the brightness, and contrast to improve the picture.

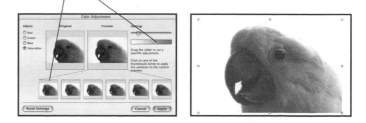

Symbols and Click and Type

Create a Temperature Conversion Chart

Sometimes you need to type symbols for words (e.g., degrees, copyright, trademark). In this activity you'll learn how easy it is to insert symbols into a document. You'll also learn about the Click and Type feature of *Word*.

> **This Activity Covers the Following Topics**
> - Inserting a Symbol
> - Using Click and Type  XP, 2000 and X, 2001 only

Inserting a Symbol

1. Open the file "Convert Temp" from the "Learning Word" folder on the CD-ROM that came with this book.

2. This file shows temperatures in both Farenheit and Celsius. The temperatures on the scale show the degrees symbol. You're going to insert the symbols for Freezing and the Human Body. Click to the **right of the 2 in 32**.

3. Click the **Insert menu** and choose **Symbol**.

4. Click the **Font** choices and choose **Symbol**.

5. Click the **degrees symbol**, click **Insert**, and then **Close**.

6. Insert degree symbols for the remaining Freezing temperature and the Human Body temperatures.

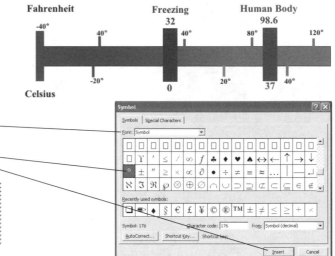

Using Click and Type  XP, 2000 and X, 2001 only

1. This file needs a title. **Double-click** in the **center at the top of the page**. The cursor blinks in the center of the page.

2. Choose **48** from the **Font Size box**.

3. Click the **Bold button**.

4. Type **Temperature Conversions**.

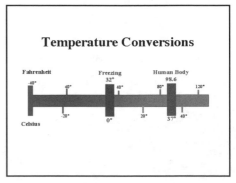

Insert a Picture from a File

Create a Graphic Study Guide

A picture is worth a thousand words. This is especially true when you're trying to teach a complicated topic. This activity will teach you to create a graphic worksheet for your students.

> ### This Activity Covers the Following Topics
> - Inserting a Picture from a File
> - Labeling the Picture
> - Creating Arrowhead Lines

Inserting a Picture from a File

1. Create a new *Word* document.

2. Click the **Font Size box** and choose **48**. ⌷48 ▾⌷

3. Click the **Center** button. Type **Parts of a Flower**. ☰

4. Press ⌨ENTER (Windows) ⌨RETURN (Macintosh) **twice** to move the cursor down.

5. Click the **Insert menu**, choose **Picture**, then **From File**.

6. Navigate to the **Pictures** folder on the CD-ROM that came with this book. Double-click the **Lily** picture.

7. **Right-click** (Macintosh users ⌨CTRL-click) the picture and choose **Format Picture**. Click the **Layout tab** (**Wrapping** in ⊞ 97 and 98) and choose **In front of text**. Center the picture on the page as shown in the screen shot.

Parts of a Flower

⊞ *XP, 2000, 97*

 98   *X, 2001*

Labeling the Picture

1. Click the **Text Box** icon from the **Drawing** toolbar or click the **Insert menu** and choose **Text Box**. Drag to draw a text box below the picture on the left side.

3. Choose **22** from the **Font Size** box.

4. Type **Petal** in the text box.

5. The text box is outlined with a thin line. Choose **No Line** from the **Line Color icon**.

6. Using this method, create labels reading **Stigma** and **Stamen**.

Creating Arrowhead Lines

⊞ *XP, 2000, 97*

 98   *X, 2001*

1. Click the **black Arrow** tool on the **Drawing toolbar**.

2. Hold ⌨SHIFT and drag to draw a line from the label **Petal** to a petal in the picture.

3. Click the **Line Style** icon and choose **2 1/4 pt**. ☰

4. Click the **Line Color** icon and choose a contrasting color.

5. **Draw arrows** from the **other two labels** to their corresponding parts.

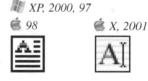

Parts of a Flower

Petal   Stigma   Stamen

Insert a Movie

Create a Self-Study Sheet with a Movie

As teachers, we're always trying to find new ways to motivate students. Why not make a self-study sheet to teach students a concept? In this activity you'll make a study sheet about butterflies and pollination that includes a movie of a butterfly getting nectar from a sunflower. You won't believe how easy it is to add a movie to a document!

> ### This Activity Covers the Following Topics
> - Preparing the File
> - Inserting a Movie into a File
> - Playing the Movie
> - Saving the File

Preparing the File

1. Open the file "Butterfly" from the "Learning Word" folder on the CD-ROM that came with this book. This file is a study sheet to teach students about butterflies. You're going to insert a movie into the space between the paragraphs.

2. **Place the cursor one line down** from the bottom of the first paragraph and **double-click**. Click the **Center justification button** on the **Formatting toolbar**.

Inserting a Movie into a File XP, 2000, 97

1. Click the **Insert menu**, and choose **Object**.

2. Click the **Create from File tab**.

3. Click **Browse.** Navigate to the **Movies** folder on the CD-ROM that came with this book.

4. Select **Butterfly.avi**, and click **Insert**. The movie appears in the middle of the page.

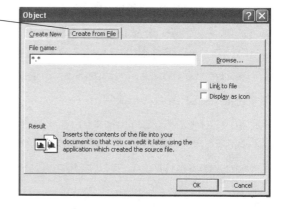

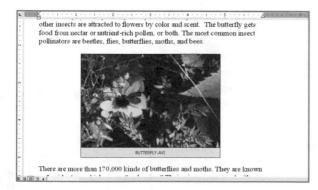

5. Go to **Playing the Movie** section on the next page.

Inserting a Movie into a File X, 2001, 98

1. Click the **Insert** menu and choose **Movie**.

2. Navigate to the **Movies** folder on the CD-ROM that came with this book.

3. Double-click the **Movies** folder.

4. Double-click the **"Butterfly Movie"** file.

5. Place the movie so that it is **centered on the page**.

Playing the Movie

1. Windows users **click the movie** to play.

2. Macintosh users **click the "filmstrip"** icon on the movie, then click the **Play** button on the strip.

Saving the File

The movie file must be loaded on the computer or the movie won't play. It's a good idea to place the file and the movie in the same folder.

1. **Create a folder** named **Butterfly files** on your hard drive.

2. **Copy** the **Butterfly** movie **into** the **folder**.

3. Go back to the **Butterfly** file you have open in *Word*.

4. Click the **File** menu, choose **Save As,** and save the file in the newly created folder.

Windows

Macintosh

Internet Pictures in a Report

Create a Worksheet with Internet Pictures

It is easy to include graphics from the Internet in *Word* documents. All you do is copy the picture from the Internet and paste it into the *Word* file. Not all browsers allow you to copy and paste a picture, but you can save the pictures and insert them later. Both methods are shown below.

> ### This Activity Covers the Following Topics
> • Copying an Image
> • Pasting an Image
> • Downloading the Image

Copying an Image

1. Open "Polar Bear Report" from the "Learning Word" folder on the CD-ROM that came with this book. You're going to put an Internet picture of a polar bear under the paragraph.

2. **Open Internet Explorer** or **other browser**. If you don't have enough memory to have both *Word* and the browser open, quit *Word* and open your browser. You can open *Word* again.

3. **Type the address of a Web site** and press [ENTER] (Windows) [RETURN] (Macintosh). (http://www.omahazoo.com has a great picture.) Scroll through the site until you **find a picture**.

4. **Right-click** (Macintosh users click and hold) **the picture**. A box of choices appears. **Note:** If your browser won't do this, skip to the Downloading the Image section below.

5. Choose **Copy Image**. You won't see anything happen, but the picture is copied into the clipboard of the computer.

6. Click in the **Taskbar** at the bottom of the screen to choose *Word* (Macintosh users choose *Word* from the **Dock** or **Applications menu** in the upper right corner of your screen), or launch it again.

Pasting an Image

1. Press [CTRL][V] (Windows) [⌘][V] (Macintosh) or right-click to paste it.

2. **Right-click** (Macintosh users [CTRL]-click) the picture and choose **Format Picture**. Click the **Layout tab** (wrapping in 97 and 98) and choose **In front of text** (**Through** in 97 and 98). Center the picture on the page.

Be sure to cite the source of your picture. You can type the Web address in a text box. If you need help, turn to page 42.

Downloading the Image

You may need to save the image to a disk instead of copying it onto the clipboard.

1. Choose **Save Picture As** or **Download Image to Disk**. Choose **where to save the image**.

2. With the Polar Bear Report open, click the **Insert menu**, choose **Picture**, and then **From File**. Navigate to the saved image and insert it.

AutoShapes

Use AutoShapes in Your Documents

Word has all kinds of geometric shapes built into the program for your use. It also has arrows, banners, conversation balloons, flowchart symbols, and basic drawing tools. Once you've drawn the shapes, you can add shadows, 3-D effects, and color. The flexibility of these tools is amazing!

> ### This Activity Covers the Following Topics
> - Creating an Arrow
> - Rotating the Arrow
> - Creating a Banner
> - Drawing a Basic Shape
> - Changing the Color of an AutoShape
> - Creating a Shadowed Shape
> - Creating a 3-D Shape
> - Formatting a 3-D Shape
> - Adding Multiple AutoShapes

Creating an Arrow

1. Create a new *Word* document. XP users, click the **Tools menu** and choose **Options**. Click the **General tab** and then click to remove the check from **Automatically create drawing canvas when inserting AutoShapes**. Click **OK**.

2. Choose **AutoShapes** from the **Drawing toolbar**, or click the **Insert** menu, choose **Picture**, and then **AutoShapes**.

3. Choose **Block Arrows** and **drag to the right** until the palette tears off and stays on the screen.

4. Click the **Curved Down Arrow** shape.

5. Place the **+** shaped cursor on the upper left corner of the page. **Click and drag** to draw the arrow.

XP, 2000, 97
98   *X, 2001*

Rotating the Arrow

1. XP users, skip to the next step. Other users, click the **Free Rotate icon** on the **Drawing toolbar**.

2. XP users, drag the **green handle** (other users drag the **upper right handle**) **down** to change the direction of the arrow.

3. **Click in the white area** around the arrow to deselect the rotate cursor function. **Click the arrow** to select it, then **click the first yellow diamond** and **drag right** to make the arrow thinner.

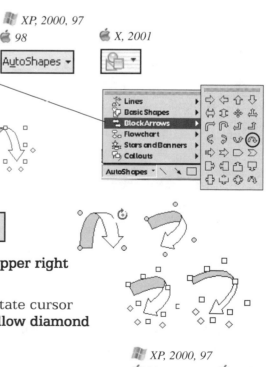

Creating a Banner

1. Choose **Stars and Banners** from **AutoShapes** and drag the palette onto the page.

2. Click the **Up Ribbon** shape. Place the **+** shaped cursor on the upper left corner of the page. **Click and drag** to draw the banner across the page.

3. Click the **Text Box** icon and draw a text box across the center of the banner. Type **Congratulations**.

XP, 2000, 97
98   *X, 2001*

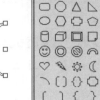

Drawing a Basic Shape

1. Choose **Basic Shapes** from **AutoShapes** and drag the palette onto the page.

2. Click the **Moon** shape.

3. Place the **+** shaped cursor on the upper left corner of the page. **Click and drag** to draw a moon on the page.

Changing the Color of an AutoShape

1. Click the **Moon** shape.

2. Click the **Fill Color** arrow on the **Drawing toolbar**.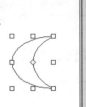

3. Click **More Fill Colors**.

4. Choose a **Yellow** color. Click **OK**.

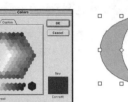

Creating a Shadowed Shape

1. Click the **Shadow** icon. 🍎 X, 2001 users, click the Drawing button on the Drawing toolbar first.

2. **Click a shadow**.

Creating a 3-D Shape

1. Draw another **Basic Shape** (a flat one, not a 3-D one).

2. **Fill the shape** with a **color**.

3. Click the **3-D icon**. 🍎 X, 2001 users, click the Drawing button on the Drawing toolbar first.

4. Click a **3-D shape**.

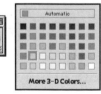

Formatting a 3-D Shape

1. Click the **3-D icon**, then choose **3-D Settings**.

2. Click the **arrow** next to the **3-D Color** icon.

3. **Click a color** or click **More 3-D Colors** for more choices.

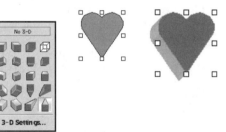

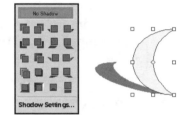

Sometimes it's hard to see the 3-D effect because of the color. Experiment with colors and other 3-D settings to get just the effect you want.

Adding Multiple AutoShapes

1. **Double-click** the **Triangle shape**. **Draw a small triangle**.

2. Notice that the cursor is still a **+**. This means you can keep drawing triangles until you click another shape. **Draw two more triangles**.

3. **Click elsewhere on the page**. A triangle is drawn every time you click. **Draw a few more triangles on the page by clicking**. Click the **Arrow** on the **Drawing toolbar**, then drag to move the triangles.

🍎 *X, 2001*

🪟 *XP, 2000, 97*

🍎 *98*

Diagrams: XP only

Use AutoShapes in Your Documents

Diagrams can help you explain difficult-to-understand concepts. In this activity you'll learn to create six types of diagrams and how to use each one. The diagrams will be inserted into a table.

> ### This Activity Covers the Following Topics
> - Creating an Organization Chart
> - Creating a Cycle Diagram
> - Creating a Venn Diagram
> - Creating a Target Diagram
> - Creating a Radial Diagram
> - Creating a Pyramid Diagram

Creating an Organization Chart

1. Open the file "Types of Diagrams" from the "Learning Word" folder on the CD-ROM that came with this book. You're going to put an organization chart in this table. As the table tells you, organization charts are used to show hierarchical relationships. A plant classification chart is an example of an organization chart.

2. Click the **empty cell** in the **top row**. Click the **Insert Diagram or Organization Chart button** on the **Drawing toolbar**.

3. **Double-click** the **Organization Chart button**.

4. Click the **top box** and type **Flowering Plants**.

5. Click the **bottom left** box and type **Monocotyledons**, then click the **bottom right** box and type **Dicotyledons**.

6. Click the **middle box** until handles appear. Press the **Delete key** to remove the box.

7. Click the **Text Wrapping** button and choose **Through**. Drag the chart to the **middle of the cell**.

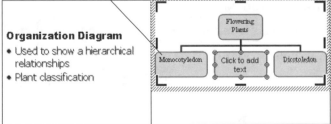

Creating a Cycle Diagram

1. Click the **second empty cell** in the table. You're going to put a cycle diagram in this table. As the table tells you, cycle diagrams are used to show a process that has a continuous cycle. An example of a continuous cycle is the water cycle. Click the **Insert Diagram or Organization Chart button** on the **Drawing toolbar**.

2. **Double-click** the **Cycle Diagram button**. A cycle diagram appears, but it is too large for the table. **Right-click** the diagram and choose **Format Diagram**.

3. Click the **Size tab**. Type **4** in the **Height** box and click **OK**.

4. Click **Insert Shape** from the **Diagram toolbar** to add another shape.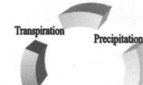

5. Click **Autoformat** from the **Diagram toolbar** and choose **3-D Color**.

6. You're going to add WordArt text because the built-in text is hard to read when the diagram is this small. Click each **Click to add text** box and press the **Spacebar**. This makes a blank area for the WordArt.

7. Click the **WordArt icon, pick a WordArt Style** that is simple and easy to read, and type **Precipitation**.

8. Rather than creating this three more times, you can duplicate this WordArt object and then change the word. Make sure the Word Art object is selected, then press [CTRL][D] three times. **Double-click** an object, type **Evaporation**, and click **OK**. **Drag** the object to a shape (see above). Repeat this process for **Condensation** and **Transpiration**.

9. Click the **Text Wrapping** button and choose **Through**. **Drag** the chart to the **middle of the cell**.

Creating a Venn Diagram

1. Click the **third empty cell** in the table. You're going to put a Venn diagram in this cell. As the table tells you, Venn diagrams are used to show areas of overlap among and between elements. A color wheel is an example of a Venn diagram.

2. Click the **Insert Diagram button** on the **Drawing Toolbar**. The **Diagram Galley** appears. **Double-click** the **Venn diagram**. A Venn diagram appears, but it is too large for the table. **Right-click** the diagram and choose **Format Diagram.** Click the **Size tab**. Type **4** in the **Height** box and click **OK**.

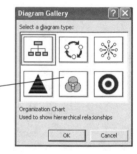

3. Click the **top circle**. Click the **Fill icon** on the **Drawing toolbar** and choose **red**. The circle changes to a transparent red.

4. Using this method, change the **left circle** to **blue**, and the **right circle** to **yellow**.

5. You're going to create text for each circle. Click the **Text Box icon** on the **Drawing toolbar**.

6. Type **Red**, make it **Boldface**, and **drag it outside the red circle**.

7. Create **text boxes** for the **blue** and **yellow** circles.

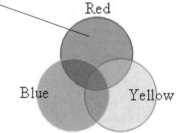

8. Click the **Text Wrapping** button and choose **Through**. **Drag** the chart to the **middle of the cell**.

Creating a Target Diagram

1. Click the **fourth empty cell** in the table. You're going to put a Target diagram in this cell. As the slide tells you, target diagrams are used to show steps toward a goal. Narrowing a search is an example of a target diagram.

2. Click the **Insert Diagram button** on the **Drawing Toolbar**. **Double-click** the **Target diagram** from the **Diagram Galley**. The diagram is too large for the table, so **right-click** it and choose **Format Diagram.** Click the **Size tab**. Type **4** in the **Height** box and click **OK**.

3. Click the **AutoFormat button** on the **Diagram toolbar** and choose **Primary Colors** from the **Design Style Gallery**. Click **Apply**.

4. Click **Insert Shape** from the **Diagram toolbar** to add a ring.

5. **Drag** the **side handles** of the target box to make it **wider** so that there's room to type multiple words.

6. Create a Word Art or Text Box and type **World War II** in the box for the **outside ring**. Type **United States** in the box for the **next ring**.

7. Type **Vehicles** in the box for the **next-to-the-inside ring**. Type **Tanks** in the box for the **inside ring**.

8. Click the **Text Wrapping** button and choose **Through**. **Drag** the diagram to the **middle of the cell**.

Creating a Radial Diagram

1. Click the **fifth empty cell** in the table. You're going to put a radial diagram on this table. As the table tells you, radial diagrams are used to show relationships of elements to a core element. A family diagram is an example of a radial diagram.

2. Click the **Insert Diagram button** on the **Drawing Toolbar**. The **Diagram Galley** appears. **Double-click** the **Radial diagram**. Right-click the diagram and choose **Format Diagram**. Click the Size tab. Type **4** in the **Height** box and click **OK**.

3. Type **Jenny** in the **center** circle. Jenny is the student creating the diagram.

4. Click **Insert Shape** from the **Diagram toolbar**.

5. You can color-code the diagram. You're going to make the parents' circles yellow. Click the **top circle**. Click the **Fill icon** on the **Drawing toolbar** and choose **yellow**. **Repeat** this process for the **bottom** circle.

6. Click the **top circle** and type **Pat Dad**. Click the **bottom circle** and type **Mary Mom**.

7. Change the **left** and **right circles** to **another color**. These circles will contain the names of siblings. Type **Nate and Missy**.

8. Click the **Text Wrapping** button and choose **Through**. **Drag** the chart to the **middle of the cell**.

Creating a Pyramid Diagram

1. Click the **last empty cell** in the table. You're going to put a pyramid diagram on this table. As the table tells you, pyramid diagrams are used to show foundation-based relationships. A color frequency diagram is an example of a pyramid diagram.

2. Click the **Insert Diagram button** on the **Drawing Toolbar**. **Double-click** the **Pyramid diagram** from the **Diagram Galley**. The diagram is too large for the table, so **right-click** it and choose **Format Diagram**. Click the **Size tab**. Type **4** in the **Height** box and click **OK**.

3. Click **Insert Shape** from the **Diagram toolbar** until you have **seven layers**.

4. Give **each layer the color name shown in the table**: Change the **colors of the layers to match the table and names**.

1	Top	Violet
2		Indigo (blue-purple)
3		Blue
4		Green
5		Yellow
6		Orange
7	Bottom	Red

Insert a Table

Create a Rubric and an Assignment Sheet

If you have data that you want to organize into columns, creating a table can be the best way to go. Tables are ideal if you have a single line of data in one column and several lines in the second. You'll learn to do this in the first part of this activity as you make a rubric. In every class there are a few kids who need a little help getting organized. In the second part of this activity, you'll draw a table and make an assignment sheet for them.

> ### This Activity Covers the Following Topics
> - Setting Up the Page
> - Creating the Title
> - Creating a Table
> - Adding Text
> - Setting Up the WordArt Heading
> - Formatting the WordArt
> - Drawing the Name Line
> - Drawing the Table
> - Distributing the Columns and Rows
> - Entering Text in the Table
> - Adding Clip Art

Setting Up the Page

Rubrics are frequently laid out on a horizontal page.

1. Create a *Word* **document**.

⊞ XP, 2000, 97

2. Click the **File** menu and choose **Page Setup**.

3. Type **.5** for each margin.

4. Click the **Landscape button**. ⊞ XP, 2000, 97 users, click the **Paper Size** tab first. Click **OK**. Turn to the next page, Creating the Title.

🍎 X, 2001, 98

2. Click the **Format** menu and choose **Document**.

3. Type **.5** for each margin.

4. Click the **Page Setup** button.

5. Click the **Landscape icon** next to **Orientation**.

6. Click **OK**, then **OK** again. Turn to the next page, Creating the Title.

Creating the Title

1. Choose **50% or 75%** from the **Zoom Control box** so that you can see the width of the entire page.

2. Press ENTER (Windows) RETURN (Macintosh) **7** times. When you insert WordArt or a table, it's a good idea to add some hard returns, so things won't move when you create the rest.

3. You're going to create a rubric for a beginning *PowerPoint* user. Create the **WordArt** title **PowerPoint Presentation Rubric**. **Center** it on the page.

4. Press ENTER (Windows) RETURN (Macintosh) **twice** and type **Student or Group**. Draw a line for the students to write their name(s) on. Type **Date** and draw another line.

Creating a Table

1. Press ENTER (Windows) RETURN (Macintosh) **twice**, then click the **Table menu** and choose **Insert**, then **Table**.

2. Type **7** in **Number of Columns** and click **OK**. You can set the number of rows, but you're going to learn to create rows as you decide you need them. Click **OK**.

Adding Text

1. Click in the **first cell** and type **Categories**. Press ENTER (Windows) RETURN (Macintosh) and type **5 Points Each**.

2. Press TAB and type **Fabulous!**. Press ENTER (Windows) RETURN (Macintosh) and type **25 Points**.

3. Press TAB and type **Great!**. Press ENTER (Windows) RETURN (Macintosh) and type **20 Points**. **Type the remaining text in the screen shot** below.

Categories 5 Points Each	Fabulous! 25 Points	Great! 20 Points	Good Job! 15 Points	Work Harder! 10 Points	Self Evaluation	Teacher Evaluation

4. This row really needs to stand out, so you're going to format the text. **Select** the entire **row**. Click the **View menu**, choose **Toolbars**, and then **Tables and Borders**. Click the **Shading Color** icon and choose **Black**. Click the **Bold button** on the **Formatting toolbar**.

Categories 5 Points Each	Fabulous! 25 Points	Great! 20 Points	Good Job! 15 Points	Work Harder! 10 Points	Self Evaluation	Teacher Evaluation

5. Press TAB until the cursor moves to the second row. Type **Title Card**. Press TAB. Type **Design is attractive and colorful; shows creativity**. The row grows in height so that the text fits in the cell.

Categories 5 Points Each	Fabulous! 25 Points	Great! 20 Points	Good Job! 15 Points	Work Harder! 10 Points	Self Evaluation	Teacher Evaluation
Title Card	Design is attractive and colorful; shows creativity	Design is attractive and colorful	Design is OK, could be more colorful	Design is unacceptable, shows little effort		

6. Press TAB. Type the text in the screen shot above.

7. Press ⌨TAB **until a new row is created**. Create the **remaining rows in the screen shot below**. Press ⌨TAB at the end of a row to create another one.

PowerPoint Presentation Rubric

Student or Group _____ Date _____

Categories 5 Points Each	Fabulous! 25 Points	Great! 20 Points	Good Job! 15 Points	Work Harder! 10 Points	Self Evaluation	Teacher Evaluation
Title Card	Design is attractive and colorful; shows creativity	Design is attractive and colorful	Design is OK, could be more colorful	Design is unacceptable, shows little effort		
Mechanics	There are no spelling, punctuation, or grammatical errors.	Errors in spelling, punctuation, and grammatical are minor and few.	Errors in spelling, punctuation, and grammatical are minor and evident.	Errors in spelling, punctuation, and grammatical are distracting.		
Sounds	Sounds enhance the quality of the presentation.	Sounds are appropriate.	Some sounds are inappropriate and/or distract from the presentation	Many sounds are inappropriate and/or distract from the presentation		
Graphics	Graphics enhance the quality of the presentation.	Graphics are appropriate.	Some graphics are inappropriate and/or distract from the presentation	Many graphics are inappropriate and/or distract from the presentation		
Teamwork	Team members worked well together, planned, discussed, assumed roles, and solved problems	Team members worked together most of the time, planned, discussed, assumed roles, and solved problems	Team members sometimes worked together; one or two members felt they did most of the work.	Team members needed teacher help to divide tasks, solve problems; one or two members felt they did most of the work.		

8. **Select** the text in the **first column** and click the **Bold button** on the **Formatting toolbar**.

9. All right! **Save** the file on your hard drive or floppy disk and **Print** it.

Tables can also be drawn. The steps below will help you create an assignment sheet.

Setting Up the WordArt Heading

1. Create a new *Word* document.

2. Press ⌨ENTER (Windows) ⌨RETURN (Macintosh) seven times.

3. Click the **Insert WordArt icon** or choose **Picture**, then **WordArt** from the **Insert** menu. Double-click a style.

4. Type **Assignments** and click **OK**. Drag it to the top.

5. Use the same WordArt style and type the word "**for**."

Formatting the WordArt

1. Click the **WordArt** shape icon in the WordArt toolbar.

2. Click the **straight line** shape.

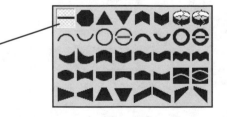

Drawing the Name Line

1. From the Drawing toolbar, click the **Straight Line** icon and **draw a line** under the word **for**.

2. Choose a **wider line** from the **Line Style** icon.

Drawing the Table

1. Click the **Table** menu and choose **Draw Table**. The cursor changes to a pencil shape.

2. Using the pencil tool, **draw a box under the heading**.

3. **Draw horizontal lines** to create **7 rows**. Make the first row much smaller than the rest.

4. Draw **vertical lines** to create **6 columns**.

The rows and columns aren't even. We'll fix that next.

Distributing the Columns and Rows

1. Move the cursor to the **second row outside the table on the left side**. It changes to an arrow. Click and **drag down to select all the rows**.

2. Click the **Distribute Rows Evenly** icon from the **Tables and Borders** palette.

3. Click the **Distribute Columns Evenly** icon.

Entering Text in the Table

1. Click the **top left cell**. Type **Assignment**.

2. Press [TAB] to move to the cell on the right. Type the **days of the week** in the first row.

3. **Select** the entire row. **Boldface** the text. Click the **Center** button.

4. Click the **Format** menu and choose **Borders and Shading**.

5. Click the **Shading** tab and select a **light** color. Click **OK**.

6. **Select all the rows**. Click the **Center** button. This centers the text in the middle of the cells.

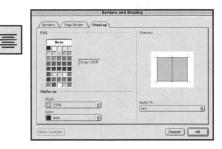

Assignment	Monday	Tuesday	Wednesday	Thursday	Friday

Adding Clip Art

Adding pictures to the assignment sheet can make it more appealing to kids.

1. In some versions it is easier to draw a **Text Box** in the cell where you'd like to insert clip art (this lets you predetermine placement and allows you to move it as a graphic).

2. Click the **Clip Art** icon or click the **Insert** menu, choose **Picture**, and then **Clip Art**.

3. Insert **clip art for each assignment**.

Reading

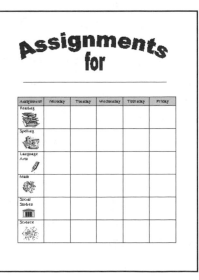

Footnotes

Use Footnotes in a Letter

We struggled to make footnotes with typewriters but it's so easy to make them with *Word*. Footnotes aren't just used in term papers, they can also be used in letters to insert information.

> ### This Activity Covers the Following Topics
> * Inserting a Footnote
> * Removing a Footnote

Inserting a Footnote

1. Open the file "Field Trip Letter Done" from the "Learning Word" folder on the CD-ROM that came with this book.

2. Click at the **end** of the word **Zoo** because that's where you want the first footnote number to appear. You're going to write the address for the zoo as a footnote.

3. XP users, click the **Insert menu** and choose **Reference**, and then **Footnote**. All other users click the **Insert menu** and choose **Footnote**. The Footnote section gives you choices about the location and numbering of footnotes. Click **OK**.

 XP

 2000, 97

 X, 2001, 98

The number "1" appears in superscript above the second "o" in Zoo. Subsequent notes are numbered in sequence.

At the same time, *Word* drops the cursor into the footnote panel at the bottom, inserts the note number, and leaves the cursor blinking.

> We're going on a field trip May 20! The students have been working very hard learning about the animal kingdom. They have researched where animals live, about their families, and their hunting and feeding habits. Now it's time to see some of these animals up close. We will visit the *Lied Jungle at Henry Doorly Zoo¹* and Educational Service Unit #3's *Gifford Farm.²* Would you like to go with us?

4. In the footnote panel, **type the text of the first footnote in the screen shot to the right**.

5. When you have finished the note, **click anywhere in the letter** to resume work on the main document.

> ¹ Henry Doorly Zoo, Deer Park Blvd. at 10th
> ² Gifford Farm, 700 Camp Gifford Rd.

6. Click after the period following the words **Gifford Farm** and insert a **Footnote**. **Type** the **second footnote** shown in the **screen shot above**.

Removing a Footnote

1. In the text, select the **reference number** of the **first footnote**.

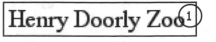

2. Press **Delete**. *Word* removes the note, rearranges the pages, and renumbers remaining notes in the text and in the footnote panel.

Leading in a Document

Tighten Up the Text

The leading (pronounced like lead in a pencil) is the white space between lines of text. This can be changed to make a document more compact or to expand it vertically on a page. If you have a document that won't quite fit on one page, and it has to be a single-page document, tightening up the leading can make it fit on one page.

This Activity Covers the Following Topic
- Changing the Leading

Changing the Leading

1. Open the file "Field Trip Letter" from the "Learning Word" folder on the CD-ROM that came with this book.

2. Highlight the **first paragraph**.

3. Click the **Format** menu and choose **Paragraph**.

4. Click the **Indents and Spacing** tab.

5. The paragraph dialog box appears. The default of line spacing is **Single**. Click the arrow under **Line spacing:** and choose **Exactly**.

6. Click the **Down Arrow** under **At:** to choose **11 pt**.

7. Click **OK**.

The first paragraph in the screen shot below is still in 12 pt. Times, but the leading has been changed to 11 pt. The second paragraph still has **Single** line spacing. Notice how much closer the lines are in the first paragraph compared with the second paragraph.

> Dear Parents:
>
> We're going on a field trip May 20! The kids have been working very hard learning about the animal kingdom. They have researched where animal live, about their family, and their hunting and feeding habits. Now it's time to see some of these animals up close. We will visit the Lied Jungle at Henry Doorly Zoo and Educational Service Unit #3's Gifford Farm. Would you like to go with us?
>
> Both Mrs. Fischer's and Mr. Harper's classes will be going on this day-long field trip. We would like to have one sponsor for every five students, so we need ten parent volunteers. Students have a great time learning about animals on this field trip so you'll have a great time, too.

When you are changing leading, you would be wise to vary the leading only one or two points at a time. Check to make sure the tops (ascenders) and bottoms (descenders) of each letter are showing, especially capital letters and the lower part of letters (e.g., "g").

Merged Letter: 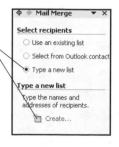 XP Only

Merge Names and Addresses in a Letter

You can create a personalized letter for students by using *Word*'s merge function. You'll learn how to create a new data source and merge it into a letter to parents. You'll also learn to merge an *Excel* document into a certificate.

> ### This Activity Covers the Following Topics
> * Opening the Letter
> * Choosing the Main Document (Step 1)
> * Creating the Data Source (Step 2)
> * Completing the Main Document (Step 3)
> * Previewing the Merged Document
> * Choosing the Main Document (Step 1)
> * Choosing the Data Source (Step 2)
> * Completing the Main Document (Step 3)

Opening the Letter

Open the file "Science Fair Letter" from the "Learning Word" folder on the CD-ROM that came with this book. It reads strangely because there are blanks where words from the data source will be merged. It needs to be sent to all students who were picked to go to the Regional Science Fair. Mail merge will insert student information using data from a data source you create.

Choosing the Main Document (Step 1)

1. Click **Zoom** and choose **75%**. Place the pointer on the **left edge** of the **Task Pane** and **drag right** to make it more **narrow**.

2. Click the **Tools menu** and choose **Letters and Mailings**, then **Mail Merge**.

3. Click **Letters** in **Select document type**.

4. Click **Next: Starting document** from the bottom of the pane.

5. From the top of the **Task pane,** click **Use the current document**, then from the bottom of the pane, **Next: Select recipients**.

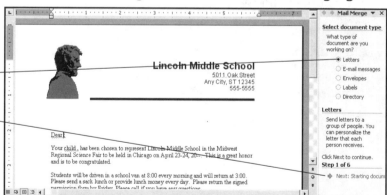

6. Click **Type a new list** from the top of the **Task pane**, and then **Create**.

Creating the Data Source (Step 2)

You're going to create a list (data source) of names and addresses. A data source contains fields and records. A **field** is a category name, e.g., First Name. There can be several different fields in a data source. A **record** is all the information about one person. This information will be merged into the main document (in this case, Science Fair Letter) modified in step 1. A data source can be used in any document once you have created it. This information will be merged with the letter.

1. The **New Address List** window contains fields (categories) you don't need. It will be faster to enter data if you delete these fields. Click the **Customize button**.

2. Click **Company Name** and click the **Delete button**. Delete **E-mail Address, Work Phone, Home Phone,** and **Country**.

2. Click the **Add button**. Type **Combined Name** and click **OK**. Click the **Move Up** button until the field is under **Last Name,** Click **OK**.

3. Type the **three records below**, pressing the Tab key to move between fields. Click **New Entry** to add a new name.

Title	First Name	Last Name	Combined Name	Address	City, State, Zip
Mr. & Mrs. Jose Martinez	Jose	Martinez	Jose Martinez	1234 Oak Street	Any City, AS 12345
Ms. Linda Smith	Lisa	Jenkins	Lisa Jenkins	3457 Pine Street	Any City, AS 12345
Mr. & Mrs. Alexjandro Gonzales	Adriana	Gonzales	Adriana Gonzales	348 S 13 Ave	Any City, AS 12345

4. Click **Close**. Name the file **Student Addresses**.

5. Click **Select All** and then **OK**.

Completing the Main Document (Step 3)

1. From the **bottom** of the **Task pane,** click **Next: Write your letter**.

2. **Click** the cursor to the **left of the colon in the greeting**. Click **More items** on the **Task Pane**.

3. **Double-click** the field **Title**, then click **Close**. The field marker <<Title>> appears in the greeting.

4. It would be easier to read if you could see the data (in this case, a name) instead of the field marker. Click the **Tools menu** and choose **Letters and Mailings,** then **Show Mail Merge Toolbar**. Click the **View Merged Data button**. The name in the first record appears.

5. Merge **First Name** to the left of the comma after **Your child,** in the first line.

Dear Mr. and Mrs. Jose Martinez:

Your child (Jose) has been chosen to Regional Science Fair to be held in and (Jose) is to be congratulated.

6. Merge **First Name** in the last sentence of the first paragraph. Press the **Spacebar**.

7. Merge **First Name** in the last line before the closing, **I am so proud of !**

8. **Scroll down** to the **permission form** and merge **Combined Name** at the beginning of the first sentence. Press the **Spacebar**.

I am so proud of (Jose)

Amy Schenk

(Jose Martinez) has my permission to attend the Midwest Regional Science Fair to be held in Chicago on April 23-24, 2003.

Daytime phone _____

Signature _____

Previewing the Merged Document

1. From the bottom of the **Task Pane,** click **Next: Preview your letters**.

2. Click the **Recipient buttons** to view the merged letters. You can also click the buttons on the **Mail Merge toolbar**.

3. From the bottom of the **Task Pane,** click **Next: Complete the merge**.

4. Click **Print** on the **Task Pane** to merge a letter to each person in the database.

Now you'll learn to merge a Word document with an Excel document.

Choosing the Main Document (Step 1)

1. Open the file "Birthday" from the "Learning Word" folder on the CD-ROM that came with this book. You're going to merge the student names into a birthday certificate.

2. Click the **Tools menu** and choose **Letters and Mailings,** then **Mail Merge**.

3. Click **Letters** in **Select document type**.

4. From the bottom of the **Task Pane,** click **Next: Starting document**.

5. From the top of the **Task Pane,** click **Use the current document,** then, from the bottom of the **Task Pane,** click **Next: Select recipients**.

Choosing the Data Source (Step 2)

You're going to use a list (data source) of names, addresses, and phone numbers from the *Excel* worksheet "Student Information." This information will be merged with the birthday certificate.

1. From the top of the **Task Pane,** click **Use an existing list,** and then, from the bottom of the **Task Pane,** click **Browse**.

2. **Navigate** to the CD-ROM that came with this book and **double-click** "Student Information" from the "Learning Word" folder. Click **OK when the Sheet1$** is selected on the new window.

3. Click **Select All** and then **OK**.

Completing the Main Document (Step 3)

1. From the bottom of the **Task Pane,** click **Next: Write your letter**.

2. **Click** the cursor to the left of the **period in the first sentence.** Click **More items** on the **Task Pane**.

3. **Double-click** the field **Combined Name,** then click **Close**.

4. Click the **Tools menu** and choose **Letters and Mailings,** then **Show Mail Merge Toolbar**. Find the toolbar and click the **View Merged Data button**. The name in the first record appears.

5. Merge **First Name** in the last sentence.

Merged Letter:  X, 2001 Only

Merge Names and Addresses in a Letter

You can create a personalized letter for students by using *Word*'s merge function. You'll learn how to create a new data source and merge it into a letter to parents. You'll also learn to merge an *Excel* document into a certificate.

> ### This Activity Covers the Following Topics
> * Opening the Letter
> * Choosing the Main Document (Step 1)
> * Creating the Data Source (Step 2)
> * Completing the Main Document (Step 3)
> * Previewing the Merged Document
> * Choosing the Main Document (Step 1)
> * Choosing the Data Source (Step 2)
> * Completing the Main Document (Step 3)

Opening the Letter

Open the file "Science Fair Letter" from the "Learning Word" folder on the CD-ROM that came with this book. It reads strangely because there are blanks where words from the data source will be merged. It needs to be sent to all students who were picked to go to the Regional Science Fair. Mail merge will insert student information using data from a data source you create.

Choosing the Main Document (Step 1)

1. Click the **Tools** menu and choose **Data Merge Manager**.

2. Click the **Create button** and choose **Form Letters**.

Creating the Data Source (Step 2)

You're going to create a list (data source) of names and addresses. A data source contains fields and records. A **field** is a category name, e.g., First Name. There can be several different fields in a data source. A **record** is all of the information about one person. This information will be merged into the main document (in this case, Science Fair Letter) modified in step 1. A data source can be used in any document once you have created it. This information will be merged with the letter.

Notice that Science Fair Letter is now identified as the Main document.

1. Click the **Get Data button** and choose **New Data Source**.

2. The **Create Data Source** window contains fields (categories) you don't need. It will be faster to enter data if you delete these fields. Click **JobTitle** and click the **Remove Field Name button**. **Delete Company, Work Phone, Home Phone**, and **Country**.

3. Type **CombinedName** (no space between the words) and click the **Add Field Name button**. Click the **Move Up** button until the field is under **Last Name**.

4. Click **OK**. Name the file **Student Addresses**.

5. Type the **three records below**, pressing the Tab key to move between fields. Click **Add New** to add a new record. Click **OK** when you're finished.

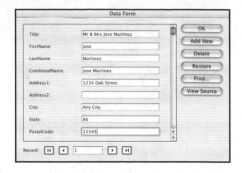

Title	First Name	Last Name	Combined Name	Address	City, State, Zip
Mr. & Mrs. Jose Martinez	Jose	Martinez	Jose Martinez	1234 Oak Street	Any City, AS 12345
Ms. Linda Smith	Lisa	Jenkins	Lisa Jenkins	3457 Pine Street	Any City, AS 12345
Mr. & Mrs. Alexjandro Gonzales	Adriana	Gonzales	Adriana Gonzales	348 S 13 Ave	Any City, AS 12345

Completing the Main Document (Step 3)

1. Drag **Title** from the **Insert Merge Field** section of the palette to the left of the **colon** in the greeting. The field marker <<Title>> appears in the greeting.

2. It would be easier to read if you could see the data (in this case, a name) instead of the field marker. Click the **View Merged Data button**. The name in the first record appears.

3. **Merge First Name** to the left of the comma after **Your child ,** in the first line.

4. **Merge First Name** in the last sentence of the first paragraph. Press the **Spacebar**.

5. **Merge First Name** in the last line before the closing, **I am so proud of !**

6. **Scroll down** to the **permission form** and **merge Combined Name** at the beginning of the first sentence. Press the **Spacebar**.

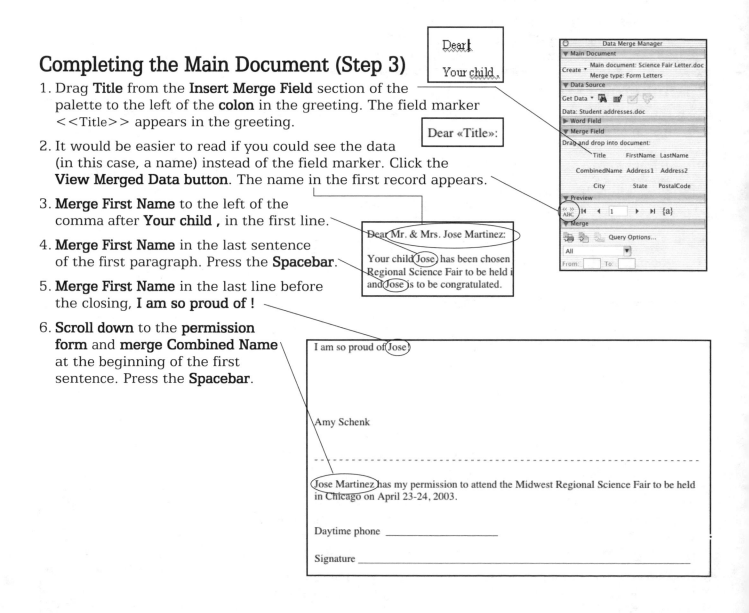

Previewing the Merged Document

1. Click the **Next Record** button to see the data for the next record inserted into the letter.

2. Click the **Merge to Printer button** to merge a letter to each person in the database.

Now you'll learn to merge a Word document with an Excel document.

Choosing the Main Document (Step 1)

1. Open the *Word* file "Birthday" from the "Learning Word" folder on the CD-ROM that came with this book. You're going to merge the student names into a birthday certificate.

2. Click the **Tools** menu and choose **Data Merge Manager**.

3. Click the **Create button** and choose **Form Letters**.

Choosing the Data Source (Step 2)

You're going to use a list (data source) of names, addresses, and phone numbers from the *Excel* worksheet "Student Information." This information will be merged with the birthday certificate.

1. Click the **Get Data button** and choose **Open Data Source**.

2. **Navigate** to the CD-ROM that came with this book and **double-click** "Student Information" from the "Learning Word" folder. Click **OK** when **Student Information** is selected on the new window.

Completing the Main Document (Step 3)

1. **Merge CombinedName** to the left of the **period in the first sentence**.

2. **Merge FirstName** to the left of the **period in the last sentence**.

3. Click the **Preview button** and click the **View Merged Data button**.

Merged Letter: 2000, 97 and 98 Only

Merge Names and Addresses in a Letter

You can create a personalized letter for students by using *Word*'s merge function. You'll learn how to create a new data source and merge it into a letter to parents. You'll also learn to merge an *Excel* document into a certificate.

> ### This Activity Covers the Following Topics
> * Opening the Letter
> * Choosing the Main Document (Step 1)
> * Creating the Data Source (Step 2)
> * Completing the Main Document (Step 3)
> * Previewing the Merged Document
> * Choosing the Main Document (Step 1)
> * Choosing the Data Source (Step 2)
> * Completing the Main Document (Step 3)

Opening the Letter

1. Open the file "Science Fair Letter" from the "Learning Word" folder on the CD-ROM that came with this book. It reads strangely because there are blanks where words from the data source will be merged. It needs to be sent to all students who were picked to go to the Regional Science Fair. Mail merge will insert student information using data from a data source you create.

Choosing the Main Document (Step 1)

1. Click the **Tools menu** and choose **Mail Merge**.

2. Click the **Create button** and choose **Form Letters**.

3. Choose **Active Window** to indicate you want the current file "Science Fair Letter" to be the document you use as a merge document.

> **Microsoft Word**
>
> To create the form letters, you can use the active document window SCIENCE_FAIR_LETTER2000.DOC or a new document window.
>
> [Active Window]   [New Main Document]

> **Mail Merge Helper**
>
> Use this checklist to set up a mail merge. Begin by choosing the Create button.
>
> 1 Main document
> [Create ▼]
> Form Letters...
> Mailing Labels...
> 2 Envelopes...
> Catalog...
> Restore to Normal Word Document...
>
> 3 Merge the data with the document
> [Merge...]
>
> [Cancel]

Creating the Data Source (Step 2)

You're going to create a list (data source) of names and addresses. A data source contains fields and records. A **field** is a category name, e.g., First Name. There can be several different fields in a data source. A **record** is all the information about one person. This information will be merged into the main document (in this case, Science Fair Letter) modified in step 1. A data source can be used in any document once you have created it. This information will be merged with the letter.

Notice that Science Fair Letter is now identified as the Main document.

1. Click the **Get Data button** and choose **New Data Source**.

2. The **Create Data Source** window contains fields (categories) you don't need. It will be faster to enter data if you delete these fields. Click **JobTitle** and click the **Remove Field Name button**.
   Delete **Company**,
   Work Phone,
   Home Phone,
   and **Country**.

3. Type
   CombinedName
   (no space between
   the words) and
   click the **Add Field
   Name button**.
   Click the **Move Up**
   button until the field is under **Last Name**.

4. Click **OK**. Name the file **Student Addresses**.

5. A message telling you there are no data records appears. Click **Edit Data Source** to add student records.

6. Type the **three records below**, pressing the Tab key to move between fields. Click **Add New** to add a new record. Click **OK** when you're finished.

Title	First Name	Last Name	Combined Name	Address	City, State, Zip
Mr. & Mrs. Jose Martinez	Jose	Martinez	Jose Martinez	1234 Oak Street	Any City, AS 12345
Ms. Linda Smith	Lisa	Jenkins	Lisa Jenkins	3457 Pine Street	Any City, AS 12345
Mr. & Mrs. Alexjandro Gonzales	Adriana	Gonzales	Adriana Gonzales	348 S 13 Ave	Any City, AS 12345

Completing the Main Document (Step 3)

1. Click to the **left of the colon** in the greeting.

2. Click the **Insert Merge Field button** on the **Mail Merge toolbar**. The field marker <<Title>> appears in the greeting.

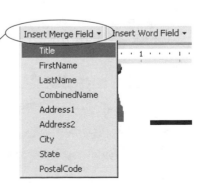

3. It would be easier to read if you could see the data (in this case, a name) instead of the field marker. Click the **View Merged Data button**. The name in the first record appears.

| Insert Merge Field ▾ | Insert Word Field ▾ | « » ABC | I◀ ◀ | 1 | ▶ ▶I | | | | | Merge... | | |

4. **Merge First Name** to the left of the comma after **Your child ,** in the first line.

Dear Mr. and Mrs. Jose Martinez:

Your child Jose, has been chosen t Regional Science Fair to be held in and Jose is to be congratulated.

5. **Merge First Name** in the last sentence of the first paragraph. Press the **Spacebar**.

6. **Merge First Name** in the last line before the closing, **I am so proud of !**

I am so proud of Jose!

7. **Scroll down** to the **permission form** and **merge Combined Name** at the beginning of the first sentence. Press the **Spacebar**.

Amy Schenk

Previewing the Merged Document

1. Click the **Next Record** button to see the data for the next record inserted into the letter.

Jose Martinez has my permission to attend the Midwest Regional Science Fair to be held in Chicago on April 23-24, 2003.

2. Click the **Merge to Printer button** to merge a letter to each person in the database.

Daytime phone _____

| Insert Merge Field ▾ | Insert Word Field ▾ | « » ABC | I◀ ◀ | 1 | ▶ ▶I | | | | | Merge... | | |

Merge to Printer button

Choosing the Main Document (Step 1)

1. Open the *Word* file "Birthday" from the "Learning Word" folder on the CD-ROM that came with this book. You're going to merge the student names into a birthday certificate.

Now you'll learn to merge a Word document with an Excel document.

2. Click the **Tools** menu and choose **Data Merge Manager**.

3. Click the **Create button** and choose **Form Letters**.

Choosing the Data Source (Step 2)

You're going to use a list (data source) of names, addresses, and phone numbers from the *Excel* worksheet "Student Information." This information will be merged with the birthday certificate.

Happy Birthday

This certifies that today is the birthday of «Combined_Name». Have a great day, «First_Name»!

1. Click the **Get Data button** and choose **Open Data Source**.

2. **Navigate** to the CD-ROM that came with this book and **double-click** "Student Information" from the "Learning Word" folder. Click **OK when Student Information** is selected on the new window.

Happy Birthday

This certifies that today is the birthday of Jose Martinez. Have a great day, Jose!

Completing the Main Document (Step 3)

1. **Merge CombinedName** to the left of the **period in the first sentence**.

2. **Merge FirstName** to the left of the **period in the last sentence**.

3. Click the **Preview button** and click the **View Merged Data button**.

Envelopes and Labels

Create Envelopes the Easy Way

Why should you use *Word* to create a great-looking letter and then handwrite the envelope?
You don't have to—just use the *Word* Labels and Envelopes feature to print the envelopes!

> **This Activity Covers the Following Topics**
> * Creating Multiple Labels and Envelopes
> * Creating A Single Envelope
> * Creating an Envelope from a Letter
> * Creating a Label

Creating Multiple Labels and Envelopes

If you want to print envelopes and labels for several people, use the merge function of *Word*
explained in the previous activity. Use the directions to Create the Main Document, but choose
Labels or Envelopes instead of Form Letter. **Hint:** #10 envelopes and Avery 2160 labels are the
most commonly used. This activity teaches you to create a single envelope or label.

Creating a Single Envelope

1. Create a new *Word* document.

2. XP users, click the **Tools** menu and choose **Letters and Mailings**,
   then **Envelopes and Labels**. 2000, 97 and 98 users,
   click the **Tools** menu and choose **Envelopes**. X, 2001 users,
   click the **Tools** menu and choose **Envelopes and Labels**.

3. Click the **Envelopes** tab.

4. **Type the name and address** of the person you're
   sending the letter to in the **Delivery Address** box.

5. Type **your name and address** in the **Return Address** box.

6. Click **Print**. Click **Yes** if you want the return address to appear each time you create an envelope.

Creating an Envelope from a Letter

1. Create a new *Word* document and **type a letter including
   the inside address** (who the letter is to).

2. Click the **Tools** menu and choose Envelopes as you did
   above. The inside address from the letter will be visible in
   the **Delivery Address** box. Click **Cancel** to close the window.

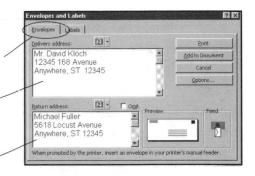

Creating a Label

1. Click the **Tools** menu and choose **Envelopes and Labels**.

2. Click the **Labels** tab. **Type** the **label data** in the window.

3. Click **Print**. A sheet of labels with that data is printed. This will be great for labeling materials
   (especially at conferences).

Languages

Create a Spanish Sing-Along Sheet

Word will check a document that contains both English and text from other languages, and it knows which dictionary to use for each word.  XP also will translate a foreign word into English or an English word into a foreign language. Several languages are available, but we'll focus on Spanish from Mexico in this activity. You'll install the language when it asks you to.

> ### This Activity Covers the Following Topics
> - Choosing a Proofing Language
> - Translating a Word  XP Only
> - Using the Thesaurus
> - Writing Using International Characters

Choosing a Proofing Language

1. Open the file "Spanish songs" from the "Learning Word" folder on the CD-ROM that came with this book. This file is a combination of Spanish and English words, some of which are spelled incorrectly.

2. Click the **Tools menu** and choose **Language**, then **Set Language**. ⬛ X, 2001 and 98 users must first select the Spanish text in the first song. Scroll to **Spanish (Mexico)**. You may be prompted to install this option.

3. Click the **Spelling and Grammar button** on the **Standard toolbar**.

4. **Check the spelling and grammar** for the document. *Word* identifies the language it is checking at the top of the window.

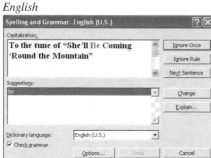

When the grammar for a Spanish word is being checked, the explanation for the error is given in Spanish.

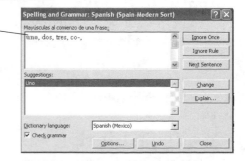

Macintosh users will save time if they put the Set Language button on their Formatting toolbar. Turn to page 50 for instructions on adding buttons. Click Tools in the Commands tab to find the Set Language command.

Macintosh users must select the Spanish text in the document before setting the language. You can select all the Spanish text and then check the Grammar.

Translating a Word ⊞ XP Only

This section is for Word XP users only. Users of other versions go to the Using the Thesaurus section of this activity.

1. **Double-click** the word **adios** in the last song.

2. Click the **Tools menu** and choose **Language**, then **Translate**. The **Translate** options appear on the **Task Pane**.

3. Click **Current selection** in the **Translate what?** portion of the pane.

4. Click the **Dictionary** menu and choose **Spanish (Spain-Modern Sort) to English (U.S.)** and click **Go**. The English translation of adios appears.

5. **Double-click** the word **Tune** in the last song.

6. Click the **Dictionary** menu and choose **English (U.S.) to Spanish** and click **Go**. The Spanish translation of tune appears.

Using the Thesaurus

1. **Double-click** the word **amigos** in the last song.

2. Click the **Tools menu** and choose **Language**, then **Thesaurus**.

3. Click **camaradas (s.)** in the **Meanings** column.

4. Synonyms appear in the right side with the selected word in the **Replace with Synonym** box. Click the **Replace button**. The word from the box appears in the document (in this case, camaradas).

Writing Using International Characters

1. Click after the last character on the page and press ⌨ENTER (Windows) ⌨RETURN (Macintosh) two times. You're going to type the word adios as it appears in the last song using the proper characters for the letter **o**.

2. Type **adi**.

3. ⊞ XP, 2000 and 97 users, press ⌨CTRL, and **while it is pressed**, type **apostrophe**, then **os**.

   X, 2001 and 98 users, press ⌨OPTION, and **while it is pressed**, type **e** then **os**.

The table shows you how to type many international characters. If you type extensively in another language, you may prefer to switch to a different keyboard instead. The Help feature in your operating system will help you do this.

Keyboard Shortcuts for International Characters

WINDOWS KEYS	MACINTOSH KEYS	CHARACTER YOU GET
CTRL+` (ACCENT GRAVE), *the letter*	OPTION+` (ACCENT GRAVE), *the letter*	à, è, ì, ò, ù, À, È, Ì, Ò, Ù
CTRL+' (APOSTROPHE), *the letter*	OPTION+e, *the letter*	á, é, í, ó, ú, _ Á, É, Í, Ó, Ú, _
CTRL+SHIFT+^ (CARET), *the letter*	OPTION+i, *the letter*	â, ê, î, ô, û Â, Ê, Î, Ô, Û
CTRL+SHIFT+~ (TILDE), *the letter*	OPTION +n, *the letter*	ã, ñ, õ Ã, Ñ, Õ
CTRL+SHIFT+: (COLON), *the letter*	OPTION +u *the letter*	ä, ë, ï, ö, ü, ÿ, Ä, Ë, Ï, Ö, Ü, Ÿ
CTRL+SHIFT+@, a or A	OPTION +a OR OPTION +SHIFT+a	å, Å
CTRL+SHIFT+&, a or A	OPTION+' (SINGLE QUOTATION MARK) OR OPTION +SHIFT+' (SINGLE QUOTATION MARK)	æ, Æ
CTRL+SHIFT+&, o or O	OPTION +q or OPTION +SHIFT+q	œ, Œ
CTRL+, (COMMA), c or C	OPTION +c or OPTION +SHIFT+c	ç, Ç
CTRL+' (APOSTROPHE), d or D		–, _
CTRL+/, o or O	OPTION +o or OPTION +SHIFT+o	ø, Ø
ALT+CTRL+SHIFT+?	OPTION +SHIFT+?	¿
ALT+CTRL+SHIFT+!	OPTION +1	¡
CTRL+SHIFT+&, s	OPTION+s	ß

Screen Shots

Create a Computer Worksheet

Teachers make worksheets to help students through a computer process that requires many steps. They also make packets of self-paced learning exercises. Screen snapshots can make these worksheets easier to follow. This exercise will explain how to do it.

> ### This Activity Covers the Following Topics
> * Creating the Title and Directions
> * Creating a Screen Shot
> * Creating Arrowhead Lines
> * Printing the File

Creating the Title and Directions

You're going to make a "How-to" worksheet with a screen shot that shows students how to insert a picture into *Word*.

1. Create a new *Word* document. Press ⌤ (Windows) ⌤ (Macintosh) seven times.

2. Click the **WordArt icon** or click the **Insert** menu, choose **Picture**, and then **WordArt**.

3. **Double-click** a **WordArt style** you like.

4. Type **Inserting a Picture** in the highlighted text box. If it has black handles, **right-click the screen shot**, choose **Format WordArt**, click the **Layout tab** (**Wrapping** in 🪟 97), and choose **In front of text** (**None** in 🪟 97). Click **OK**. Drag the WordArt object to the center at the top of the page.

5. **Click 3 lines below** the **WordArt** and type **1**. Press the Tab key. Type **Click the Insert menu and choose Picture**, then **From File**. You may want to boldface the commands **Insert menu, Picture**, and **From File** because those are the important instructions.

6. **Click below the directions** or click after the instruction and press ⌤ (Windows) ⌤ (Macintosh).

7. Save the file as **Picture worksheet**.

Creating a Screen Shot

1. Now that you have the directions for inserting a picture from a file, you need to make a screen shot that will illustrate it. *You'll need the Picture worksheet file, so don't close it.* Create a **Word** document. You won't want the text you just created to be in the screen shot, so you are creating a new document to use for the screen shot. You'll come back to the Picture worksheet file in a minute.

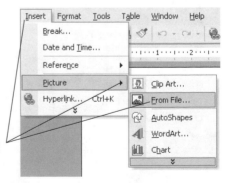

2. Follow your directions exactly; **Click the Insert menu and choose Picture, then From File**. *Don't click!* Leave the menu on your screen by not clicking the mouse.

XP, 2000, 97   *This section is for Word XP, 2000 and 97 users only.*
Users of other versions go to your section of this activity.

1. Press the **Print Screen** button on your keyboard. Nothing appears to happen, but the screen was copied into the clipboard of the computer.

2. Click **Picture worksheet** in the **Taskbar** at the bottom of the screen. The Picture worksheet file reappears. You can also click the **Window** menu and choose **Picture worksheet**.

3. Click the **Zoom Box** and choose **Whole Page**. `50%` ▼

4. **Right-click** below the directions and choose **Paste** or press `CTRL` `V`. The screen shot appears.

5. You need white handles around the screen shot to drag and resize it properly. Click the screen shot. If it has black handles, **right-click the screen shot**, choose **Format Picture**, click the **Layout (Wrapping** in 97), and choose **In front of text (None** in 97). Click **OK**.

6. It needs to be made smaller. Click the **Arrow** tool and **drag a corner to shrink** it. Drag it to the center of the page.

7. Go to Creating Arrowhead Lines on the next page.

Windows users: Third-party software like FullShot allows you to draw a box around the portion of the screen you want to snap. You don't have to snap the entire screen this way. Their web address is www.fullshot.com/.

X, 2001, 98   *This section is for Word X, 2001 and 98 users only.*
Users of other versions go to your section of this activity.

1. Press `SHIFT` `⌘` `3`. You'll hear a camera shutter sound to tell you that the screen was copied.

2. Click the **Window** menu and choose **Picture worksheet**. Click the **Zoom Box** `50%` ▼ and choose **Whole Page**.

3. A file named "Picture 1" was created on the hard drive. Click **below the directions**. Click the **Insert menu**, choose **Picture,** and then **From file**.

4. Navigate to the hard drive and choose **Picture 1**. The screen shot appears on the page.

5. You need white handles around the screen shot to drag and resize it properly. Click the screen shot. If it has black handles, `CTRL`**-click the screen shot**, choose **Format Picture**, click **Layout (Wrapping** in 98), and choose **In front of text (None** in 98).

6. It needs to be made smaller. Click the **Arrow** tool and **drag a corner to shrink** it. Drag it to the center of the page.

7. Go to Creating Arrowhead Lines on the next page.

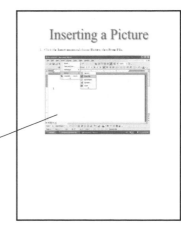

Macintosh users: If you press `SHIFT` `⌘` `4`, the cursor will change to a +. Then you can draw a box around the portion of the screen you want to snap. You don't have to snap the entire screen this way. System X users can use the Snapz Pro X program that comes with the system.

Creating Arrowhead Lines

1. Click the **Zoom Box** and choose **100%**.

2. 🪟 XP users, click the **Tools menu**, click **Options**, click the **General tab**, and click **Automatically create drawing canvas when inserting AutoShapes** to remove the check. This prevents the Drawing Canvas from appearing.

🪟 *XP, 2000, 97*
🍎 *98*   🍎 *X, 2001*

3. Click the **black arrow** tool on the **Drawing toolbar**.

4. **Draw a line** from the word **Insert** to the **Insert menu**.

5. **Draw arrows** from **Picture** and **From File** to their corresponding parts.

6. Press ⌨ENTER (Windows) ⌨RETURN (Macintosh) until the cursor is below the screen shot. If the screen shot moves down, drag it back up to its original location.

7. Type **2.** and press the Tab key. Type **Navigate to the place you saved the file. Double-click the icon next to the file name.**

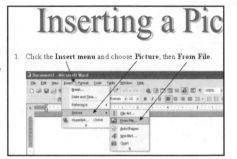

Printing the File

Print the file to see how cool it looks. Worksheets with screen shots and labels can make teaching computer skills much easier.

If you're going to use this worksheet, you might want to include a screen shot showing how to navigate to the picture file, directions on formatting the picture, and anything else you want your students to know.

Keeping a copy of the finished worksheet next to the computer may save you answering questions on inserting pictures from a file.

Create a Newsletter

Send a Newsletter Home Every Week

Newsletters are a terrific way to organize information in an attractive format. The *Word* Newsletter Assistant is a quick and easy way to make a newsletter template. It takes you step-by-step through the process of creating a standard newsletter. You can also create a newsletter on your own from scratch. You'll learn to create both in this activity.

> ### This Activity Covers the Following Topics
> - Changing the Margins
> - Setting the Columns
> - Viewing the Column Boundaries
> - Creating the Banner
> - Separating the Banner from the Text
> - Saving As a Template
> - Inserting the Stories
> - Formatting the Headings
> - Inserting Clip Art
> - Inserting a Watermark
> - Inserting a Border
> - Saving This Issue

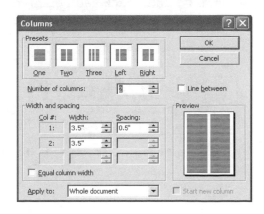

Changing the Margins

1. Create a *Word* document. Newsletters never have large margins, so the first thing you're going to do is change the default margins.

2. ⊞ XP, 2000 and 97 users, click the **File** menu and choose **Page Setup**.

   🍎 X, 2001 and 98 users, click the **Format** menu and choose **Document**.

3. Click the **Margins** tab. Choose **.5"** margins on all sides. Click **OK**. If you see a warning that the margins are set outside the printable area, click **Ignore**.

Setting the Columns

Click the **Columns** button and drag to choose **2 Columns**.

or

Click the **Format** menu and choose **Columns**. Click **Two** and click **OK**. **Note:** You may click **Line Between** if you want a line separating the columns.

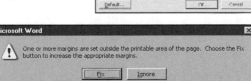

Viewing the Column Boundaries

1. 🪟 XP users, click the **Tools menu** and choose **Options** (Preferences in 98). X users, click the **File menu** and choose **Preferences**. 2001 users, click the **Edit menu** and choose **Preferences**.

2. Click the **View tab** and click **Text Boundaries**. Click **OK**.

The boundaries won't print; they're just to help you see where the columns are while you're writing.

Creating the Banner

1. 🪟 XP users, click the **Tools menu**, click **Options**, click the **General tab**, and click **Automatically create drawing canvas when inserting AutoShapes** to remove the check. This prevents the Drawing Canvas from appearing.

2. Click the **Rectangle button** on the **Drawing toolbar** and draw a rectangle across the top of the page to mark the banner location. Cover both columns as shown in the newsletter on page 114. Click the **arrow** next to the **Fill Color button** on the **Drawing toolbar** and choose **None**.

3. Click the **WordArt button** or click the **Insert menu**, choose **Picture,** and then **WordArt**. Type the name of your newsletter, e.g., 5th Grade News.

4. Click the **Clip Art icon** or click the **Insert** menu, choose **Picture,** and then **Clip Art**. **Choose a picture** for the banner.

🪟 *XP, 2000, 97*

 98   *X*   *2001*

5. Click the **Text Box icon** or click the **Insert** menu and choose **Text Box**. **Draw a text box** and **type your professional name**. Move it to the **bottom of the banner**.

🪟 *XP, 2000, 97*

 98   *X, 2001*

Mr. Michael Rodriques

6. Click the **Line Color icon** and choose **No Line**.

7. Create another text box. Click the **Insert** menu and choose **Date and Time**. Choose a date style. **Note:** Be sure Update Automatically is not checked so that the date won't change. You'll want to keep the date constant for this issue of the newsletter. Click the **Line Color** icon and choose **No Line**.

8. Insert or draw any other **graphics or text for the banner**.

🪟 *XP, 2000, 97*

 98   *X, 2001*

9. Press [SHIFT] and **click each element of the banner** to select it. Don't forget to click the rectangle. Click the **Draw button** and choose **Group**.

Draw

Ungrouped - many handles   *Grouped - 8 handles*

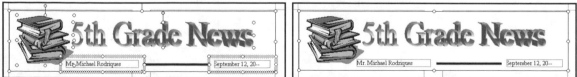

The banner shows only eight handles to indicate it is one object.

If you start typing your newsletter stories now, they will move behind the banner. You need the banner to force the text to stay below it. You'll do that next.

Separating the Banner from the Text

1. **Right-click** the banner (Macintosh users [CTRL]-click) or click the **Format** menu and choose **Format Object**.

2. Click the **Layout** tab and then **Advanced**. ⊞ 97 and 🍎 98 users, skip this step and go to step 3.

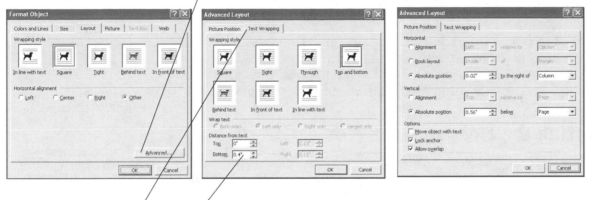

3. Click the **Text Wrapping** tab.

4. Click **Top and bottom**. Type **.4** in the box next to **Bottom** to allow white space between the banner and the text.

5. Click the **Picture Position** tab and remove the check mark from **Move object with text**. Click **Lock anchor**. Click **OK** twice.

Saving As a Template

You are going to save this newsletter as a template. Newsletters are ideal documents to save as templates, so you can open up a blank document formatted as a newsletter. You'll be able to insert stories for this issue and save it without accidentally overwriting the previous issue.

1. Click the **File** menu and choose **Save As**.

2. Give the file the name **Newsletter**.

3. Click the **Save as type** menu and choose **Document Template**. The default place to save is in the *Office* Templates folder.

To use a template, you must click the **File menu** *and choose* **New**, *then click the Templates tab.*

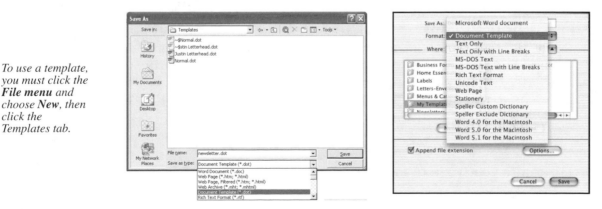

Inserting the Stories

1. Open the file **Newsletter Stories** from the "Learning Word" folder on the CD-ROM that came with this book. You could type your newsletter, but you can also share the responsibility with students. This part of the activity shows you how to copy and paste stories that were typed and saved earlier.

2. Press ⌃A (Windows) ⌘A (Macintosh) or click the **Edit** menu and choose **Select All** to select the entire document.

3. Press ⌃C (Windows) ⌘C (Macintosh) or click the **Edit** menu and choose **Copy**.

4. Click the **Window** menu and choose **Newsletter** (the newsletter you just saved).

5. **Click the top of the first column**. Press ⌃V (Windows) ⌘V (Macintosh) or click the **Edit** menu and choose **Paste**. The new stories flow into both columns. **Hint:** If the banner moves, just drag it back up. You aren't doing anything wrong, it just happens.

Formatting the Headings

1. Select the first heading, **It's Back to School Time** and **boldface** the text.

2. Press ⌃] (Windows) ⌘] (Macintosh) to increase the text size to **16**. Make every heading **boldfaced** and **16 point**.

Inserting Clip Art

1. Choose a **clip art** picture to enhance the **first story**.

2. Choose **Tight** as the text wrap option from **Format Picture**.

Inserting a Watermark

1. Insert a clip art picture into the **Grading Scale** story.

2. Click the **Draw button**, choose **Order** (**Arrange** in X, 2001), and then **Send Behind Text** (**Behind Text** in X, 2001). 97 and 98 users, click the **Draw** button on the **Drawing toolbar**, choose **Order**, and then **Send Behind Text**.

3. Click the **Format** menu and choose **Picture**. Click the **Picture** tab and choose **Watermark** (**Washout** in XP). Click **OK**.

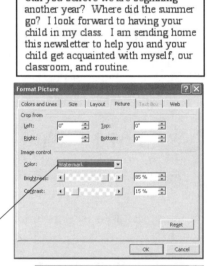

Inserting a Border

1. **Select** the **text at the bottom of the Schedule** reminding parents to **send library books to school**. Using any method you've learned, **decrease the font size** until it **all fits on two lines**. This will draw the eye to the paragraph.

3. **Select all the text** in the **schedule**.

4. Click the **Format** menu and choose **Borders and Shading**.

5. Make sure you are in the **Borders** tab.

6. Choose **Shadow** from the **Setting** choices.

7. Click the **Width** menu and choose **4 1/2 pt.** Click **OK**.

Saving This Issue

You're all done! **Save** the file with a name that identifies it as the newsletter with the date so that you can find it next month or next year, e.g., Oct_12_02News.

Create a Brochure

Create a Great-Looking Informational Brochure

Brochures draw the eye. When we see a brochure, we automatically pick it up and look at it. That's why they are such a good idea in education. Teachers can use the brochure format to present information in a new way to grab kids' attention. Assigning a brochure as a report will allow students to show creativity, as well as what they have learned.

> ### This Activity Covers the Following Topics
> - Setting Up the Page
> - Setting the Columns
> - Viewing the Text Boundaries
> - Inserting a Page Break
> - Understanding the Brochure Layout
> - Creating the Cover
> - Inserting a Text Box
> - Inserting a Picture from a File
> - Creating the Folded-to-the-Inside Page
> - Creating the Back
> - Creating the Inside Page
> - Saving the File
> - Printing the File

Setting Up the Page

⊞ XP, 2000, 97   *This section is for Word XP, 2000 and 97 users only. Users of other versions go to your section of this activity.*

Brochures have very small margins and are frequently laid out on a horizontal page.

1. Create a new *Word* document.

2. Click the **File menu** and choose **Page Setup**.

3. Type **.5** for each margin.

4. Click **Landscape**. ⊞ 2000, 97 users, click the **Paper Size** tab. Click **OK**.

⬤ X, 2001, 98   *This section is for Word X, 2001, and 98 users only. Users of other versions go to your section of this activity.*

1. Create a new *Word* document.

2. Click the **Format menu** and choose **Document**.

3. Type **.5** for each margin.

4. Click the **Page Setup** button.

5. Click the **Landscape** icon.

6. Click **OK**, then **OK** again.

Setting the Columns

Click the **Columns** button and drag to choose **3 Columns**. **Note:** More information on setting columns can be found in the newsletter activity.

Viewing the Text Boundaries

The default for *Word* is for the boundaries to be hidden, but you may find it helpful to see the column boundaries as you are working.

1. XP users, click the **Tools menu** and choose **Options** (**Preferences** in 98). X users, click the **Word menu** and choose **Preferences**. 2001 users, click the **Edit menu** and choose **Preferences.**

2. Click the **View tab**, and then **Text Boundaries** and **OK.**

Inserting a Page Break

Click the **Insert** menu and choose **Break** and then **Page Break**. Click **OK**. Now you have two pages with three columns on each.

Understanding the Brochure Layout

One of the most confusing things about creating a brochure is understanding where everything goes. Below is a template for a typical two-page brochure. The outside must have three separate columns of information. On the inside, however, the data can cover one, two, or three columns.

All text in this activity will be graphic text—you'll be able to click and drag it to a new location with the arrow tool. The columns in the document will be used as guides; text will not be typed directly into them. Instead, WordArt and Text Boxes will be created.

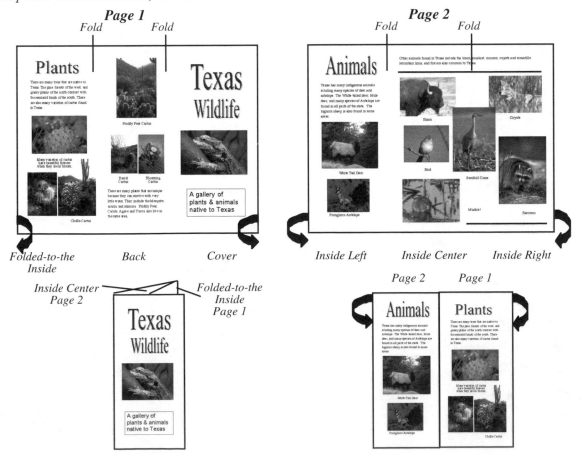

Creating the Cover

1. Click the **WordArt** icon and choose a style from the gallery.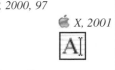

2. Type **Texas** and click **OK**. If it has black handles, **right-click the WordArt**, choose **Format WordArt**, click the **Layout**, and choose **In front of text**. Move the word to the front cover (right column) using the text boundaries to guide you.

3. Click the **WordArt** button again. Pick the same style, and type **Wildlife**. Move it under the word "Texas."

XP, 2000, 97
98
X, 2001

Inserting a Text Box

1. Click the **Text Box** icon or click the **Insert** menu and choose **Text Box**.

2. Drag to **draw a text box** in the **lower left corner of the cover** and type **A gallery of plants & animals native to Texas**.

3. Choose a **font** and **font size** to contrast with the WordArt text.

Inserting a Picture from a File

1. Make sure nothing is selected, then click the **Insert** menu, choose **Picture,** and then **From File**.

2. Navigate to the **Pictures** folder on the CD-ROM that came with this book. Double-click a picture of a plant or animal from Texas. If it has black handles, **right-click the screen shot**, choose **Format Picture**, click the **Layout** (**Wrapping** in 97), and choose **In front of text** (**None** in 97).

Creating the Folded-to-the-Inside Page

1. Make a WordArt title called **Plants** and place it on the panel that will be folded to the inside.

2. Draw a **Text Box** and write text about the trees of Texas. Sample text might read **There are many trees that are native to Texas. The pine forests of the west, and grassy plains of the north contrast with the semiarid brush of the south. There are also many varieties of cactus found in Texas**.

3. Insert pictures of plants from Texas and **create text boxes** to label them.

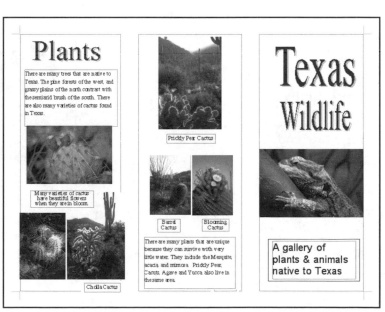

Creating the Back

The folded-to-the-inside panel and the back panel will both show when the brochure is folded flat, so they may coordinate as in the example above, or the back may be a completely separate panel.

1. Insert a **Text Box describing the plants** native to Texas.

2. Insert **pictures** and **text boxes to label them**.

If you don't want a line around the text box, it's easy to remove. Click the box. Click the Line Color button and choose No Line. The dotted box will remain, however. It is a text boundary that you turned on early in this activity.

Creating the Inside Page

Because the first panel of the previous page will be folded over the center and right panels of this page, it is important to create the left panel to coordinate with that page.

1. **Scroll down** to **page 2**.

2. Make a **WordArt** title reading **Animals** and place it on the left panel.

3. Draw a **Text Box** and write text about the animals of Texas and insert pictures.

4. **Create the rest of the page**. You can make two separate panels or spread the information across two panels.

5. Let's look at the brochure as it will look when printed by turning off the Text Boundaries. 🔳 XP users, click the **Tools menu** and choose **Options** (**Preferences** in 98). X users, click the **Word menu** and choose **Preferences**. 2001 users, click the **Edit menu** and choose **Preferences**. Click the **View tab**, and then **Text Boundaries** and **OK**.

Saving the File

After all this work, you want to be sure to save it! **Save** the file and give it a name you can identify with the project.

Printing the File

1. **Print** the file.

2. Place the **blank sides** of the pages **together** and **fold** the brochure.

3. You may need to change the margins or widen the column guides. To widen the space between the columns, click the **Format** menu, choose **Columns**, and increase the numbers in the **Spacing** box.

Note: This is just one way to create a brochure. Instead of making all the text into graphics (WordArt and Text Boxes), you could type as you normally do—directly onto the page instead of using the columns as guides.

Turn to page 147 to see student-created brochures.

Create Linked Pages

Create an Interactive Activity

Most schools allow students to use the Internet for research. To prepare students, teachers can create *Word* files with hypertext that looks similar to Internet pages. Students click blue, underlined text (hypertext) to navigate to other *Word* documents to learn about a subject in a controlled environment. When they have opened and read the files created by the teacher, they can open a teacher-created hotlinks page that takes them directly to selected Web sites. You'll learn to link *Word* documents in this activity, and then make a related Web page in the next one.

> ### This Activity Covers the Following Topics
> - Learning How Hyperlinks Between Files Work
> - Creating a Hyperlink
> - Adding an Internet Link
> - Creating a Hotlist
> - Using the Hotlist
> - Creating an Internet Worksheet
> - Hyperlinking to *PowerPoint*
> - Learning How Hyperlinks Within a Document Work
> - Creating a Bookmark
> - Creating a Hyperlink Within the Document

Learning How Hyperlinks Between Files Work

1. Drag the "Animals" folder from the "Learning Word" folder on the CD-ROM that came with this book onto your hard drive. Windows users, **right-click the folder** and choose **Properties**. If there is a check in the **Read-only** box, remove it. Click **Apply**. This allows you to save the files.

2. Open the file "Homepage" from this folder.

3. Place the **pointer** on the word **Mammals**. The word is blue and underlined to show it is linked and the cursor changes to a hand (a double-crosshair in ⊞ XP).

4. **Click** (⊞ XP users ⌨-click). "Mammals" opens because it was linked to the "Homepage" file.

5. Place the **pointer** on the **arrow** at the **bottom of the page**. The cursor changes to a hand (a double-crosshair in ⊞ XP).

6. **Click** (⊞ XP users ⌨-click). The file "Homepage" appears. Notice that the word Mammals is now purple to indicate that you have opened that link (just like on a Web page).

7. Click the word **Rodents** (⊞ XP users ⌨-click), and then click the **arrow** on the Rodents page to return to the Homepage. Click **Amphibians**, then the **arrow** to get back to the **Homepage**.

This section is for Word XP, and 2000 users only.
Users of other versions go to your section of this activity.

Creating a Hyperlink

1. **Select** the word **Fish** on the **Homepage** file. **Click** the **Insert Hyperlink** button on the **Standard toolbar** or click the **Insert menu** and choose **Insert Hyperlink**. You can also press ⌨CTRL⌨K.

2. Navigate to the **Animals folder** that you dragged to the hard drive. **Double-click Fish.**

3. The text becomes blue and underlined. ⌨CTRL-click the word **Fish**. The Fish file opens.

4. Click the **blue arrow** at the bottom of the Fish page.

5. **Click** the Insert Hyperlink button on the **Standard toolbar** or click the **Insert menu** and choose **Insert Hyperlink**.

6. **Link the arrow** to the **Homepage** file.

7. **Save** the file. **Click outside the arrow** to deselect it, then **click the arrow** to test the link.

8. **Link** the **Birds** file and the **Homepage** file and **Save** both of them.

Adding an Internet Link

1. Click **after the word Birds** and press ⌨ENTER. Type **San Diego Zoo**. See the screen shot below. **Select** the words.

2. **Click** the Insert Hyperlink button on the **Standard toolbar** or click the **Insert menu** and choose **Insert Hyperlink**. You can also press ⌨CTRL⌨K.

3. Type **www.sandiegozoo.org** in the **Address** box. ⊞ 2000 users, type in the **Type the file or Web page name** box at the **top** of the window. Click **OK**.

4. The text becomes blue and underlined. ⌨CTRL-click the words. Your browser opens to the San Diego Zoo homepage.

5. Click **Homepage.doc** from the **Taskbar** at the bottom of the screen. Turn to Creating a Hotlist on page 122.

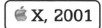

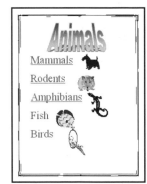

This section is for Word X and 2001 users only.
Users of other versions go to your section of this activity.

Creating a Hyperlink

1. **Select** the word **Fish** on the **Homepage** file. **Click** the **Insert Hyperlink** button on the **Standard toolbar** or click the **Insert menu** and choose **Insert Hyperlink**. You can also press ⌨⌘⌨K.

2. Click the **Documents tab**. Click the **Select** button. Navigate to the **Animals folder** that you dragged to the hard drive. **Double-click Fish**. Fish.doc appears at the top of the window in **Link to** to show you the document it is linked to. Click **OK**.

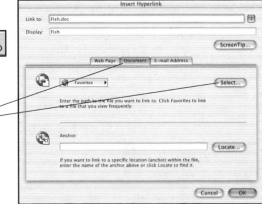

3. The text becomes blue and underlined. Click the word **Fish**. The Fish file opens.

4. Click the **blue arrow** at the bottom of the Fish page.

5. **Click** the **Insert Hyperlink** button on the **Standard toolbar** or click the **Insert menu** and choose **Insert Hyperlink**. You can also press ⌘K.

6. **Link the arrow** to the **Homepage** file.

7. **Save** the file. **Click outside the arrow** to deselect it, then **click the arrow** to test the link.

8. **Link** the **Birds** file and the **Homepage** file and **Save** both of them.

Adding an Internet Link

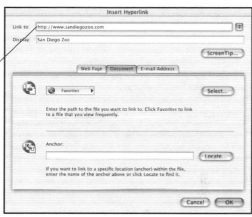

1. Click **after the word Birds** and press RETURN. Type **San Diego Zoo**. See the screen shot below. **Select** the words.

2. **Click** the **Insert Hyperlink** button on the **Standard toolbar** or click the **Insert menu** and choose **Insert Hyperlink**. You can also press CTRL K.

3. Type **www.sandiegozoo.org** in the **Link to** box. ⊞ 2000 users, type in the **Type the file or Web page name** box at the top of the window. Click **OK**.

4. The text becomes blue and underlined. **Click the words**. Your browser opens to the San Diego Zoo homepage.

5. Choose **Word** from the **Dock** or **Application menu** (the application menu is in the upper right corner of the screen. Turn to Creating a Hotlist on the next page.

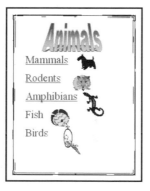

 *This section is for Word 97 and 98 users only. Users of other versions go to your section of this activity.*

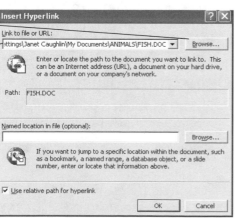

Creating a Hyperlink

1. **Select** the word **Fish** on the **Homepage** file. **Click** the **Insert Hyperlink** button on the **Standard toolbar** or click the **Insert menu** and choose **Insert Hyperlink**. You can also press CTRL K (Windows) ⌘K (Macintosh).

2. Click the **Browse button** at the **top of the screen**. Navigate to the **Animals folder** that you dragged to the hard drive. **Double-click Fish**. The path of the Fish file appears at the top of the window to show you the document it is linked to. Click **OK**.

3. The text becomes blue and underlined. It also reverts to a font size of 12. Click to the **right of the word** and **drag left** to **select** it. Change the size to **48**.

4. Click the word **Fish**. The Fish file opens.

5. Click the **blue arrow** at the bottom of the Fish page.

6. **Click** the **Insert Hyperlink** button on the **Standard toolbar** or click the **Insert menu** and choose **Insert Hyperlink**. You can also press CTRL K (Windows) ⌘K (Macintosh).

Adding an Internet Link

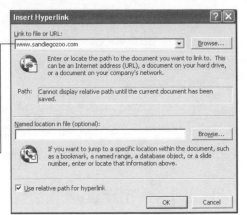

1. Click **after the word Birds** and press [ENTER] (Windows) [RETURN] (Macintosh). Type **San Diego Zoo**. See the screen shot below. **Select** the words.

2. **Click** the **Insert Hyperlink** button on the **Standard toolbar** or click the **Insert menu** and choose **Insert Hyperlink**. You can also press [CTRL][K].

3. Type **www.sandiegozoo.org** in the **Link to title or URL** box. Click **OK**.

4. The text becomes blue and underlined. **Click the words**. Your browser opens to the San Diego Zoo homepage.

5. [Windows] 97 users, choose **Homepage.doc** from the **Taskbar** at the bottom of the screen. [Apple] 98 users, choose **Word** from the **Dock** or **Application menu** (the application menu is in the upper right corner of the screen). Turn to Creating a Hotlist below.

Creating a Hotlist

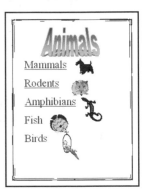

Students have limited computer time, so when you assign them to do research on the Internet, they can't waste time surfing. Using the link option in *Word*, you can create a worksheet that includes Web sites you have already researched. Students click the link and *Word* launches the browser to the chosen site.

1. Open the file "Zoos" from the "Learning Word" folder on the CD-ROM that came with this book.

2. Click the **blank line under San Diego Zoo**.

3. Type **http://www.sandiegozoo.org** and press the **Spacebar**. The text becomes blue and underlined.

4. Using this method, type the following zoo URL addresses, followed by a space: Woodland Park Zoo **http://www.zoo.org/** Los Angeles Zoo **http://www.lazoo.org/** American Zoo & Aquarium Association **http://www.aza.org/FindZooAquarium/**

You don't really have to type the entire address. Typing www.zoo.org will open the Woodland Park Zoo site.

Using the Hotlist

1. Place the **mouse pointer on the web address for the San Diego Zoo**. The cursor is shaped like a pointer finger (a double-crosshair in [Windows] XP) to indicate that a hyperlink has been created.

2. **Click** the text ([Windows] XP users [CTRL]-click). Your browser launches and the San Diego Zoo homepage appears.

3. Windows users, click **Zoos** in the **Taskbar** at the bottom of the screen. Macintosh users, choose **Microsoft *Word*** from the **Dock** or **Application Icon** in the upper right corner of the menu bar.

4. Click the **other zoo sites using this method**.

Creating an Internet Worksheet

You can create a worksheet with an Internet link that students can use for research and for taking notes or writing answers. You'll make one that students can use to research inventors.

1. Open the file "Inventors" from the "Learning Word" folder on the CD-ROM that came with this book.

2. Click the **Biography.com** icon.

3. Click the **Insert** menu and choose **Insert Hyperlink**.

4. Type **http://biography.com/**. Click **OK**. **Save** the file.

5. Now you're going to be the student and use the worksheet. Click the newly created **link**. Your Web browser will launch and go to the Biography.com homepage.

6. Type **Alexander Graham Bell** in the search box and press [ENTER] (Windows) [RETURN] (Macintosh) or click **Find**.

7. Read the biography of Bell. When you discover what he invented, go back to *Word* to type the answer.

   Windows users, click **Inventors** in the **Taskbar** at the bottom of the screen.

   Macintosh users, choose **Microsoft** *Word* from the **Dock** or the **Application Icon** in the upper right corner of the menu bar.

8. Type the answer in the blank area under Alexander Graham Bell.

9. Using the **Taskbar** (Windows) or the **Dock** or **Application Icon** (Macintosh) to move between your browser and the Inventors file, answer the rest of the questions.

Hyperlinking to *PowerPoint*

1. Open the file "Balanced Diet" from the "Learning Word" folder on the CD-ROM that came with this book. This file is the beginning of a worksheet that is being created for use with students.

2. Drag to select the words **Food Pyramid Guide** in the last sentence. You're going to link this to the *PowerPoint* file "Eat Right."

3. Click the **Insert** menu and choose **Hyperlink**.

4. **Link** the **Eat Right** file from the Learning *Word* folder.

5. Type **#2** after the link (**Eat Right.ppt#2**) to indicate you want students to look at the second slide in the presentation.

6. Click **OK**. The text is underlined and blue in color to indicate it has been linked.

8. Click the **linked text**. The *PowerPoint* program opens to the second slide of the "Food Pyramid" presentation showing the Food Pyramid.

9. Students will return to the "Nutrition" worksheet for further reading after the PowerPoint presentation is finished. Windows users, click **Nutrition** in the **Taskbar** at the bottom of the screen. Macintosh users, choose **Microsoft** *Word* from the **Dock** or **Application Icon** in the upper right corner of the menu bar.

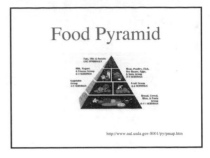

Learning How Hyperlinks Within a Document Work

Hyperlinks and bookmarks work together in lengthy documents to save you time. Instead of scrolling through a long document looking for a certain section, you can set bookmarks and hyperlink to the bookmarks. This allows the reader to jump directly to a section, read it, and then jump back to the top. You've probably experienced this in lengthy Web pages.

1. Open the file "Amphibians Information" from the "Animals" folder you copied to the hard drive. Notice that the words **Frogs** and **Top** are **hyperlinked**.

2. Click the hyperlinked word **Frogs** in the **first paragraph**. (XP users [CTRL]-click.) You jump to the Frog paragraph.

3. Click the word **Top** (XP users [CTRL]-click).

XP, 2000   *This section is for Word XP and 2000 users only.*
Users of other versions go to your section of this activity.

Creating a Bookmark

1. **Scroll** down to **page 2**.

2. Select the large word **Toad** at the top of the page.

3. Click the **Insert** menu and choose **Bookmark**.

4. Type **Toad** and click the **Add button**.

Creating a Hyperlink Within the Document

1. Scroll to **page 1**. Select the word **toads** in the first paragraph.

2. Click the **Insert Hyperlink** button.

3. Click the **Bookmark** button.

4. **Double-click Toad,** then click **OK**.

5. **Click the newly linked word toads** in the first paragraph (XP users [CTRL]-click). The Toad story appears.

6. Using this method, link the word **Top**. The bookmark for Top has been created for you.

7. **Link** the **Salamander** information.

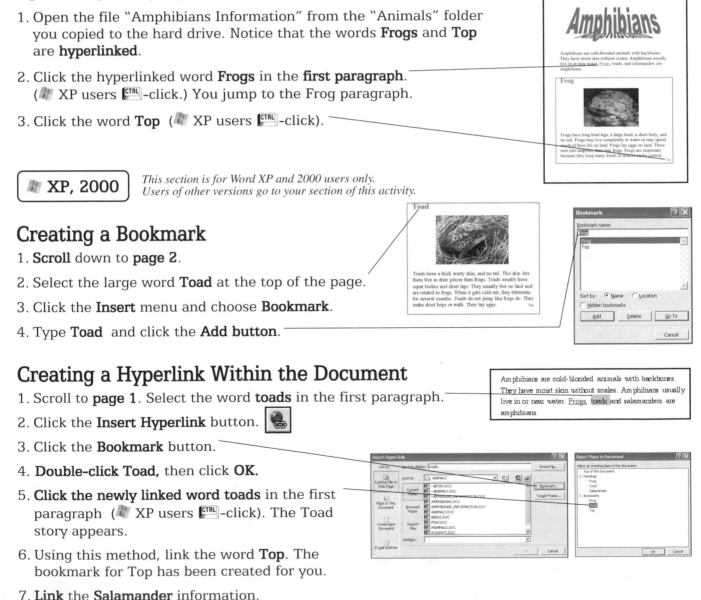

X, 2001 *This section is for Word X and 2001 users only.*
Users of other versions go to your section of this activity.

Creating a Bookmark

1. **Scroll** down to **page 2**.

2. Select the large word **Toad** at the top of the page.

3. Click the **Insert** menu and choose **Bookmark**.

4. Type **Toad** and click the **Add button.**

Creating a Hyperlink Within the Document

1. Scroll to **page 1**. Select the word **toads** in the first paragraph.

2. Click the **Insert Hyperlink** button.

3. Click the **Locate** button in the **Anchor** section.

4. **Double-click Toad,** then click **OK.**

5. **Click the newly linked word toads** in the first paragraph. The Toad story appears.

6. Using this method, **link** the word **Top**. The bookmark for Top has been created for you.

7. **Link** the **Salamander** information.

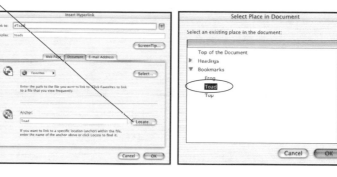

---

97 98 *This section is for Word X and 2001 users only.*
Users of other versions go to your section of this activity.

Creating a Bookmark

1. **Scroll** down to **page 2**.

2. Select the large word **Toad** at the top of the page.

3. Click the **Insert** menu and choose **Bookmark**.

4. Type **Toad** and click the **Add button.**

Creating a Hyperlink Within the Document

1. Scroll to **page 1**. Select the word **toads** in the first paragraph.

2. Click the **Insert Hyperlink** button.

3. Click the **Browse** button in the **Named location in file** section.

4. **Double-click Toad,** then click **OK.**

5. **Click the newly linked word toads** in the first paragraph. The Toad story appears.

6. Using this method, **link** the word **Top**. The bookmark for Top has been created for you.

7. **Link** the **Salamander** information.

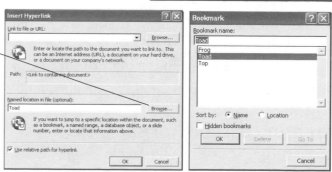

Create a Web Page

Create an Animals Web Page

Hopefully, you have learned to create hyperlinked pages from the previous activity. Now you're ready to create a related Web page. Since the linked pages taught the students about animals, this Web page will take the students to good zoo sites so that they can learn more about animals. *Word* 2000 has a much improved Web page interface. Virtually anything you create in *Word* will look the same on the Web. Earlier versions will take a few other steps.

> ### This Activity Covers the Following Topics
> - Creating the Title for the Page
> - Inserting Pictures
> - Creating a Table for the Text
> - Creating a Table for the Web Sites
> - Adding Lines for Interest
> - Saving the File
> - Saving as a Web Page
> - Viewing the Page as a Web Page

Creating the Title for the Page

1. Create a *Word* document. Press ⌨ENTER (Windows) ⌨RETURN (Macintosh) 5 times.

2. ⊞ XP, 2000 and X, 2001 users, create a **WordArt** title for your Web page.

   ⊞ 97 and 98 users, **type the title into the document**. Use a great color, a large size, and boldface. WordArt won't show in your browser if you are using these versions of *Word*.

3. **Center** the title at the top of the page.

Inserting Pictures

1. Click two spaces below the title. Choose **16** from the **Font Size** menu and a black color if you have changed it.

2. Click the **Insert** menu, choose **Picture**, and then **From file**. Navigate to the "Pictures" folder on the CD-ROM that came with this book.

3. **Double-click** the "Pictures" folder, then "Animals" and the "Zoo" folder, then on a picture.

4. **Drag** a handle **to make the picture smaller**.

5. **Insert another picture**. Make it small enough to fit on the same line.

Creating a Table for the Text

To be sure that text appears where you want it to be, and margins are just as you want them to look, you can type text into a table.

1. **Press** ⌤ (Windows) ⏎ (Macintosh) until the cursor is blinking two lines below the pictures. You're going to draw a table at this position.

2. Click the **Table** menu and choose **Draw Table**.

3. The cursor turns into a pencil. Drag the pencil diagonally down and to the right to **draw a rectangle**.

4. **Type text below** into the table.

   Both wild and domesticated animals live in captivity in a zoo. The keeping of wild animals in captivity began in ancient times. As wild populations continue to shrink in their dwindling habitats, zoos must now fill the roles of breeding grounds and reservoirs of genetic diversity for the many species in danger of becoming extinct. Sometimes there are larger populations of some endangered species in zoos than in the wild. Visit the famous zoos below and check out the animals.

5. Click the **Tables and Borders button** on the **Standard toolbar**. Click the **Outside Borders button** and choose **No Border**. If you don't see this button, click the **Table menu** and choose **Borders**, then **None**. Click outside the table.

Creating a Table for the Web Sites

Data on the Web are frequently presented in a table format, especially if the information is lined up. You'll be entering Web site names and addresses in a table format.

1. **Press** ⌤ (Windows) ⏎ (Macintosh) until the cursor is **blinking two lines below the text**.

2. Click the **Table** menu and choose **Insert**, then **Table**. ⊞ 97 and 98 users, click the **Table** menu and choose **Insert Table.**

3. Choose **2 columns** and **4 rows**. Click **OK**.

4. Enter the **data in the table below**.

San Diego Zoo	http://www.sandiegozoo.org
Woodland Park Zoo	http://www.zoo.org/
Los Angeles Zoo	http://www.lazoo.org/
Smithsonian National Zoological Park	http://natzoo.si.edu

Adding Lines for Interest

Drawing lines can add interest to a Web page and clearly separate sections of a page. ⊞ 97 and 98 users, skip this step and turn to Saving the File because the lines won't show in your browser.

1. Click the **Straight Line** icon and drag to draw a line between the text and the table. **Hint:** Holding down ⇧ while you draw forces a straight line.

2. Choose a **coordinating color** from the **Line Color** icon.

3. Choose a **wider line** from the **Line Style** icon.

4. **Click** the finished **line** and **copy it**.

5. **Paste this line below the table**.

Saving the File

Whenever you create a Web page in *Word*, you need to save it in two ways. You need to save it as a *Word* document and then you need to save it as a Web page.

1. Click the **File** menu and choose **Save**.

2. Save the file as you would any *Word* document and name it **zoopage**. **Note:** It's a good idea to create a web page folder and save any web pages in that folder.

Saving as a Web Page

1. Click the **File** menu and choose **Save As Web Page**. ⊞ 97 and 98 users, choose Save as HTML. Click **Save**.

2. Depending on the version you are using, a warning may appear informing you about the changes that will occur when you save the page. Click **Continue** because you've already saved the page as a *Word* file.

Viewing the Page as a Web Page

1. Click the **Web Layout View** icon or click the **View** menu and choose **Web Layout**. ⊞ 97 and 98 users, choose **Web Page Preview**.

2. **Launch** your **browser** (Internet Explorer, Netscape Navigator, etc.).

3. Click the **File menu**, choose **Open file** or **Open**, and then navigate to the location where you saved the file as a Web page. Depending on the version of *Word* and your browser, your Web page may look very much like the *Word* version, or it may have some differences. If you want to make changes, open the *Word* version of the file and make your changes, then save it both as a *Word* file and as a Web file.

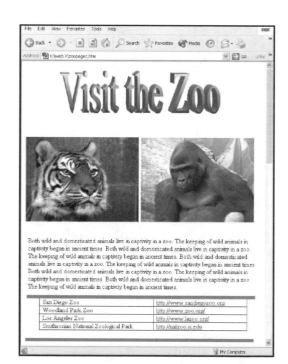

The next two sections of the book contain *Word* files created by teachers and students for use in the classroom. You can use them as examples or modify them to meet your needs. The How Teachers Use *Word* section contains slide shows made by teachers for use as teaching tools. The How Students use *Word* section contains slide shows made by students as part of a curriculum project. The cartoon characters and their captions indicate the grade level and subject of the lesson. Read the summary to see if the lesson fits into your curriculum. The slide shows and support materials are found on the CD-ROM that is included with this book. To view the materials, match the section title in the book with a folder on the CD-ROM, e.g., Teachers use *Word*. Open that folder and match the teacher name in the book and on the CD-ROM.

Section title

Teacher(s) who contributed the lesson

Grade level

Contact information for the teacher(s)

Lesson summary

Objectives or Standards

Sample materials on the CD-ROM

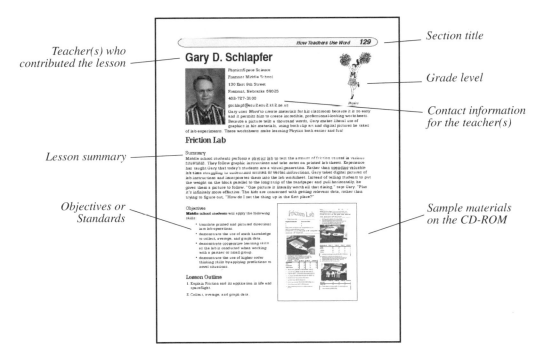

Primary *Intermediate* *Middle School* *High School*

How Teachers Use *Word*

Detailed Contents

Each activity shows pages from its accompanying Word *file.*
The complete Word *files are included on the CD-ROM that comes with this book.*

Gary D. Schlapfer

Physics

Physics and Space Science

Fremont Middle School

130 East 9th Street

Fremont, NE 68025

402-727-3100

gschlapf@esu2.esu2.k12.ne.us

Gary uses *Word* to create materials for his classroom because it is so easy and it permits him to create incredible, professional-looking worksheets. Because a picture tells a thousand words, Gary makes liberal use of graphics in his materials, using both clip art and digital pictures he takes of lab experiments. These worksheets make learning physics both easier and fun!

Friction Lab

Summary

Middle school students perform a physics lab to test the amount of friction caused in various situations. They follow graphic instructions and take notes on printed lab sheets. Experience has taught Gary that today's students are a visual generation. Rather than spending valuable lab time struggling to understand written or verbal instructions, Gary takes digital pictures of lab instructions and incorporates them into the lab worksheet. Instead of telling students to put the weight on the block parallel to the long strip of the sandpaper and pull horizontally, he gives them a picture to follow. "One picture is literally worth all that dialog," says Gary. "Plus it's infinitely more effective. The kids are concerned with getting relevant data, rather than trying to figure out, "How do I set the thing up in the first place?"

Objectives

Middle school students will apply the following skills:

- translate printed and pictured directions into lab operations.
- demonstrate the use of math knowledge to collect, average, and graph data.
- demonstrate cooperative learning skills as the lab is conducted when working with a partner or small group.
- demonstrate the use of higher-order thinking skills by applying predictions to novel situations.

Lesson Outline

1. Explain friction and its application in life and spaceflight.

2. Collect, average, and graph data.

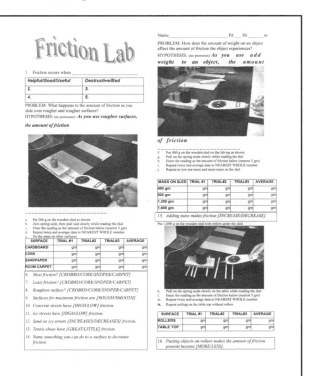

Simple Machines - Inclined Planes

Physics

Summary

Middle school students complete a worksheet to show they can apply concepts they have learned in labs and teaching situations. Gary makes this worksheet graphic because, "I want kids to actually see it and then try and take it to a little bit higher level in Bloom's Taxonomy. They take the information I give them, see it in a novel circumstance, and apply it." In this worksheet they see a drawing of an inclined plane. Then they see it made longer, made shorter, and made taller. Gary asks, "What will that do to your effort?" In the levers section, students identify the effort arm and the load arm, and they are asked, "If you pull down here, what goes up? How do you pull harder? How do the distances compare?" Students then apply these concepts in space.

Objectives

Middle school students will apply the following skills:

- translate printed and pictured directions into lab operations.
- demonstrate the use of math knowledge to complete tasks on the worksheet.
- if working with a partner or small group, demonstrate cooperative learning skills as the lab is conducted.
- verbally explain components of simple machines and their application through an explanation of the lab work conducted.
- demonstrate the use of higher-order thinking skills by applying predictions to novel situations.

Lesson Outline

1. Teach inclined planes and levers with concrete examples like teeter-totters; squeezing a kid's hand with your hand, and then with a pair of pliers; discuss bicycles and the gear ratios, the differences when you get force and when you get speed.

2. Assign this worksheet.

Additional worksheet files are available on the CD-ROM.

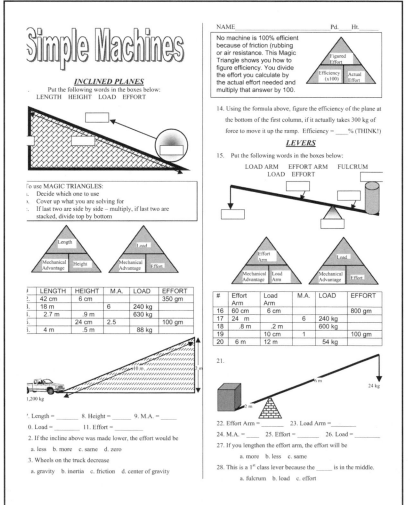

Krista Mead

Elementary Instructional Technology Specialist

Banfield Elementary School

301 17th St SW

Austin, MN 55912

507-437-6623

kmead@austin.k12.mn.us

All Subjects

Krista thinks the hyperlinking feature of *Word* is fabulous! Kids like the Internet, so if you create a linked set of pages, it's like using the Internet, and kids are automatically eager to do the lesson.

Search the Internet

Summary
As students work through a set of hyperlinked pages, they learn about the myths and realities of researching on the Internet.

Objectives
Minnesota Electronic Curriculum Repository Inquiry and Research Standards that are addressed include:

> B. media sources, including selecting a topic and framing a question; accessing information from any or all of electronic media, print, interviews, and other sources; recording and organizing information; and reporting findings in written, oral, or visual presentation;

Lesson Outline
1. Copy the folder "Search the Internet" onto each computer or onto the server. This folder is inside the Krista Mead folder inside the Teacher folder.

2. Instruct students to open the homepage file.

3. Instruct students to click the Common SEARCH myths link, and then follow all the other links.

Learn to create linked documents on page 119.

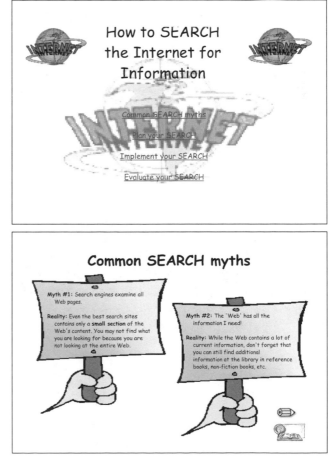

Diane Johnson

Seventh Grade Science Teacher

Fremont Middle School

130 East 9th Street

Fremont, NE 68025

402-727-3100

dlj@etecknetwork.com

Botany

Diane uses *Word* because it is the program that has been chosen by her school. She has her own computer in her classroom and appreciates the ease with which she can create materials to make it easier for her students to complete tasks she wants them to do. Anything she makes in *Word* looks so professional that she's proud to hand it out!

Moss/Liverwort Lab

Summary

Middle school students organize their data on mosses and liverworts while they rotate through lab stations. Students look at the sheet to determine which station to go to, what to do while they're there, where to write their data, and where to draw their observations. Diane says, "This lab sheet helps them stay organized in their data collection. They don't have to try to organize the data on their own, or waste lab time while I tell them where to put their information."

Objectives

Middle school students will apply the following skills:

- translate lab activities into organized written notes using forms provided.
- if working with a partner or small group, demonstrate cooperative learning skills as the lab is conducted.
- verbally describe the physical attributes of moss and liverworts.
- compare and contrast moss and liverworts to other plants.

Name_____ Date_____ Period_____

🔍 MOSS/LIVERWORT LAB

STATION 1: MOSS
Examine a piece of moss. Use a hand lens and draw 2 fields of view. Record your observations.

(⃝)   (⃝)

| Top view
Name_____
Power_____x | 2/3 Moss pieces pulled from the soil
Name_____
Power_____x |

Tell 3 things you learned from your moss observations.

1._____

2._____

3._____

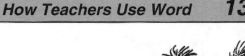

Botany

Great State Lakes Activity

Summary

This activity is a three-part curriculum field trip to Fremont State Lakes. It correlates with the students' unit on plants, leaves, etc. and allows them to apply their knowledge in a practical way. Diane's class made their first field trip in October. One activity was to "adopt" a tree. Students drew a map to their tree and noted wildlife and landmarks around it. In February, students will use their maps to find their tree and repeat the Great State Lakes activity to see changes in the environment, plant life, and wildlife around it. This will be repeated again during Earth Week.

Students work in pairs to fill in the lab sheets. Whenever the teacher blows a whistle, students move to the next activity. The activity includes tree, moss, liverwort, lichen identification, and real-life use of data collection in data tables. Back in class students make a bar graph of the data they collected. Students also make a leaf print T-shirt with leaves they collect and write poetry about the tree they adopted. The rubric is a scoring device to aid students in determining grades and goals of the activity.

Objectives

Middle school students will apply the following skills:

- use of lab sheets to complete "in the field" activities.
- demonstrate the use of math knowledge to complete bar graphs and other tasks.
- work with a partner or small group, and demonstrate cooperative learning skills as the activities are conducted.
- demonstrate learning through different modalities including data collection, T-shirt design, and poetry.
- demonstrate the ability to use a rubric to self-assess attainment of activity objectives.

Name:_____
Partner:_____

GREAT STATE LAKES ESCAPE
7th Grade Science Activity Requirements

ACTIVITY 1: ADOPT A TREE

Find a tree that appeals to you and your partner. It can be any type of tree within our exploration area. You will need to collect data about this tree, so pay attention to where you are.

1. MAP THE LOCATION OF YOUR TREE. Draw a map below indicating the location of your tree from the bus. Fill in any blanks with your data.

# of paces from bus_____

Direction from bus_____

Landmarks on your way to your tree: (list below)

2. Using your Tree Identification Pamphlet, determine what type of tree you have adopted. Write its name here: _____

3. Calculate the height of your tree. Our tree is _____m.

4. Calculate the diameter of your tree at breast height (DBH). Measure 137 cm above the ground. Our tree's DBH is _____cm.

5. Measure a 2-meter radius from the base of your tree in four directions.

NAME_____ DATE_____ PERIOD____

GREAT STATE LAKES ESCAPE RUBRIC

ACTIVITY	TOTAL POINTS	YOURS
ACTIVITY 1: ADOPT A TREE		
***all tasks completed correctly	70	_____
***neatness, effort, time	10	_____
ACTIVITY 2: SCAVENGER HUNT		
***all tasks completed correctly	20	_____
***neatness, effort, time	10	_____
ACTIVITY 3: ANIMAL DATA TABLE		
***all tasks completed correctly	10	_____
***neatness, effort, time	10	_____
ACTIVITY 4: SIGNS OF HUMAN PRESENCE		
***all tasks completed correctly	10	_____
***neatness, effort, time	10	_____
TOTAL POINTS	150	_____

Paula Grinvalds

Sixth Grade Teacher

Valley Elementary School

301 South Pine Street

Valley, NE 68064

402-359-2151

pgrinvalds@esu3.org

Language Arts and School Community Relations

Paula uses *Word* for everything she possibly can because, "It's so easy to use! Everything I make looks *so* professional! You can insert any kind of graphic and then turn it into a watermark in 2 seconds flat. It's simple to make columns or tables or anything you want. As far as I'm concerned, it's just about the perfect word-processing program!"

Newsletter

Summary

Paula sends home a newsletter on a regular basis to keep parents informed about what's happening in her classroom. The newsletter is written in three columns with a WordArt title. The sample below has a special watermark in the background. Paula took a picture of her class with a digital camera, inserted it into the newsletter document, turned it into a watermark, and sent it behind the text. As the year progresses, Paula turns the newsletter writing and layout over to her students.

Objectives

Sixth grade students will apply the following skills:

- demonstrate writing and editing skills.
- demonstrate cooperative learning skills as the newsletter is developed when working with a partner or small group.
- demonstrate the ability to conduct interviews and to organize information used in the newsletter.
- demonstrate the ability to develop and adjust newsletter layout.

Learn to create a newsletter on page 111.

Sharon Carlson

Sixth Grade English Teacher

Fremont Middle School

130 East 9th Street

Fremont, NE 68025

402-727-3100

Self-Esteem

Sharon has used computers in her classroom for many years. She finds they make her job easier and more fun. She not only uses the computer herself, she assigns her students to use them, too.

A Penny for Luck

Summary

Moving to the middle school is a whole new world for the sixth graders in Fremont Community Schools. To help students with the transition, Sharon makes a certificate for each student, glues a penny between the hands, and tapes it onto his/her locker. This helps them find their locker during that first rushed day, it gives them important school information, and it assures students that this new school has a caring environment. Sharon says that students usually keep the certificate inside their locker for the entire year hoping the penny brings them luck. The merge feature in *Word* makes it easy to create a certificate for each student quickly.

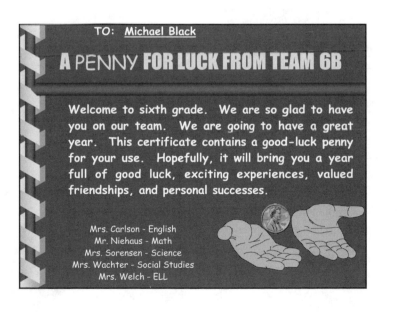

TO: Michael Black

A PENNY FOR LUCK FROM TEAM 6B

Welcome to sixth grade. We are so glad to have you on our team. We are going to have a great year. This certificate contains a good-luck penny for your use. Hopefully, it will bring you a year full of good luck, exciting experiences, valued friendships, and personal successes.

Mrs. Carlson - English
Mr. Niehaus - Math
Mrs. Sorensen - Science
Mrs. Wachter - Social Studies
Mrs. Welch - ELL

Learn to merge documents on page 96.

Joanne Lehman

Fifth Grade Teacher

Clarkson Elementary School

1005 N. Clarkson

Fremont, NE 68025

402-727-3178

jlehman@esu2.esu2.k12.ne.us

School Community Relations

Joanne uses *Word* because it's quick and fun to use. "You know how sometimes you get in a rut, so you try some new and different things? Then your kids get excited and so do you? *Word* lets me do that," Joanne says. Also her kids have no problem using *Word*; they love it!

Class Memory Book

Summary

Joanne takes digital pictures of her students throughout the year while they perform their daily work. She also takes pictures of their special activities and events. These pictures are inserted into *Word* documents, and then bound into a "yearbook" that is given to each student at the end of the year. These "yearbooks" will be especially meaningful since this is the last year Joanne's kids will be in their neighborhood school.

Objectives

Fifth grade students will apply the following skills:

- utilize *Word* and its mail merge function to provide positive communication between school and home to keep parents informed.
- encourage student performance through recognition with parents.

Favorite Things Joanne Does With *Word*

1. Mail merge for her beginning-of-the-year letter and holiday greetings.

2. Use tables to make her schedules.

3. Use the Comment function to give feedback on student writing projects instead of handwriting comments.

4. Use Format Painter when writing papers to facilitate formatting.

5. Use columns and WordArt to enhance weekly newsletters.

6. Insert clip art from www.hoxie.org/clipart.htm or www.geocities.com/Heartland/Meadows/7597.

Favorite Things Joanne's Students Do With *Word*

1. Reinforce keyboarding skills by typing curriculum-related papers.

2. Learn new *Word* techniques as they practice keyboarding.

Thanksgiving

School Community Relations

Summary

Thanksgiving is a very special holiday in the United States that inspires people to think about their blessings and appreciate their lives and families. "I truly appreciate the opportunity to work with so many wonderful children, to get to know them and their families," Joanne says, "So I send them a letter every Thanksgiving to say thanks. Using the merge option in *Word* lets me make each letter a personal one."

Objectives

- utilize *Word* and its mail merge function to provide positive communication between school and home to keep parents informed.
- encourage student performance through recognition with parents.

Greetings to the «LastName» Family,

I am so thankful to you for sharing your child, «Child», with me this year. We have had a wonderful year here at Clarkson. Thanks for your help and cooperation, Mr. and Mrs. «LastName», whenever I've needed assistance and support. I am hoping you enjoy this break with your family at «Address1».

«Child», be sure to eat plenty of turkey, enjoy the football games and parades, and be ready to work hard when you return.

This is such a busy time of year Mr. and Mrs. «LastName». Please continue to encourage «Child» to do «HisOrHer» best. Again, thank you!.

Mrs. Lehman

Learn to merge documents on page 96 and how to create borders on page 69.

Ruth Follen

Nutrition

Physical Education Teacher

Fremont Elementary Schools

957 N. Pierce St.

Fremont, NE 68025

402-727-3000

"It's hard to think of teaching without computers to plan, organize, and now, interact with students. *Word* has helped add to lessons in creative ways. This in no way takes the place of a creative or inspirational teacher. Computers don't come up with ideas, strategies, or plans for you. But they sure make a lot of ideas come to life for you and your students. *Word* has expanded lessons allowing for more information and learning processes to be used."

Weekly Journal of Snacks for the Week

Summary
Students are assigned to keep track of snacks they eat for a week, "so they know what they're putting in their mouth." They bring the journals back to class and analyze their eating habits.

Objectives
Elementary students will apply the following skills:
- use of snack journal sheet to track eating habits.
- use of higher-order thinking skills to analyze eating habits.

5-A-DAY
EAT THE HEALTHY WAY

EATING HEALTHY IS NOT MAGIC

WEEKLY JOURNAL OF SNACKS FOR THE WEEK

1.	1.	1.	1.	1.
2.	2.	2.	2.	2.
3.	3.	3.	3.	3.
4.	4.	4.	4.	4.
5.	5.	5.	5.	5.

HOW WOULD YOU JUDGE YOUR SNACKING HABITS?

HOW CAN YOU IMPROVE YOUR SNACKS TO MAKE THEM HEALTHIER?

Examining Your School Lunch

Summary

Students fill in the foods they ate for lunch on a *Word*-created pyramid form that resembles the USDA Food Pyramid. Students determine which food group each food fits into and write it on the line representing that food group on the USDA Food Pyramid. When each food has been listed, students analyze their lunch and decide if they ate a balanced meal.

Nutrition

Objectives

Elementary school students will apply the following skills:

- demonstrate knowledge of the USDA Food Pyramid.
- use higher-order thinking skills to analyze individual lunch items.
- categorize food items into the USDA Food Pyramid.
- if working with a partner or small group, demonstrate use of cooperative learning skills.

Learning Webs

Summary

Elementary students map out health-related issues using a web to organize their thoughts. If they are studying fruits and vegetables, Ruth instructs them to write "fruit" in the center oval, and then list fruits in the outside shapes. If they are studying smoking, students write "smoking" in the center oval and write effects of smoking in the other shapes.

Objectives

Elementary students will apply the following skills:

- demonstrate use of the "learning web" sheet to organize research.
- demonstrate effective collection of research information for given topics.

Information Collection and Organization

- create written report or presentation on the topic.
- if working with a partner or small group, demonstrate use of cooperative learning skills.

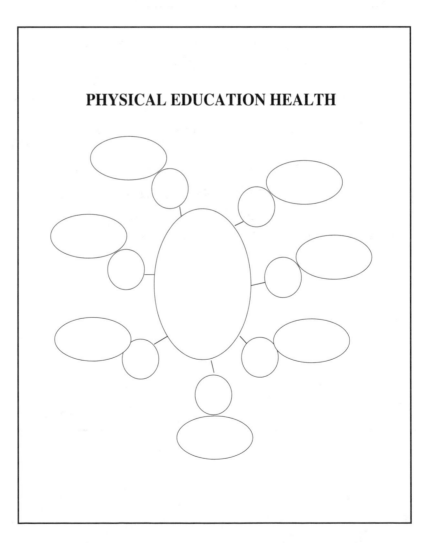

PHYSICAL EDUCATION HEALTH

Additional worksheet files are available on the CD-ROM.

Lorna McCloud

Coordinator of Information and Technology; School Media Specialist

Jackson Elementary School

4340 Edwinstowe Avenue

Colorado Springs, CO 80907

719-328-5824

mcclolj@d11.org

Lorna McCloud says, "I use *Word*, *Excel*, *PowerPoint*, and *Outlook* quite often in my job as Coordinator of Info and Tech. I use *Word* whenever I write newsletters to the staff or letters to parents, and I also use it in conjunction with a paint program to create technical documents and directions for my staff. I use *PowerPoint* for presentations, and plan to help my staff train their older students to use it for projects soon. I use *Excel* CONSTANTLY to keep track of purchases, laptop configurations, etc. I haven't learned *Access* yet, but am anxious to do so. *Outlook* not only keeps me in communication with everyone in the district, its Calendar and Tasks help me keep my world somewhat in order."

How-To Worksheets

Summary

In her job as technology coordinator, Lorna creates graphic worksheets to help her staff learn to use the myriad of hardware and software available to them. Each teacher in her district received a laptop, so she often does after-school trainings to help teachers get more use out of their machines. Using *Word*, she creates step-by-step handouts like this laptop fax worksheet.

Objectives

- demonstrate the use of Microsoft *Office* products for planning and training purposes.

Learn to create screen shots on page 108.

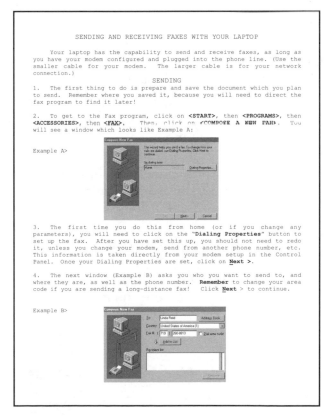

Diane Wolfe

Distance Learning Coordinator and Technology Consultant

Educational Service Unit #2

6320 N. Colorado Avenue

Fremont, NE 68025

402-721-7710

dmwolfe@esu2.esu2.k12.ne.us

As a special education teacher, Diane found that the icons in *Word* made it easy for her kids to use the program. She prefers *Word* because it lets her do everything she wants. "Since most of our businesses are using *Word,* it's important to introduce it to our kids. Kids can easily make the transition from any program or platform, but we should do everything we can to help them. Besides, I just think it's a good product."

All Subjects

Vocabulary Bingo

Summary

Teachers use this Vocabulary Bingo template to create curriculum-based bingo cards for students as a fun way to study vocabulary. Diane recommends just calling the words out the first time, so students can match the words on their cards. The second time she recommends reading the definition, so kids have to match the word to the definition.

Objectives

Elementary grade students will apply the following skills:

- demonstrate word recognition skills by playing bingo and matching words on card with stated words.
- demonstrate knowledge of word meaning by matching bingo card words with definitions read by teacher.
- if working with a partner or small group, demonstrate cooperative learning skills.
- use *Word* to create their own vocabulary bingo cards.

Learn to create tables on page 90.

Vocabulary Bingo
Type Name of Story Here

Use	The	Tab	Key	To
Move	From	Cell	To	Cell
And	Replace	FREE	Each	Word
With	A	Word	From	The
Story	or	Chapter	You're	In

How Students Use *Word*

Detailed Contents

Each activity shows pages from its accompanying Word *file.*
The complete Word *files are included on the CD-ROM that comes with this book.*

Sandi Snyder

Computer Teacher

Shickley High School

104 East Murray, Box 137

Shickley, NE 68436

402-627-3375

ssnyder@esu6.esu6.k12.ne.us

School and Community Cooperation

Sandi uses *Word* in her curriculum because Microsoft *Office* is the program her school has chosen to use. She says *Word* is easy to use, is functional and complete, and is user-friendly. Students enjoy using it, and if they need help, they use the online Help built into the program.

Community Brochure Project

Summary

High school students investigate local businesses and create bifold, three-column brochures. Sandi says, "This brochure project was designed to make a school-community connection. The first year, students were to create a brochure for a business, organization, activity, etc. in our community. It has since broadened to include businesses in other towns. We wanted our community to see the creativity of our students. The students were given the assignment sheet after our study of Microsoft *Word*. They fold a piece of paper as they would the brochure and then sketch where things will go. This showed that the cover was actually in the third column, minimizing cutting and pasting later. The grading rubric makes it very easy to compile points. Some of the student brochures were actually used by the businesses and organizations."

Objectives

High school students will apply the following skills:

- demonstrate the use of *Word* to create brochures.
- solicit information from area businesses to help in creating the brochure.
- demonstrate the use of higher-order thinking skills by creating a new brochure.
- demonstrate the use of time management skills.

Learn to create brochures on page 115.

Lesson Outline

1. Explain the assignment, including design principles, and show examples of student and commercially created brochures.

2. Allow students to pick their brochure topic and gather information from businesses.

3. Allow students to begin creating the brochures, emphasizing design and time management principles.

Name_____

BROCHURE GRADE SHEET

ITEM	POINTS	COMMENTS
Design		
Clip Art		
Word Art		
Spelling/Punctuation/Grammar		
Eye Appeal		

ASSIGNMENT: Trifold brochure promoting a business, community, organization, etc.

GRADING:
1. Design example–10 pts–Show a sketch of your brochure to Mrs. Snyder by September 8, 1999, to receive full points.
2. Clip Art–20 pts–Include one color clip art AND one picture taken with the Mavica Camera. You may use more.
3. Word Art–20 pts–Include at least one word art, 2 font styles, 2 font sizes. Use a variety of fonts and positioning to make your brochure attractive.
4. Spelling/Punctuation/Grammar–25 pts–
5. Eye Appeal–25 pts–Adequate use of space, placement of material, info on all 6 panels, etc.

Your brochure CAN include more.

6. Due Date–10 pts–Your final product is due September 22, 1999.

Outside of Brochure   *Inside of Brochure*

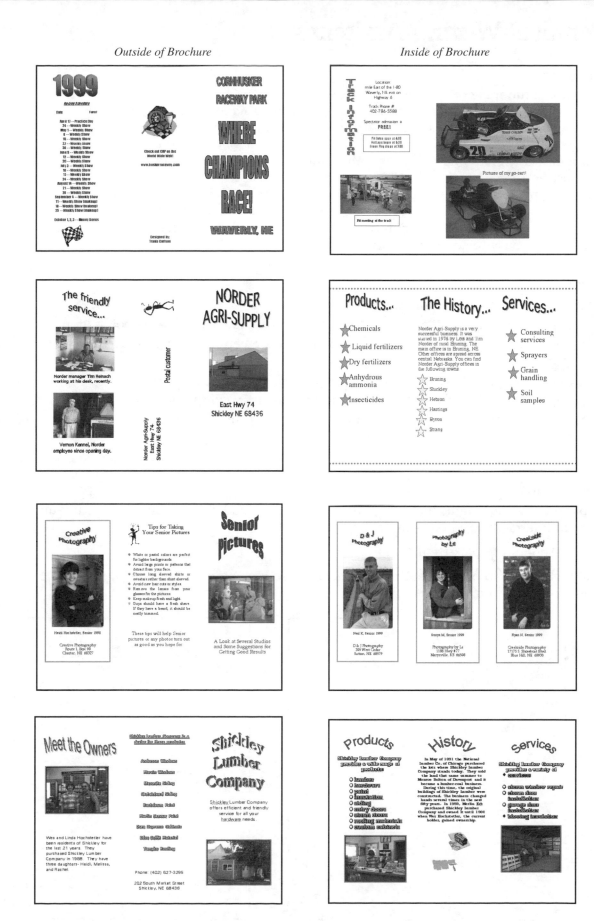

Technical Writing Assignment

Language Arts

Summary

High school students create step-by-step worksheets for students in middle school grades. "After a review of the state standards, this technical writing assignment was created. Technical writing is one skill that businesses feel employees lack. The students create a step-by-step handout geared toward 7th graders to explain one topic from Microsoft *Word*. Some examples: Saving a file, Setting tabs, Creating WordArt, etc. Students use the program *FullShot*, an image-capturing software, so they can use parts of the *Word* screen to help clarify the steps." Sandi has a great group of students, and most enjoyed this project. The students knew the grading criteria at the beginning of the project, and the scoring rubric made it easy to compile points.

Objectives

High school students will apply the following skills:

- demonstrate the use of *Word* to create worksheets for middle school students.
- demonstrate the ability to use screen-capturing commands and insert the screen shots in a *Word* document.
- demonstrate cooperative learning with other students if working in a group.
- demonstrate the use of time management skills in completing the project.
- demonstrate their understanding of the grading rubric and activities needed to compile grade points.
- demonstrate the use of technical writing skills.

Lesson Outline

1. Explain the assignment, including design principles, and show examples of student and commercially created technical writing.

2. Allow students to pick their topic.

3. Allow students to begin creating the "how-to" sheets, emphasizing design and time management principles.

Topic	Scoring			Comments
	Needs improvement	Average	Excellent	
Spelling/Grammar				
Information Correct				
Correct Sequence				
Level of Difficulty				
Incorporation of Visuals				
Peer Evaluation				
Due Date				

You are to construct a handout for the seventh graders. This handout will explain a Microsoft Word topic. The topic is yours to choose, as long as the teacher OKs it! Some ideas would be: How to make a word art, How to select a font and size, etc. Be thorough, complete and use correct grammar and punctuation. Use FullShot to help make your handout clear and easy to understand.

This activity will be due October 6, 1999. Below are the criteria for this activity:

Spelling/Grammar: 20 points
Information Correct: 20 points
Correct Sequence: 10 points
Level of Difficulty: 10 points
Incorporation of Visuals: 20 points
Peer Evaluation: 10 points
Due Date: 10 points

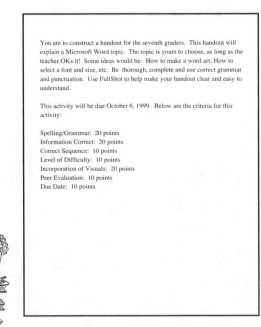

Learn to create screen shots on page 108.

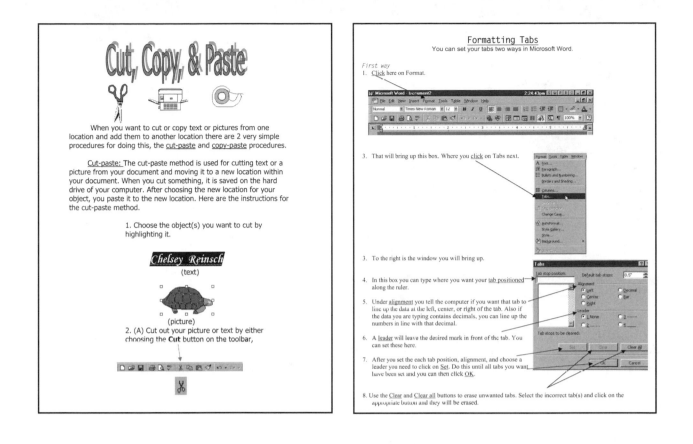

Cut, Copy, & Paste

When you want to cut or copy text or pictures from one location and add them to another location there are 2 very simple procedures for doing this, the cut-paste and copy-paste procedures.

Cut-paste: The cut-paste method is used for cutting text or a picture from your document and moving it to a new location within your document. When you cut something, it is saved on the hard drive of your computer. After choosing the new location for your object, you paste it to the new location. Here are the instructions for the cut-paste method.

1. Choose the object(s) you want to cut by highlighting it.

Chelsey Reinsch

(text)

(picture)

2. (A) Cut out your picture or text by either choosing the **Cut** button on the toolbar,

Formatting Tabs
You can set your tabs two ways in Microsoft Word.

First way

1. Click here on Format.

3. That will bring up this box. Where you click on Tabs next.

3. To the right is the window you will bring up.

4. In this box you can type where you want your tab positioned along the ruler.

5. Under alignment you tell the computer if you want that tab to line up the data at the left, center, or right of the tab. Also if the data you are typing contains decimals, you can line up the numbers in line with that decimal.

6. A leader will leave the desired mark in front of the tab. You can set these here.

7. After you set the each tab position, alignment, and choose a leader you need to click on Set. Do this until all tabs you want have been set and you can then click OK.

8. Use the Clear and Clear all buttons to erase unwanted tabs. Select the incorrect tab(s) and click on the appropriate button and they will be erased.

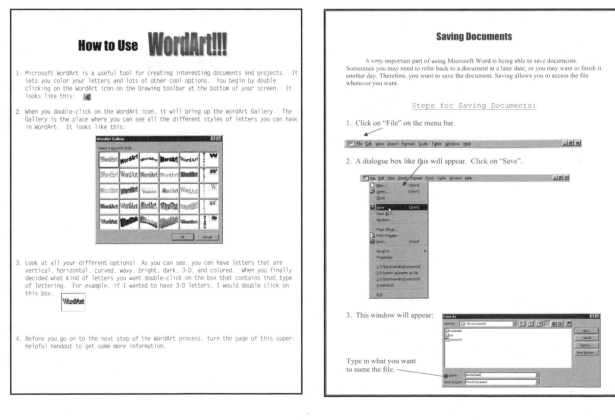

How to Use WordArt!!!

1. Microsoft WordArt is a useful tool for creating interesting documents and projects. It lets you color your letters and lots of other cool options. You begin by double clicking on the WordArt icon on the Drawing toolbar at the bottom of your screen. It looks like this:

2. When you double-click on the WordArt icon, it will bring up the WordArt Gallery. The Gallery is the place where you can see all the different styles of letters you can have in WordArt. It looks like this:

3. Look at all your different options! As you can see, you can have letters that are vertical, horizontal, curved, wavy, bright, dark, 3-D, and colored. When you finally decided what kind of letters you want double-click on the box that contains that type of lettering. For example, if I wanted to have 3-D letters, I would double click on this box:

4. Before you go on to the next step of the WordArt process, turn the page of this super-helpful handout to get some more information.

Saving Documents

A very important part of using Microsoft Word is being able to save documents. Sometimes you may need to refer back to a document at a later date, or you may want to finish it another day. Therefore, you want to save the document. Saving allows you to access the file whenever you want.

Steps for Saving Documents:

1. Click on "File" on the menu bar.

2. A dialogue box like this will appear. Click on "Save".

3. This window will appear:

Type in what you want to name the file.

Melissa Burns Johnston

Teacher of Gifted and Talented Students

Anahuac Middle School

706 Mikhaeal Ricks Drive

Anahuac, TX 77514

409-267-3421

johnstonm@anahuac.isd.esc4.net

Any Subject

Technology has been a vital part of Melissa's gifted and talented classroom for several years. "I knew I had to jump on the technology bandwagon if I was going to keep up with my G/T kids. Technology is their reality, and I wanted to be a part of it! It's a natural fit for the product-based learning that goes on in my Challenge classrooms."

Kid of the Month

Summary

Middle school students generate a personal résumé (with teacher-directed guidelines) for their portfolio. Résumés can have a theme like applying for Kid of the Month, Scientist of the Month, Inventor of the Month, etc.

Objectives

Middle school students will apply the following skills:

- demonstrate thinking skills, including analysis to determine what information will be used for "selling" one's self.
- use word-processing skills by completing the appropriate "Kid of the Month" form.
- demonstrate the understanding of *Word*'s Resume Wizard feature to create a résumé.

Lesson Outline

1. Explain the assignment and how it fits in the curriculum.

2. Discuss the concept of selling yourself, picking out your best points, defining your skills, and deciding what you want people to know about you. Discuss the importance of listing extracurricular activities, offices held, community service, etc.

3. Have students put their personal information in the appropriate form. To incorporate word processing, give students the file and allow them to enter their information. Otherwise, duplicate a printed version and allow students to handwrite their information.

4. Demonstrate the Resume Wizard in *Word* to the class. Allow students to create their own résumé, incorporating data listed in the previous step.

5. Students or a group of teachers vote on the best résumé to choose Kid of the Month. These can be posted on bulletin boards or sent to principals, counselors, etc.

Kid of the Month

You are applying for a job as "Kid of the Month." Create a resume highlighting your strengths as a kid. Be sure to include something for each category listed below.

Type your name here   Type your street address here
Your PO Box number
Your city, state, and zip code

Summary of Kid Qualifications
Type a short summary listing your overall qualifications as a kid. Be sure to include why you should be chosen "Kid of the Month."

Education

Date   School attended   City, State
Date   School attended   City, State

Experience   One of My Greatest Experiences as a Kid!
Type a paragraph telling about the greatest experience you've had as a kid.

Talents
List all the unique talents you possess as a kid. Be creative!

Activities/Clubs
List all the activities, clubs, and organizations in which you participate.

Stories That Grow

Language Arts

Summary

Middle school students in a lab or minilab situation begin typing a story in *Word* (this works especially well with Halloween or other holiday stories). The teacher gives them 3-5 minutes. On a signal from the teacher, students move to the next computer. They read what has been written and then continue the story, but they must write in a different color to distinguish what they've written. This writing and moving continues until the story comes around to the original author(s). **Note**: Melissa warns that kids love nothing more than to change the direction the authors intended when they began the story! It adds a whole new, fun element to the activity.

Objectives

Middle school students will apply the following skills:

- demonstrate the use of *Word* to write stories in a lab setting.
- demonstrate cooperative learning with other students.
- demonstrate reading skills and comprehension of previously printed story segments.
- demonstrate the use of time management skills in completing their story section.
- demonstrate use of higher-order thinking skills through their creativity in synthesizing new stories.

Lesson Outline

1. Explain the assignment and how it fits into the curriculum.

2. Assign individual students or groups to computers and have them pick a color for their writing.

3. Allow them to begin writing.

4. Print the stories when finished. The stories can be published on the school server or projected to practice editing, revising, and elaboration skills.

Tables and Vocabulary

Summary

This activity can be used in any curriculum area. The teacher creates a three-column table and inserts vocabulary words in column one. Students then type related words in the other columns or handwrite the words if the sheet is duplicated.

Any Subject

Objectives

Middle school students will apply the following skills:

- demonstrate the use of *Word* to complete the table of vocabulary words or handwrite the words.
- if working with a partner or small group, demonstrate cooperative learning with other students.
- use analysis skills to identify related words to words provided by the teacher.
- demonstrate the use of time management skills in completing the project.
- demonstrate vocabulary skills.

Learn to create tables on page 90.

Lesson Outline

1. Explain the assignment and how it fits into the previously taught curriculum.

2. To incorporate word processing into this phase of the assignment, give students the teacher-created file and allow them to type in their information. Otherwise, duplicate a printed version and allow students to handwrite their information.

DESCRIBE IT!

Choose two adjectives to describe each noun listed. Do not use any adjective more than once.

NOUN	ADJECTIVE #1	ADJECTIVE #2
Sandwich	Delicious	Satisfying
Friend	Faithful	Exciting
Automobile	Convenient	Economical
Book	Intriguing	Lengthy
Summer	Steamy	Free
Crayon	Colorful	Slender
Map	Informative	Reliable
Computer	Advanced	High-tech
Classroom	Educational	Crowded
Park	Shady	Quiet
Mountain	Rocky	Dangerous
Freedom	Unchained	Everlasting

TIME MARCHES ON

Choose two adjectives to describe each time period in America in the 20th century. Ask for help from parents, grandparents, and other family members! Use each adjective only once. Good Luck!

DATE	ADJECTIVE #1	ADJECTIVE #2
1900-1909	Tragic	Revolutionary
1910-1919	Musical	Hostile
1920-1929	Glamorous	Depressing
1930-1939	Unemployed	desperate
1940-1949	Catastrophic	Serene
1950-1959	Innovative	Scientific
1960-1969	groovy	Turmoiled
1970-1979	Scandalous	Eventful
1980-1989	Explosive	caring
1990-1999	Technological	Controversial

Laurie Holben

Third Grade Teacher

Howard Elementary School

240 North Howard Street

Fremont, NE 68025

402-727-3169

Math

Laurie incorporates technology, including Microsoft *Word*, into her curriculum as much as possible. She says, "I believe you can judge a worthwhile project in the computer lab when it spurs students to think of possible additional ways to use the skills they have just learned. That's more exciting than the actual new technology itself."

Geometric Shapes

Summary

Third grade students show their knowledge of geometric shapes by using the AutoShapes and Drawing tools to create a shapes sheet.

Objectives

Nebraska Mathematics Standards that are addressed include:

- 4.4.1 By the end of fourth grade, students will identify, describe, and create two- and three-dimensional geometric shapes.
- 4.4.2 By the end of fourth grade, students will identify and draw points, lines, line segments, rays, and angles.

Nebraska Technology Guidelines that are addressed include:

- 3. Productivity Tools - Use technology resources for problem solving, communication, and illustration of thoughts, ideas and stories

Learn to create AutoShapes on page 85.

Lesson Outline

1. Teach students about geometric shapes including the number of sides and corners.

2. Explain the assignment and how it fits in the curriculum.

3. Demonstrate the use of the drawing tools on the Drawing toolbar and the Basic Shapes palette in AutoShapes. Demonstrate the use of the Text Box tool.

4. Print and hand out Geometry Instructions.

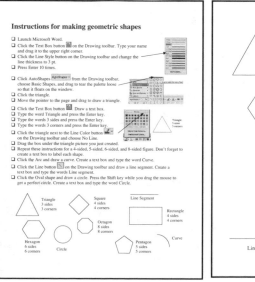

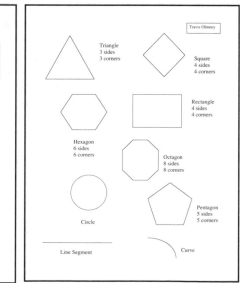

Annette Johnson

Title I and Reading Recovery Teacher

Washington Elementary School

515 South Broad Street

Fremont, NE 68025

402-727-3164

Reading

Annette says, "*Word* helps us not be confined to our own drawing ability, but opens a whole new world of pictures to us. We can insert pictures from the Internet or clip art into a *Word* document. Kids love to see their professional and published "books" and the first graders love to read them."

Read My Book

Summary
Annette uses books with a simple sentence pattern to teach Reading Recovery to struggling first graders, Her fourth and fifth grade Title I students make similar books for the Reading Recovery students to use. They create the titles using WordArt and incorporate clip art and Internet pictures for illustrations.

Objectives
Nebraska Reading/Writing Standards that are addressed include:

- 4.2.1 By the end of the fourth grade, students will write using standard English (conventions) for sentence structure, usage, punctuation, capitalization and spelling.
- 4.2.4 By the end of the fourth grade, students will demonstrate the use of multiple forms to write for different audiences and purposes.

Nebraska Technology Guidelines that are addressed include:

- 3. Productivity Tools - Use general purpose productivity tools and peripherals to support personal productivity, remediate skill deficits, and facilitate learning throughout the curriculum.
- 3. Productivity Tools - Use technology tools for individual and collaborative writing, communication, publishing activities to create knowledge products for audiences inside/outside the classroom.

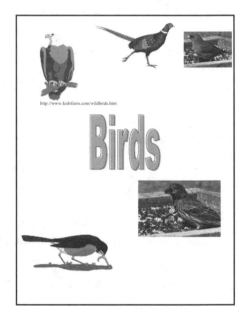

A chicken has feathers.

Paula Grinvalds

Sixth Grade Teacher

Valley Elementary School

301 South Pine Street

Valley, NE 68064

402-359-2151

pgrinvalds@esu3.org

Language Arts

Paula uses *Word* for everything she can. She says, "Kids love to publish their work. If I give them a chance to write their assignments in a word processor, they are much more willing to edit and make changes, so their work is much better."

Haiku Poetry

Summary

Middle school students write haiku poetry, and then jazz it up with graphics including watermarks and graphics from the Internet.

Objectives

Middle school students will apply the following skills:

- demonstrate their understanding of haiku structure by writing their own poems.
- demonstrate their use of different features within *Word* by inserting pictures, formatting pictures into watermarks, copying pictures from the Internet and pasting into a *Word* file.
- demonstrate the use of higher-order thinking skills by creating their haiku presentation.

Lesson Outline

1. Introduce students to haiku poetry.

2. Demonstrate how to insert pictures into a *Word* file.

3. Demonstrate how to format a picture into a watermark.

4. Demonstrate how to copy and paste or insert an Internet picture into a *Word* file.

Learn to create watermarks on page 76.

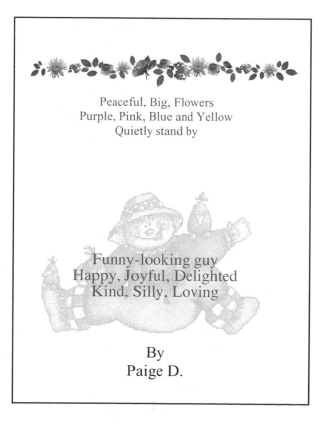

Peaceful, Big, Flowers
Purple, Pink, Blue and Yellow
Quietly stand by

Funny-looking guy
Happy, Joyful, Delighted
Kind, Silly, Loving

By
Paige D.

My Weekly Plan

Time Management

Summary

Middle school students open the "My Weekly Plan" file and enter their weekly schedule. The WordArt title can be edited to replace the word "My" with the student's name. As an alternative, teachers can print the file, duplicate it, and allow students to handwrite their schedules. As an extension of the activity, students can use the Text Box function in *Word* to create weekly schedules. Depending on their learning style, after they have created a computer-generated schedule, students can update them every week on the computer or handwrite them on duplicated schedule forms.

Objectives

Middle school students will apply the following skills:

- using Paula's schedule as a model, develop a personal weekly schedule.
- if working with a partner or small group, demonstrate cooperative learning skills as a weekly schedule is developed.
- demonstrate the ability to follow an organized framework.
- demonstrate the use of *Word* features including WordArt, text boxes, and editing features.

Lesson Outline

1. Discuss the principle and value of time management.

2. Demonstrate how to enter schedule data into the schedule.

3. Demonstrate how to edit the WordArt title to include the student's name.

4. As an extension activity, demonstrate how to create text boxes and schedule forms.

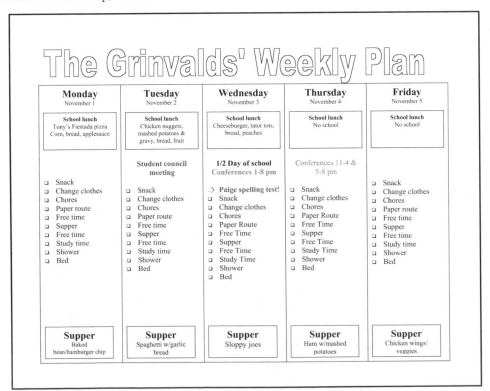

Joanne Lehman

Fifth Grade Teacher

Clarkson Elementary School

1005 N. Clarkson

Fremont, NE 68025

402-727-3178

jlehman@esu2.esu2.k12.ne.us

Art & Design

Since kids are so into technology, it is easy to take advantage of their enthusiasm by incorporating technology into lessons. Kids think they are getting to do cool stuff on the computer (and they are), but at the same time, they are reinforcing key concepts.

This is *MY* Locker!

Summary

Students will use *Word* to create name tags for their lockers. Use of WordArt, page borders, inserting clip art and pictures from the Internet will be emphasized.

Objectives

Middle school students will apply the following skills:

- use WordArt, including changing colors and sizes.
- demonstrate ability to insert clip art and pictures.
- demonstrate ability to copy and download pictures from the Internet.

Lesson Outline

1. Demonstrate WordArt, including how to change size and color.

2. Demonstrate Borders and Shading to make page borders.

Learn to create borders on page 69.

Learn to create borders on page 69.

3. Demonstrate how to insert clip art and pictures into a *Word* file.

4. Demonstrate how to copy or download pictures from the Internet.

5. Demonstrate how to paste or insert an Internet picture into a *Word* file.

6. Demonstrate how to use Drawing tools.

Jan Kruse

Media Specialist

Fremont Elementary Schools

Fremont Public School District

957 N. Pierce St.

Fremont, NE 68025

402-727-3023

Language Arts

Jan says using *Word* with primary children may seem an unlikely possibility. However, a simple and easy-to-prepare template can provide a publishing opportunity for students as young as those in first grade. It is very helpful if students bring an "edited" document to the computer so they can focus on keyboarding their stories. Illustrations may be done by hand once the story is published or when they can use the draw tools to complete their work.

Primary Publishing

Summary

Students will use *Word* to publish stories. They will use a Drop Cap to make their work look "just like a real picture book," and leave room at the top of the page to draw an illustration by hand or with draw tools.

Objectives

Primary students will apply the following skills:

- demonstrate writing and editing skills.
- demonstrate the use of Drop Caps.
- use *Word* to type stories and create space for illustrations.
- demonstrate art skills by creating illustrations.

Learn to create a Drop Cap on page 74.

Lesson Outline

1. Open the document template (landscape orientation and large type size) or demonstrate the difference in page orientation.

2. Demonstrate pressing ⌨ENTER (Windows) ⌨RETURN (Macintosh) to leave blank space at the top of the page for drawing a picture.

3. Demonstrate the use of Drop Cap to begin the first page of a story, just like a real picture book.

4. Demonstrate printing setup and sequence of printing.

I went to the zoo. I saw an elephant. It was gray. It had a long nose.

Diane Wolfe

Distance Learning Coordinator and Technology Consultant

Educational Service Unit #2

6320 N. Colorado Avenue

Fremont, NE 68025

402-721-7710

dmwolfe@esu2.esu2.k12.ne.us

Science

As a special education teacher, Diane found that the icons in *Word* made it easy for her kids to use the program. She prefers *Word* because it lets her do everything she wants. "When most of our businesses are using *Word,* it's important to introduce it to our kids. Kids can easily make the transition, but we should do everything we can to help them. Besides, I just think it's a good product."

My Internet "Bug" Project

Summary

First and second grade students use the Internet to study metamorphosis. Students use the worksheet created in *Word* to write a sentence describing what they learned about each of the four stages of metamorphosis, using the pictures as a guide.

Objectives

Primary grade students will apply the following skills:

- demonstrate the understanding of the four stages of metamorphosis.
- demonstrate use of the Internet by navigating through a Web site.
- complete the worksheets provided for the "bug" project.

Lesson Outline

Learn to insert Internet pictures on page 84.

1. Teach the four stages of metamorphosis.

2. Bookmark a butterfly Web site. This worksheet was created using photos from http://www.geocities.com/Heartland/9379/monarch.htm.

3. Go on the Web site and work with students as they go through the site.

My Internet "Bug" Project

Other Things That I Saw

Christmas Around the World

*Multicultural
Education*

Summary
Students use the Internet to search for Christmas customs from around the world. They color in their country on the map at the bottom of the worksheet and fill in the rest of the information as they research their project.

Objectives
Intermediate students will apply the following skills:
- identify various cultural celebrations of Christmas.
- search Web sites to find Christmas celebrations.
- create a "Christmas Around the World" booklet.
- if working with a partner or small group, demonstrate cooperative learning skills.

Lesson Outline
1. Discuss holidays around the world and how they vary.
2. Find good Web sites for students to use in their research.
3. Create a "Christmas Around the World" booklet from everybody's sheets.

Christmas Around the World

Name of country	Web address:

Climate in December	Foods

Interesting traditions

Learn to insert Internet pictures on page 84 and text boxes on page 42.

Rainforest Research

Ecology

Summary

Students use the Internet to find information about rainforest plants and animals. They pick an interesting plant and animal; record where in the rainforest they live; record neat information about them; draw a picture of them; and write what the animal eats. Students also give bibliographic information about the Web site. Reading *The Great Kapok Tree, A Tale of the Amazon Rainforest* by Lynne Cherry incorporates literature into the lesson as well as adds to student understanding. Penmanship could also be incorporated.

Objectives

Intermediate students will apply the following skills:

- demonstrate ability to access the Internet and locate appropriate Web sites.
- ability to collect information about their rainforest plant or animal.
- if working with a partner or small group, demonstrate cooperative learning skills.
- demonstrate completion of worksheets for assignment.

Lesson Outline

1. Read *The Great Kapok Tree, A Tale of the Amazon Rainforest* by Lynne Cherry.

2. Discuss the rain forest.

3. Find good Web sites for students to use in their research.

4. Assign students to begin researching the rain forest.

5. Assign students to fill in the information they find.

Rainforest Information

Location of rainforest:

Web address:

Created by

Plant Information

Neat information

Name:

Other information

Size

Picture of my plant

Where in the rainforest does it live?

Animal Information

Neat information

Name:

What does it eat?

Size

Picture of my animal

Where in the rainforest does it live?

Learn to insert Internet pictures on page 84 and text boxes on page 42.

Science Fair Review

Science

Summary

Students use the Science Fair Peer Review Sheet as a guide to evaluate science fair projects of other students. The focus of this sheet is to have students help each other on science fair projects before they go to the science fair where their projects will be judged. The sheet could be changed to a self-evaluation.

Objectives

Middle school students will apply the following skills:

- use the "Peer Review Sheet" to evaluate the projects of others.
- use higher-order thinking skills to analyze and evaluate the work of peers.
- demonstrate cooperative learning skills.

Science Fair Peer Review Sheet

Project Title: _____

Student Name(s) _____

_____

School: _____

<u>To Be Completed by Judge:</u>

Category	Things Done Well	Things to Remember for Next Time
Scientific Thought/Research (planning, expert advice sought, etc.)		
Data Collection (data supports project, enough data, lab notes)		
Creative Ability (original, unique style of displaying information)		
Presentation to Judges (3-5 minutes, well organized, presenters poised and confident)		
Display (attractive, eye catching, spelling, carefully constructed)		

Additional Comments: _____

_____

_____

_____

_____

Reviewer's signature: _____

Additional worksheet files are available on the CD-ROM.

Appendix

Detailed Contents

Word Menu Differences

File   Edit   View   Insert   Format   Tools   Table   Window   Help

File Menu

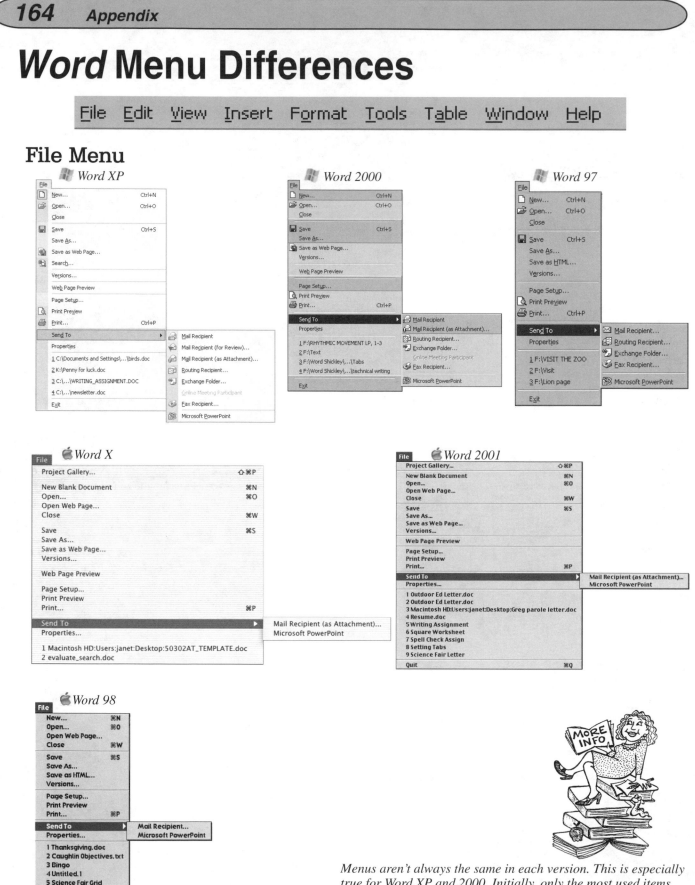

Menus aren't always the same in each version. This is especially true for Word XP and 2000. Initially, only the most used items appear. Click ≋ *to see all the menu items. If you use hidden items frequently, they will move up and unused ones will move down.*

Edit Menu

Word XP

Edit		
⌚ Undo Move Object	Ctrl+Z	
⟳ Can't Repeat	Ctrl+Y	
✂ Cut	Ctrl+X	
📋 Copy	Ctrl+C	
📋 Office Clipboard...		
📋 Paste	Ctrl+V	
Paste Special...		
Paste as Hyperlink		
Clear	▶	Formats
		Contents Del
Select All	Ctrl+A	
🔍 Find...	Ctrl+F	
Replace...	Ctrl+H	
Go To...	Ctrl+G	
Links...		
Object		

Word 2000

Edit		
⌚ Can't Undo	Ctrl+Z	
⟳ Repeat Typing	Ctrl+Y	
✂ Cut	Ctrl+X	
📋 Copy	Ctrl+C	
📋 Paste	Ctrl+V	
Paste Special...		
Paste as Hyperlink		
Clear	Del	
Select All	Ctrl+A	
🔍 Find...	Ctrl+F	
Replace...	Ctrl+H	
Go To...	Ctrl+G	
Links...		
Object		

Word 97

Edit		
⌚ Undo Typing	Ctrl+Z	
⟳ Repeat Typing	Ctrl+Y	
✂ Cut	Ctrl+X	
📋 Copy	Ctrl+C	
📋 Paste	Ctrl+V	
Paste Special...		
Paste as Hyperlink		
Clear	Delete	
Select All	Ctrl+A	
🔍 Find...	Ctrl+F	
Replace...	Ctrl+H	
Go To...	Ctrl+G	
Links...		
Object		

Word X

Edit		
Can't Undo	⌘Z	
Can't Repeat	⌘Y	
Cut	⌘X	
Copy	⌘C	
Paste	⌘V	
Paste Special...		
Paste as Hyperlink		
Clear	▶	Formats
Select All	⌘A	Contents
Find...	⌘F	
Replace...	⇧⌘H	
Go To...	⌘G	
Links...		
Object		

Word 2001

Edit		
Undo Typing	⌘Z	
Repeat Typing	⌘Y	
Cut	⌘X	
Copy	⌘C	
Paste	⌘V	
Paste Special...		
Paste as Hyperlink		
Clear		
Select All	⌘A	
Find...	⌘F	
Replace...	⌘H	
Go To...	⌘G	
Links...		
Object		
Preferences...		

Word 98

Edit		
Can't Undo	⌘Z	
Repeat New Default	⌘Y	
Cut	⌘X	
Copy	⌘C	
Paste	⌘V	
Paste Special...		
Paste as Hyperlink		
Clear		
Select All	⌘A	
Find...	⌘F	
Replace	⌘H	
Go To...	⌘G	
Links...		
Object		
Publishing	▶	

Work Menu

Work	⌘ Word X, 2001, 98
Add to Work Menu	

Font Menu

Font   ⌘ *Word X, 2001, 98*

Abadi MT Condensed Extra Bold
Abadi MT Condensed Light
AGaramond
AGaramond Bold
AGaramond BoldItalic
AGaramond Italic
AGaramond Semibold
AGaramond SemiboldItalic
Albertus Extra Bold
Albertus Medium
American Typewriter
American Typewriter Condensed
American Typewriter Light
Andale Mono
Antique Olive
Apple Chancery
Arial
Arial Black
Arial MT Condensed Light

View Menu

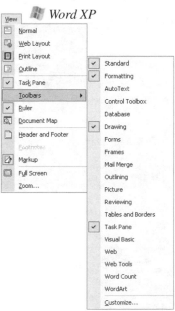

Word XP

View	
📄 Normal	
📄 Web Layout	
📄 Print Layout	
📄 Outline	
✓ Task Pane	
Toolbars	▶
✓ Ruler	
📄 Document Map	
📄 Header and Footer	
Footnotes	
📄 Markup	
📄 Full Screen	
Zoom...	

Toolbars submenu:
- ✓ Standard
- ✓ Formatting
- AutoText
- Control Toolbox
- Database
- ✓ Drawing
- Forms
- Frames
- Mail Merge
- Outlining
- Picture
- Reviewing
- Tables and Borders
- ✓ Task Pane
- Visual Basic
- Web
- Web Tools
- Word Count
- WordArt
- Customize...

Word 2000

View	
📄 Normal	
📄 Web Layout	
📄 Print Layout	
📄 Outline	
Toolbars	▶
Ruler	
📄 Document Map	
Header and Footer	
Footnotes	
📄 Comments	
📄 Full Screen	
Zoom...	

Toolbars submenu:
- ✓ Standard
- ✓ Formatting
- AutoText
- Clipboard
- Control Toolbox
- Database
- ✓ Drawing
- Forms
- Frames
- Picture
- Reviewing
- Tables and Borders
- Visual Basic
- Web
- Web Tools
- WordArt
- Customize...

Word 97

View	
📄 Normal	
📄 Online Layout	
📄 Page Layout	
📄 Outline	
📄 Master Document	
Toolbars	▶
✓ Ruler	
📄 Document Map	
Header and Footer	
Footnotes	
📄 Comments	
📄 Full Screen	
Zoom...	

Toolbars submenu:
- ✓ Standard
- ✓ Formatting
- AutoText
- Control Toolbox
- Database
- ✓ Drawing
- Forms
- Frames
- Picture
- Reviewing
- Tables and Borders
- Visual Basic
- Web
- WordArt
- Customize...

View Menu

Word X

View
Normal
Online Layout
✓ Page Layout
Outline
Master Document
Formatting Palette
Toolbars ▶
✓ Ruler
Document Map
Office Clipboard
Header and Footer
Footnotes
Comments
Reveal Formatting
Full Screen
Zoom...

Toolbars submenu:
Standard / Formatting / AutoText / Background / Contact / Database / ✓ Drawing / Forms / Movie / Picture / PowerBook / Reviewing / Tables and Borders / Visual Basic / Web / WordArt / Customize...

Word 2001

View
Normal
Online Layout
✓ Page Layout
Outline
Master Document
Formatting Palette
Toolbars ▶
✓ Ruler
Document Map
Office Clipboard
Word 5.1 Menus
Header and Footer
Footnotes
Comments
Reveal Formatting
Full Screen
Zoom...

Toolbars submenu:
✓ Standard / ✓ Formatting / AutoText / Background / Contact / Database / ✓ Drawing / Forms / Movie / Picture / PowerBook / Reviewing / Ribbon / Ruler / Tables and Borders / Visual Basic / Web / Word for Macintosh 5.1 / WordArt / Primary Toolbar / Customize...

Word 98

View
Normal
Online Layout
✓ Page Layout
Outline
Master Document
Toolbars ▶
Ruler
Document Map
Word 5.1 Menus
Header and Footer
Footnotes
Comments
Reveal Formatting
Full Screen
Zoom...

Toolbars submenu:
✓ Standard / ✓ Formatting / AutoText / Background / Database / ✓ Drawing / Forms / Movie / Picture / PowerBook / Reviewing / Ribbon / Ruler / Tables and Borders / Visual Basic / Web / Word for Macintosh 5.1 / WordArt / Customize...

Insert Menu

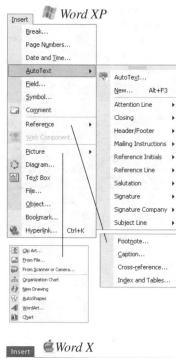

Word XP

Insert
Break...
Page Numbers...
Date and Time...
AutoText ▶
Field...
Symbol...
Comment
Reference ▶
Web Component...
Picture ▶
Diagram...
Text Box
File...
Object...
Bookmark...
Hyperlink... Ctrl+K

AutoText submenu: AutoText... / New... Alt+F3 / Attention Line ▶ / Closing ▶ / Header/Footer ▶ / Mailing Instructions ▶ / Reference Initials ▶ / Reference Line ▶ / Salutation ▶ / Signature ▶ / Signature Company ▶ / Subject Line ▶

Reference submenu: Footnote... / Caption... / Cross-reference... / Index and Tables...

Picture submenu: Clip Art... / From File... / From Scanner or Camera... / Organization Chart / New Drawing / AutoShapes / WordArt... / Chart

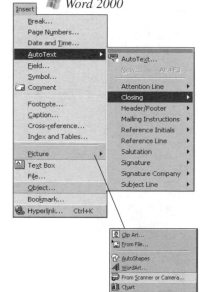

Word 2000

Insert
Break...
Page Numbers...
Date and Time...
AutoText ▶
Field...
Symbol...
Comment
Footnote...
Caption...
Cross-reference...
Index and Tables...
Picture ▶
Text Box
File...
Object...
Bookmark...
Hyperlink... Ctrl+K

AutoText submenu: AutoText... / New... Alt+F3 / Attention Line ▶ / Closing ▶ / Header/Footer ▶ / Mailing Instructions ▶ / Reference Initials ▶ / Reference Line ▶ / Salutation ▶ / Signature ▶ / Signature Company ▶ / Subject Line ▶

Picture submenu: Clip Art... / From File... / AutoShapes / WordArt... / From Scanner or Camera... / Chart

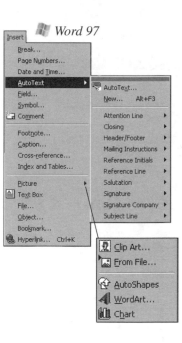

Word 97

Insert
Break...
Page Numbers...
Date and Time...
AutoText ▶
Field...
Symbol...
Comment
Footnote...
Caption...
Cross-reference...
Index and Tables...
Picture ▶
Text Box
File...
Object...
Bookmark...
Hyperlink... Ctrl+K

AutoText submenu: AutoText... / New... Alt+F3 / Attention Line ▶ / Closing ▶ / Header/Footer ▶ / Mailing Instructions ▶ / Reference Initials ▶ / Reference Line ▶ / Salutation ▶ / Signature ▶ / Signature Company ▶ / Subject Line ▶

Picture submenu: Clip Art... / From File... / AutoShapes / WordArt... / Chart

Word X

Insert
Break ▶
Page Numbers...
Date and Time...
AutoText ▶
Field...
Symbol...
Comment
Footnote...
Caption...
Cross-reference...
Index and Tables...
Picture ▶
HTML Object ▶
Text Box
Movie...
File...
Object...
Bookmark...
Hyperlink... ⌘K

Break submenu: Page Break / Column Break ⇧⌘↵ / Section Break (Next Page) / Section Break (Continuous) / Section Break (Odd Page) / Section Break (Even Page)

Picture submenu: Clip Art... / From File... / Horizontal Line... / AutoShapes / WordArt... / From Scanner or Camera... / Chart

AutoText submenu: AutoText... / New... / Attention Line ▶ / Closing ▶ / Header/Footer ▶ / Mailing Instructions ▶ / Reference Line ▶ / Salutation ▶ / Subject Line ▶

HTML Object submenu: Background Sound... / Scrolling Text... / Checkbox... / Option Button... / List Box... / Textbox... / Submit... / Reset... / Hidden...

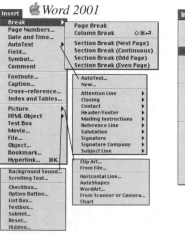

Word 2001

Insert
Break ▶
Page Numbers...
Date and Time...
AutoText ▶
Field...
Symbol...
Comment
Footnote...
Caption...
Cross-reference...
Index and Tables...
Picture ▶
HTML Object ▶
Text Box
Movie...
File...
Object...
Bookmark...
Hyperlink... ⌘K

Break submenu: Page Break / Column Break ⇧⌘↵ / Section Break (Next Page) / Section Break (Continuous) / Section Break (Odd Page) / Section Break (Even Page)

AutoText submenu: AutoText... / New... / Attention Line ▶ / Closing ▶ / Contact ▶ / Header/Footer ▶ / Mailing Instructions ▶ / Reference Line ▶ / Salutation ▶ / Signature ▶ / Signature Company ▶ / Subject Line ▶

HTML Object submenu: Background Sound... / Scrolling Text... / Checkbox... / Option Button... / List Box... / Textbox... / Submit... / Reset... / Hidden...

Picture submenu: Clip Art... / From File... / Horizontal Line... / AutoShapes / WordArt... / From Scanner or Camera... / Chart

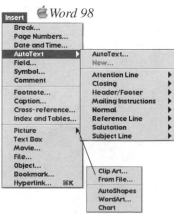

Word 98

Insert
Break...
Page Numbers...
Date and Time...
AutoText ▶
Field...
Symbol...
Comment
Footnote...
Caption...
Cross-reference...
Index and Tables...
Picture ▶
Text Box
Movie...
File...
Object...
Bookmark...
Hyperlink... ⌘K

AutoText submenu: AutoText... / New... / Attention Line ▶ / Closing ▶ / Header/Footer ▶ / Mailing Instructions ▶ / Normal ▶ / Reference Line ▶ / Salutation ▶ / Subject Line ▶

Picture submenu: Clip Art... / From File... / AutoShapes / WordArt... / Chart

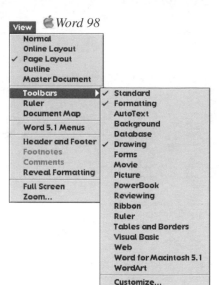

File   Edit   View   Insert   Format   Tools   Table   Window   Help

Format Menu

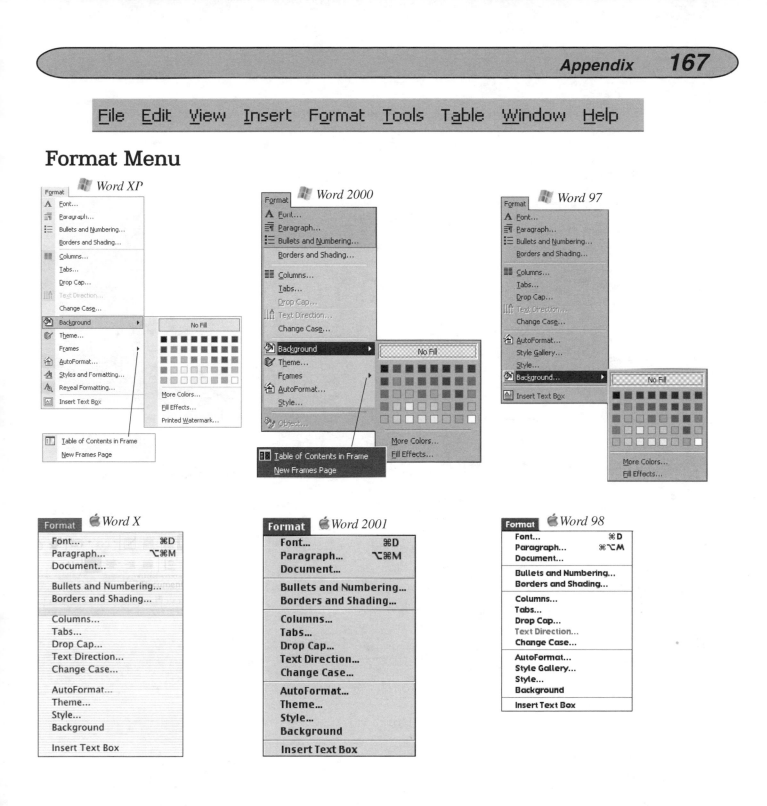

Window Menu

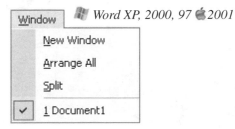

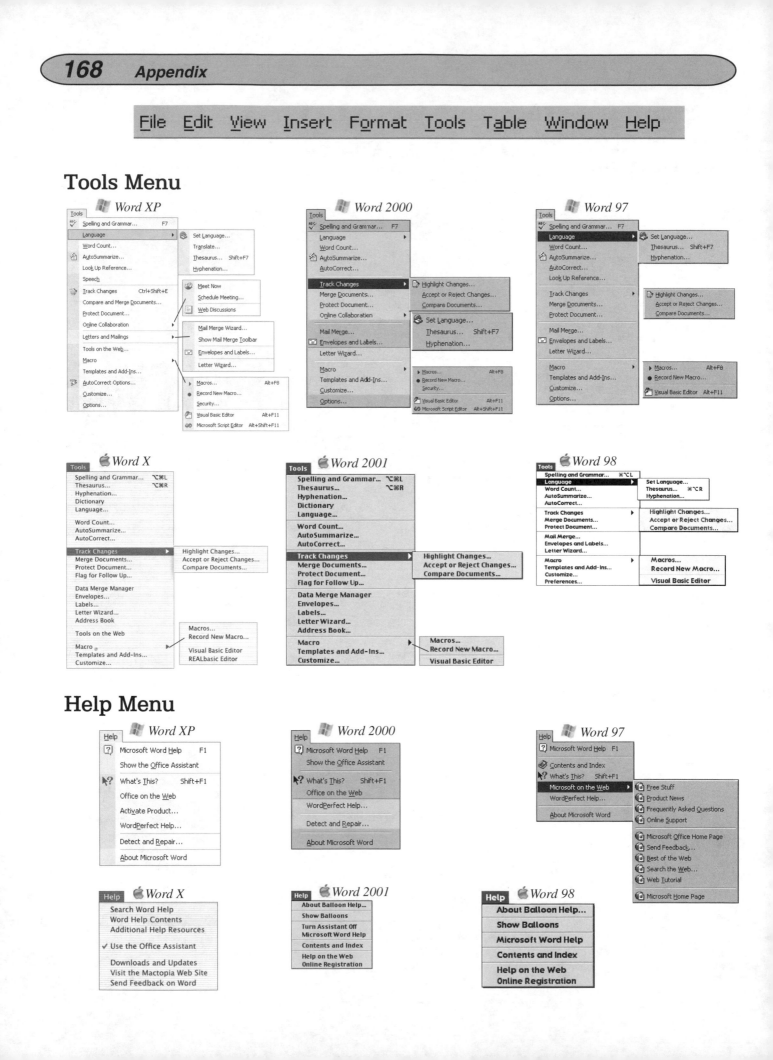

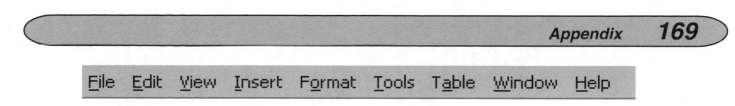

Table Menu

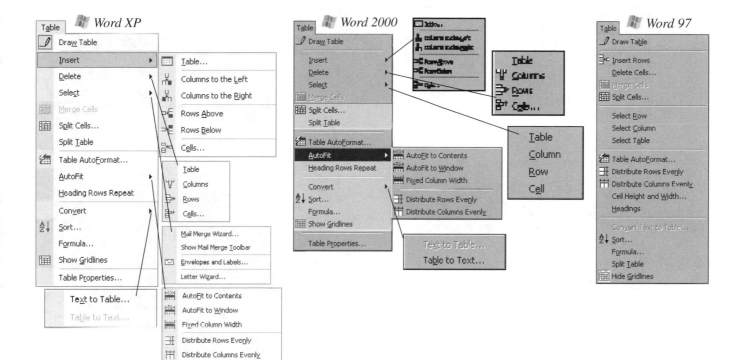

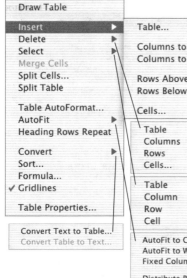

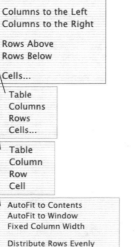

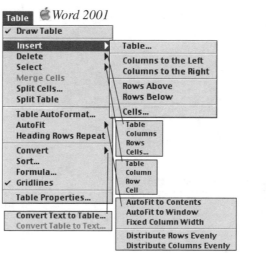

Help! I Want to Share My MS Word File...

PROBLEM:

1. Recipient Does Not Have Word, and Wants to "View Only." In other words, the person with whom you are sharing your *Word* file (the recipient) simply wants to be able to view the file in its full glory and maybe print it. The recipient does not need to be able to edit the file.

2. Recipient Has A Different Version of Word, and Wants to Both "View and Edit." In other words, your recipient has *Word* but it is a different version than the one you created the file in or the recipient is running *Word* on a different computer platform (e.g. Macintosh instead of Windows). You want your recipient to be able to view and change your *Word* file with no loss of data.

3. Recipient Uses Something other than Word, and Wants to View and/or Edit.

SOLUTION:

1. If Recipient Uses Windows, She Only Needs the Free Word Viewer.

Good news:

• If your recipient is a **Windows** user and all she wants to do is view the presentation (i.e. she will not need to edit it), then actually she does not even need to have *Word,* just the **Word Viewer**.

Bad news:

• There is no Word Viewer for **Macintosh** users. See solution 2 below if recipient has a Macintosh.

2. Be Careful When Opening Files in Different Versions of Word. Things can get a bit more complex here, but there is still reassuring news:

Good news:

• Since version 6.0 came out, Word has been a "cross-platform" application. That means that as long as the recipient of your file has the **same version** of *Word 6.0, 95, 97, or 2000* you used, but is just running it on a **different platform** (Macintosh instead of Windows, or vice versa), your file should open, with no loss of original data.

• If the recipient of your file has a **newer version** of *Word* than the one with which you created the file, then again, she can open your file with no loss of data. Note: for versions earlier than 6.0, the recipient would need to be opening the file at least on the **same platform** (i.e. Windows or Macintosh) on which you created the file.

Bad news:

• In all other situations where the recipient has an **older version** of *Word* there are a few limits on your ability to share the file. First, you will either need to save the file in an older format before sending it, or else the recipient needs to install a "post-ship converter" (see chart on next page). Second, some data from the file created with the newer version of *Word* will be lost when the recipient opens it in an older version.

3. Be Careful When Opening Word Files in Different Word Processing Programs. Your Best Bet is to Save the file as RTF Instead.

Bad news:

• In situations where the recipient uses a program **other than** *Word,* there are limits on your ability to share a *Word* file. The best way to ensure the file will open with **most formatting intact** is to save the file in **RTF** (RIch Text Format, one of options in "Save as" window) before sending the file. More risky alternatives, in terms of the file opening and data being intact, include b) relying on the recipient's program having the appropriate "converter" to read your *Word* file as is, and c) saving the file in the format the recipient uses (check the options in the Save as window).

Still confused about what happens when you open files in different versions of *Word*? The following page contains an easy-to-use chart to help you sort through compatibility issues:

Use This Chart to See What Happens When You Open a Word File Across a Platform or Version

When File Created With... → Is Opened With... ↓	MACINTOSH — Word 98/Office98 (8.0) (Power PC only)	Word 6.0	Word 5.x	Word 4.0	WINDOWS 95/98/NT — Word 2000/Office 2000 (9.0)	Word 97/Office97 (8.0)	Word 95/Office95 (7.0)	WINDOWS 3.x — Word 6.0	Word 2.0
Word 98/Office98 (8.0) (Power PC only)	OK	OK	OK	OK	OK	OK	OK	OK	OK
Word 6.0 (Mac)	OK, if 97-2000 Import Converter installed in 6.0 folder, or if 98 file saved as 6.0 **SOME DATA LOSS***	OK	OK	OK	OK, if 97-2000 Import Converter installed in 6.0 folder, or if '00 file saved as 6.0 **SOME DATA LOSS***	OK, if 97-2000 Import Converter installed in 6.0 folder, or if 97 file saved as 6.0 **SOME DATA LOSS***	OK	OK	OK **SOME DATA LOSS**
Word 5.x (Mac)	OK, if 97-2000 Import Converter installed in 5.x folder, or if 98 file saved as 4/5 **SOME DATA LOSS***	if 6.0 Import Converter for 5.x installed in 5.x folder, or if 6.0 file saved as 4/5 **SOME DATA LOSS****	OK	OK	if 97-2000 Import Converter installed in 5.x folder, or if 2000 file saved as 4/5 **SOME DATA LOSS***	if 97-2000 Import Converter installed in 5.x folder, or if 97 file saved as 4/5 **SOME DATA LOSS***	if 6.0 Import Converter installed in 5.x folder, or if 7.0 file saved as 4/5 **SOME DATA LOSS****	if 6.0 Import Converter for 5.x installed in 5.x folder, or if 6.0 file saved as 4/5 **SOME DATA LOSS****	OK **SOME DATA LOSS**
Word 4.0 (Mac)	OK, if 98 file saved in 4/5 **SOME DATA LOSS***	OK, if 6.0 file saved in 4/5 **SOME DATA LOSS****	OK	OK	OK, if 2000 file saved as 4/5 **SOME DATA LOSS***	OK, if 97 file saved as 4/5 **SOME DATA LOSS***	OK, if 7.0 file saved as 4/5 **SOME DATA LOSS****	OK, if 6.0 file saved in 4/5 **SOME DATA LOSS****	OK **SOME DATA LOSS**
Word 2000/Office 2000 (9.0)	OK	OK VIEW ONLY	OK VIEW ONLY	OK VIEW ONLY	OK	OK	OK VIEW ONLY	OK VIEW ONLY	OK **SOME DATA LOSS**
Word 97/Office97 (8.0)	OK	OK	OK	OK	OK	OK	OK	OK	OK
Word 97-2000 Viewer for Windows 95-98 (free)	OK VIEW ONLY	OK VIEW ONLY	OK VIEW ONLY	OK VIEW ONLY	OK VIEW ONLY	OK VIEW ONLY	OK VIEW ONLY	OK VIEW ONLY	OK VIEW ONLY
Word 95/Office95 (7.0)	OK	OK	OK	OK	OK	OK	OK	OK	OK
Word 97-2000 Viewer for Windows 3.x (free)	OK VIEW ONLY	OK VIEW ONLY	OK VIEW ONLY	OK VIEW ONLY	VIEW ONLY	VIEW ONLY	VIEW ONLY	VIEW ONLY	OK VIEW ONLY
Word 6.0 (Win)	OK	OK	OK	OK	OK, if 97-2000 Import Converter installed in 6.0 folder, or if '00 file saved as 6.0 **SOME DATA LOSS***	OK, if 97-2000 Import Converter installed in 6.0 folder, or if 97 file saved as 6.0 **SOME DATA LOSS***	OK	OK	OK **SOME DATA LOSS**
Word 2.0 (Win)	OK, if 98 file saved as 2.0 for Windows **SOME DATA LOSS***	OK, if 6.0/7.0 Import Converter installed, or if 6.0 file saved as 2.0 for Windows **SOME DATA LOSS***	OK, if 5.x file saved as 2.0 for Windows **SOME DATA LOSS***	OK **SOME DATA LOSS**	OK, If 2000 file saved in 2.0 format **SOME DATA LOSS***	OK, If 2000 file saved in 2.0 format **SOME DATA LOSS***	OK, if 6.0/7.0 Converter for Win 2.0 installed, or if 7.0 file saved in 2.0 format **SOME DATA LOSS***	OK, if 6.0/7.0 Converter for Win 2.0 installed, or if 6.0 file saved in 2.0 format **SOME DATA LOSS***	OK

Safe Bets: 👈 Word 98/Office98 (8.0); Word 97/Office97 (8.0); Word 97-2000 Viewer for Windows 95-98; Word 97-2000 Viewer for Windows 3.x

*Because the file is being converted from 97-2000 to an older format, any special new features of Word 97-2000 are lost. E.g. there are over thirty features in the 97-2000 versions of Word that will not work. In the case of converting a 97-2000 file to the older 7.0 (or Word 95 or 6.0) format, lost features include: editing of charts, embedded True Type fonts, page borders, Animated text formatting, graphics effects like embossed and engraved character formatting, document backgrounds, shadows, perspective, preset shaded fills, picture and textured backgrounds, use of emf, .png & .jpg graphic formats (converted to wmf and pict), floating pictures, text box margins, text effects, embedded hyperlinks, and hyperlinks that combine Play Sound with other actions, as well as Title Master formatting changes, and editing of headers and footers, password protection, macros, and customized menu and toolbar settings. In the case of converting a 97-2000 file to the even older 4.0/5.x Macintosh or 2.0 for Windows formats, additional lost features include: variable width columns, page orientation, page size, and vertical alignment.

**6.0-specific features lost during conversion to 5.x or 2.0 for Windows include variable width columns, lines between columns, kerning, vertical alignment, automatic bullets and numbering, drawn objects, fields, revision marks, and master documents.

***The Word 97-2000 Viewer for Windows 3.1 does not support display of pictures contained in Word for Macintosh files.

****E.g. some colored text is not converted. There is a workaround for this.

Change the RAM (Memory) Allocated to *Word*

Word files with scanned pictures or movies need a lot of RAM. If you are using a Macintosh with System 9, 8, or 7, it would be advisable to bump up the amount of memory allocated to *Word* when you are creating files with lots of pictures or movies. If you don't bump up the allocation, you will likely get the error message, "Memory was too full to draw everything." This doesn't mean that your computer doesn't have enough memory; it means that not enough of the memory has been allocated to *Word*. Macintosh computers using System X and Windows computers have another allocation method, so if you're using one of those computers, you can skip this lesson.

Determining the Amount of RAM (Memory) Available

Before you bump up the allocation, you need to know how much memory is being used by your system and your screen saver.

1. To do this, choose "About This Computer" from the Apple menu in the left corner of your menu bar.

   The dialog box will tell you how much RAM (memory) is available on your computer.

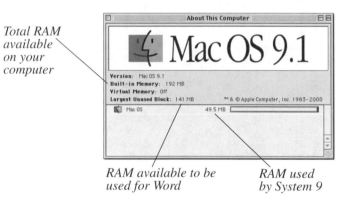

Total RAM available on your computer

RAM available to be used for Word

RAM used by System 9

Now that you know how much memory is available to be used for *Word*, it is time to see how much has been allocated for the program.

2. Open the Microsoft Office folder.

3. Click **one** time on the *Word* application icon to select it.

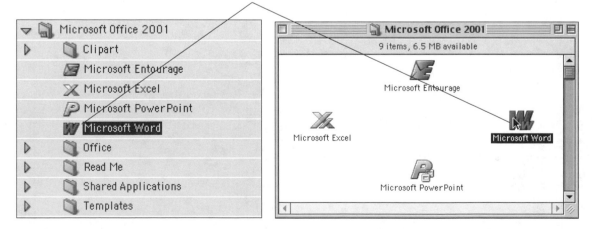

If you click twice, the application will open. The application must be closed to do this operation, so you must quit *Word* if it is open.

4. Once the application icon is selected (highlighted), click the File menu and choose Get Info, or press ⌘I. (If you have Mac OS 9 or higher you then need to choose Memory from the new menu.)

A dialog box will appear showing how much memory is needed for the application and how much has been allocated.

The system's "About This Computer" dialog box shows 141 megabytes of RAM could be used by *Word*. Don't use it all though.

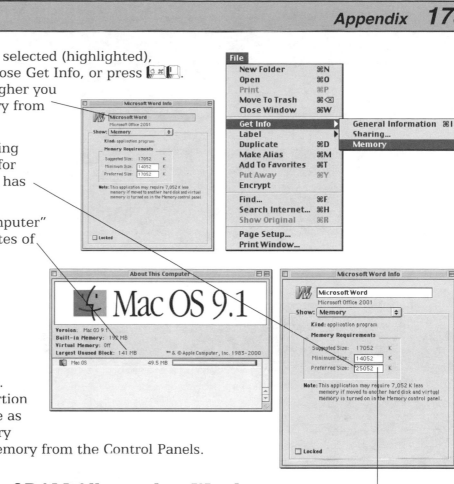

Power Macintoshes

Word operates with less RAM on Power Macintoshes if Virtual Memory is turned on. Virtual Memory allocates a portion of the hard drive storage space as RAM (memory). Virtual Memory can be changed by opening Memory from the Control Panels.

Changing the Amount of RAM Allocated to *Word*

1. Click in the box next to Preferred Size and type a larger number.

2. Click the Close Box in the upper left corner to close the window.

3. Open the *Word* program. Because you just allocated extra memory to the program, you will probably have enough memory to do most operations. If you get a memory error, save your file, quit *Word*, and allocate more memory (if available).

4. When you are finished with your work and have quit *Word*, you may need to change the memory allocation back to the suggested size. If you are working on your own computer and you frequently use large files in *Word*, you may decide to keep the allocation as you have set it.

You will not be able to have another program open at the same time you are using *Word* if all the available RAM is allocated to *Word*. If you keep your calendar program open throughout the day, as well as using *Word*, you may wish to take the memory allocation back to the suggested size so that you can have them both open. If you are using a computer that is used by many people, it would be advisable to change the allocation back to the suggested size and bump it up the next time you need to.

If you try to type a new number in the Preferred Size box and nothing happens, you probably have Word open. Quit Word and then you will be able to type in the dialog box.

Animals

Amphibians

Firebellied Toad

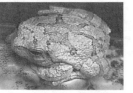
Tomato Frog

Gray Tree Frog

Woodhouse's Toad

Newt

Mud Puppy

Tiger Salamander

Salamander in Nymph Stage

Basilisk

Birds

Red-Winged Blackbird

Blue Jay

Gray Jay

Western Bluebird

Red-Bellied Woodpecker

Eastern Bluebird

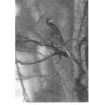
Cardinal, Male

Cardinal, Female

Black-Capped Chickadee

House Finch

Gold-Crowned Sparrow

Flamingos

Robin

Western Meadowlark

Pigeon

Crow

Hummingbird

Penguins

Penguin

Killdeer

Pelican

Ptarmigan

Anhinga

Purple Gallinule

Roseate
Spoonbill

Great Blue
Heron

Great American
Egret

White and Scarlet Ibis

Wood Stork

Seagull

Swan

Mallard, Female

Mallard, Male

Ring-Necked Pheasant

Red-Tailed Hawk

Ostrich

Sandhill Crane

Canada Goose

Chicken

Wild Turkey

Sharp-Tailed
Grouse

Greater Prairie
Chicken

Cockatoo

Victoria Crowned Pigeon

Scarlet Macaw

Yellow-Headed Parrot

Fish

Hepatus Tang

Catfish

Clown Fish

Pompano

Grouper

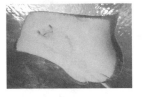
Stingray

Yellow Tang

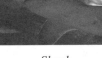
Shark

Zoo Animals

Tapir

Tiger

Hippo

Giraffe Baby

Giraffe

Bear

Bear, Wet

Gorilla, Black

Rhinoceros

Gorilla

Gorilla Eating

Lion

Rhino

Elephant

Marmoset

Mountain Lion

Polar Bear

Panda with Baby

Mammals

Elk 2

Pronghorn

Moose

Deer

Elk

Elk Herd

Bison

Mountain Sheep

Mountain Goat

Coyote

Raccoon

Raccoon 2

Rabbit

Snowshoe Hare

Rodents

Muskrat

Pika

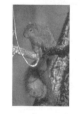
Guinea Pig

Fox Squirrel

Fox Squirrel 2

Ground Squirrel

Marmot

Reptiles

Alligator

Bearded Dragon

Turtles

Monitor Lizard

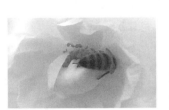

Rat Snake

Insects

Bee

Hunter's Butterfly/
American Painted Lady

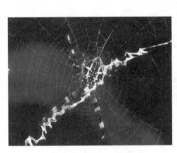

Spider

Dragonfly

Monarch Butterfly

Pipevine Swallowtail

Cloudless Sulphur

Eastern Swallowtail

Plants

Cacti

Arizona
Hedgehog

Barrel Cactus

Cholla and Saguaro

Prickly Pear Cactus2

Prickly Pear Cactus3

Prickly Pear Cactus

American Lotus

Flowers

Bachelor Button

Bird of Paradise

Bougainvillea

Clematis

Columbine

Coneflower

Fireweed

Goblin Gaillardia

Hollyhock

Jack-in-
the-Puplit

Mandevilla

Pasqueflower

Purple Coneflower

Rose

Flowers

Rose2

Siberian Iris

Sneezeweed

Thistle

Tiger Lily

Tiger Lily

Tiger Lily

Fruits, Berries & Seeds

Acorns

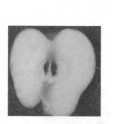

Apple Seeds

Apples

Dandilion Seeds

Evergreen Berries

Milkweed Seeds

Rasberry

Mushrooms

Antler Jelly

Blue cheese Polypore

Common Morel

Destroying Angel

Flecked-flesh Polypore

Graying Yellow Russula

Lichen Aagaric

Luminescent Panellus

Orange Pinwheel

Rosy Gomphidius

Shelf Mushroom

Stalked Hairy Fairy Cup

Tree Volvariella

Witches Butter

Index

Tom Snyder Productions®

80 Coolidge Hill Road • Watertown, MA 02472-5003 • USA
Phone 1-800-342-0236 • Fax 1-800-304-1254 • www.tomsnyder.com

XJAN WW2 U 02